Nutsh

WEST PUBLIS

P.O. Box 3526

St. Paul, Minnesota 55165

August, 1981

Administrative Law and Process, 2nd Ed., 1981, approx. 440 pages, by Ernest Gellhorn, Professor of Law, University of Virginia and Barry B. Boyer, Professor of Law, SUNY, Buffalo.

Agency-Partnership, 1977, 364 pages, by Roscoe T. Steffen, Late Professor of Law, University of Chicago.

American Indian Law, 1981, 288 pages, by William C. Canby, Jr., former Professor of Law, Arizona State University.

Antitrust Law and Economics, 2nd Ed., 1981, 425 pages, by Ernest Gellhorn, Professor of Law, University of Virginia.

Church-State Relations—Law of 1981, 305 pages, by Leonard F. Manning, Professor of Law, Fordham University.

Civil Procedure, 1979, 271 pages, by Mary Kay Kane, Professor of Law, University of California, Hastings College of the Law.

Civil Rights, 1978, 279 pages, by Norman Vieira, Professor of Law, University of Idaho.

Commercial Paper, 2nd Ed., 1975, 361 pages, by Charles M. Weber, Professor of Business Law, University of Arizona.

Conflicts, 3rd Ed., 1974, 432 pages, by Albert A. Ehrenzweig, Late Professor of Law, University of California, Berkeley.

NUTSHELL SERIES

Constitutional Analysis, 1979, 388 pages, by Jerre S. Williams, former Professor of Law, University of Texas.

Constitutional Power—Federal and State, 1974, 411 pages, by David E. Engdahl, former Professor of Law, University of Denver.

Consumer Law, 2nd Ed., 1981, 418 pages, by David G. Epstein, Dean and Professor of Law, University of Arkansas and Steve H. Nickles, Professor of Law, University of Arkansas.

Contracts, 1975, 307 pages, by Gordon D. Schaber, Dean and Professor of Law, McGeorge School of Law and Claude D. Rohwer, Professor of Law, McGeorge School of Law.

Contract Remedies, 1981, approx. 325 pages, by Jane M. Friedman, Professor of Law, Wayne State University.

Corporations—Law of, 1980, 379 pages, by Robert W. Hamilton, Professor of Law, University of Texas.

Corrections and Prisoners' Rights—Law of, 1976, 353 pages, by Sheldon Krantz, Professor of Law, Boston University.

Criminal Law, 1975, 302 pages, by Arnold H. Loewy, Professor of Law, University of North Carolina.

Criminal Procedure—Constitutional Limitations, 3rd Ed., 1980, 438 pages, by Jerold H. Israel, Professor of Law, University of Michigan and Wayne R. LaFave, Professor of Law, University of Illinois.

Debtor-Creditor Law, 2nd Ed., 1980, 324 pages, by David G. Epstein, Dean and Professor of Law, University of Arkansas.

Employment Discrimination—Federal Law of, 2nd Ed., 1981, 402 pages, by Mack A. Player, Professor of Law, University of Georgia.

NUTSHELL SERIES

Energy Law, 1981, approx. 330 pages, by Joseph P. Tomain, Professor of Law, Drake University.

Estate Planning—Introduction to, 2nd Ed., 1978, 378 pages, by Robert J. Lynn, Professor of Law, Ohio State University.

Evidence, Federal Rules of, 1981, 428 pages, by Michael H. Graham, Professor of Law, University of Illinois.

Evidence, State and Federal Rules, 2nd Ed., 1981, 514 pages, by Paul F. Rothstein, Professor of Law, Georgetown University.

Family Law, 1977, 400 pages, by Harry D. Krause, Professor of Law, University of Illinois.

Federal Estate and Gift Taxation, 2nd Ed., 1979, 488 pages, by John K. McNulty, Professor of Law, University of California, Berkeley.

Federal Income Taxation of Individuals, 2nd Ed., 1978, 422 pages, by John K. McNulty, Professor of Law, University of California, Berkeley.

Federal Income Taxation of Corporations and Stockholders, 2nd Ed., 1981, 362 pages, by Jonathan Sobeloff, Late Professor of Law, Georgetown University and Peter P. Weidenbruch, Jr., Professor of Law, Georgetown University.

Federal Jurisdiction, 2nd Ed., 1981, 258 pages, by David P. Currie, Professor of Law, University of Chicago.

Future Interests, 1981, 361 pages, by Lawrence W. Waggoner, Professor of Law, University of Michigan.

Government Contracts, 1979, 423 pages, by W. Noel Keyes, Professor of Law, Pepperdine University.

Historical Introduction to Anglo-American Law, 2nd Ed., 1973, 280 pages, by Frederick G. Kempin, Jr., Professor of Business Law, Wharton School of Finance and Commerce, University of Pennsylvania.

Injunctions, 1974, 264 pages, by John F. Dobbyn, Professor of Law, Villanova University.

Insurance Law, 1981, 281 pages, by John F. Dobbyn, Professor of Law, Villanova University.

International Business Transactions, 1981, 393 pages, by Donald T. Wilson, Professor of Law, Loyola University, Los Angeles.

Judicial Process, 1980, 292 pages, by William L. Reynolds, Professor of Law, University of Maryland.

Jurisdiction, 4th Ed., 1980, 232 pages, by Albert A. Ehrenzweig, Late Professor of Law, University of California, Berkeley, David W. Louisell, Late Professor of Law, University of California, Berkeley and Geoffrey C. Hazard, Jr., Professor of Law, Yale Law School.

Juvenile Courts, 2nd Ed., 1977, 275 pages, by Sanford J. Fox, Professor of Law, Boston College.

Labor Arbitration Law and Practice, 1979, 358 pages, by Dennis R. Nolan, Professor of Law, University of South Carolina.

Labor Law, 1979, 403 pages, by Douglas L. Leslie, Professor of Law, University of Virginia.

Land Use, 1978, 316 pages, by Robert R. Wright, Professor of Law, University of Arkansas, Little Rock and Susan Webber, Professor of Law, University of Arkansas, Little Rock.

Landlord and Tenant Law, 1979, 319 pages, by David S. Hill, Professor of Law, University of Colorado.

Law Study and Law Examinations—Introduction to, 1971, 389 pages, by Stanley V. Kinyon, Late Professor of Law, University of Minnesota.

Legal Interviewing and Counseling, 1976, 353 pages, by Thomas L. Shaffer, Professor of Law, Washington and Lee University.

NUTSHELL SERIES

Legal Research, 3rd Ed., 1978, 415 pages, by Morris L. Cohen, Professor of Law and Law Librarian, Yale University.

Legislative Law and Process, 1975, 279 pages, by Jack Davies, Professor of Law, William Mitchell College of Law.

Local Government Law, 1975, 386 pages, by David J. McCarthy, Jr., Dean and Professor of Law, Georgetown University.

Mass Communications Law, 1977, 431 pages, by Harvey L. Zuckman, Professor of Law, Catholic University and Martin J. Gaynes, Lecturer in Law, Temple University.

Medical Malpractice—The Law of, 1977, 340 pages, by Joseph H. King, Professor of Law, University of Tennessee.

Military Law, 1980, 378 pages, by Charles A. Shanor, Professor of Law, Emory University and Timothy P. Terrell, Professor of Law, Emory University.

Post-Conviction Remedies, 1978, 360 pages, by Robert Popper, Professor of Law, University of Missouri, Kansas City.

Presidential Power, 1977, 328 pages, by Arthur Selwyn Miller, Professor of Law Emeritus, George Washington University.

Procedure Before Trial, 1972, 258 pages, by Delmar Karlen, Professor of Law, College of William and Mary.

Products Liability, 2nd Ed., 1981, 341 pages, by Dix W. Noel, Late Professor of Law, University of Tennessee and Jerry J. Phillips, Professor of Law, University of Tennessee.

NUTSHELL SERIES

Professional Responsibility, 1980, 399 pages, by Robert H. Aronson, Professor of Law, University of Washington, and Donald T. Weckstein, Professor of Law, University of San Diego.

Real Estate Finance, 1979, 292 pages, by Jon W. Bruce, Professor of Law, Stetson University.

Real Property, 2nd Ed., 1981, approx. 440 pages, by Roger H. Bernhardt, Professor of Law, Golden Gate University.

Remedies, 1977, 364 pages, by John F. O'Connell, Professor of Law, Western State University College of Law, Fullerton.

Res Judicata, 1976, 310 pages, by Robert C. Casad, Professor of Law, University of Kansas.

Sales, 2nd Ed., 1981, 370 pages, by John M. Stockton, Professor of Business Law, Wharton School of Finance and Commerce, University of Pennsylvania.

Secured Transactions, 2nd Ed., 1981, 391 pages, by Henry J. Bailey, Professor of Law, Willamette University.

Securities Regulation, 1978, 300 pages, by David L. Ratner, Professor of Law, Cornell University.

Titles—The Calculus of Interests, 1968, 277 pages, by Oval A. Phipps, Late Professor of Law, St. Louis University.

Torts—Injuries to Persons and Property, 1977, 434 pages by Edward J. Kionka, Professor of Law, Southern Illinois University.

Torts—Injuries to Family, Social and Trade Relations, 1979, 358 pages, by Wex S. Malone, Professor of Law Emeritus, Louisiana State University.

NUTSHELL SERIES

Trial Advocacy, 1979, 402 pages, by Paul B. Bergman, Adjunct Professor of Law, University of California, Los Angeles.

Trial and Practice Skills, 1978, 346 pages, by Kenney F. Hegland, Professor of Law, University of Arizona.

Uniform Commercial Code, 1975, 507 pages, by Bradford Stone, Professor of Law, Detroit College of Law.

Uniform Probate Code, 1978, 425 pages, by Lawrence H. Averill, Jr., Professor of Law, University of Wyoming.

Welfare Law—Structure and Entitlement, 1979, 455 pages, by Arthur B. LaFrance, Professor of Law, University of Maine.

Wills and Trusts, 1979, 392 pages, by Robert L. Mennell, Professor of Law, Hamline University.

Hornbook Series

and

Basic Legal Texts

of

WEST PUBLISHING COMPANY

P.O. Box 3526

St. Paul, Minnesota 55165

August, 1981

———

VIII

HORNBOOKS & BASIC TEXTS

Common Law Pleading, Koffler and Reppy's Hornbook on, 1969, 663 pages, by Joseph H. Koffler, Professor of Law, New York Law School and Alison Reppy, Late Dean and Professor of Law, New York Law School.

Common Law Pleading, Shipman's Hornbook on, 3rd Ed., 1923, 644 pages, by Henry W. Ballantine, Late Professor of Law, University of California, Berkeley.

Constitutional Law, Nowak, Rotunda and Young's Hornbook on, 1978 with 1979 Pocket Part, 974 pages, by John E. Nowak, Professor of Law, University of Illinois, Ronald D. Rotunda, Professor of Law, University of Illinois, and J. Nelson Young, Professor of Law, University of Illinois.

Contracts, Calamari and Perillo's Hornbook on, 2nd Ed., 1977, 878 pages, by John D. Calamari, Professor of Law, Fordham University and Joseph M. Perillo, Professor of Law, Fordham University.

Contracts, Corbin's One Volume Student Ed., 1952, 1224 pages, by Arthur L. Corbin, Late Professor of Law, Yale University.

Contracts, Simpson's Hornbook on, 2nd Ed., 1965, 510 pages, by Laurence P. Simpson, Late Professor of Law, New York University.

Corporate Taxation, Kahn's Handbook on, 3rd Ed., Student Ed., Soft cover, 1981, 614 pages, by Douglas A. Kahn, Professor of Law, University of Michigan.

Corporations, Henn's Hornbook on, 2nd Ed., 1970, 956 pages, by Harry G. Henn, Professor of Law, Cornell University.

Criminal Law, LaFave and Scott's Hornbook on, 1972, 763 pages, by Wayne R. LaFave, Professor of Law, University of Illinois, and Austin Scott, Jr., Late Professor of Law, University of Colorado.

HORNBOOKS & BASIC TEXTS

Damages, McCormick's Hornbook on, 1935, 811 pages, by Charles T. McCormick, Late Dean and Professor of Law, University of Texas.

Domestic Relations, Clark's Hornbook on, 1968, 754 pages, by Homer H. Clark, Jr., Professor of Law, University of Colorado.

Environmental Law, Rodgers' Hornbook on, 1977, 956 pages, by William H. Rodgers, Jr., Professor of Law, University of Washington.

Equity, McClintock's Hornbook on, 2nd Ed., 1948, 643 pages, by Henry L. McClintock, Late Professor of Law, University of Minnesota.

Estate and Gift Taxes, Lowndes, Kramer and McCord's Hornbook on, 3rd Ed., 1974, 1099 pages, by Charles L. B. Lowndes, Late Professor of Law, Duke University, Robert Kramer, Professor of Law Emeritus, George Washington University, and John H. McCord, Professor of Law, University of Illinois.

Evidence, Lilly's Introduction to, 1978, 486 pages, by Graham C. Lilly, Professor of Law, University of Virginia.

Evidence, McCormick's Hornbook on, 2nd Ed., 1972 with 1978 Pocket Part, 938 pages, General Editor, Edward W. Cleary, Professor of Law Emeritus, Arizona State University.

Federal Courts, Wright's Hornbook on, 3rd Ed., 1976, 818 pages, including Federal Rules Appendix, by Charles Alan Wright, Professor of Law, University of Texas.

Future Interest, Simes' Hornbook on, 2nd Ed., 1966, 355 pages, by Lewis M. Simes, Late Professor of Law, University of Michigan.

X

HORNBOOKS & BASIC TEXTS

Income Taxation, Chommie's Hornbook on, 2nd Ed., 1973, 1051 pages, by John C. Chommie, Late Professor of Law, University of Miami.

Insurance, Keeton's Basic Text on, 1971, 712 pages, by Robert E. Keeton, former Professor of Law, Harvard University.

Labor Law, Gorman's Basic Text on, 1976, 914 pages, by Robert A. Gorman, Professor of Law, University of Pennsylvania.

Law Problems, Ballentine's, 5th Ed., 1975, 767 pages, General Editor, William E. Burby, Professor of Law Emeritus, University of Southern California.

Legal Writing Style, Weihofen's, 2nd Ed., 1980, 332 pages, by Henry Weihofen, Professor of Law Emeritus, University of New Mexico.

New York Practice, Siegel's Hornbook on, 1978, with 1979-80 Pocket Part, 1011 pages, by David D. Siegel, Professor of Law, Albany Law School of Union University.

Oil and Gas, Hemingway's Hornbook on, 1971 with 1979 Pocket Part, 486 pages, by Richard W. Hemingway, Professor of Law, University of Oklahoma.

Partnership, Crane and Bromberg's Hornbook on, 1968, 695 pages, by Alan R. Bromberg, Professor of Law, Southern Methodist University.

Poor, Law of the, LaFrance, Schroeder, Bennett and Boyd's Hornbook on, 1973, 558 pages, by Arthur B. LaFrance, Professor of Law, University of Maine, Milton R. Schroeder, Professor of Law, Arizona State University, Robert W. Bennett, Professor of Law, Northwestern University and William E. Boyd, Professor of Law, University of Arizona.

HORNBOOKS & BASIC TEXTS

Property, Boyer's Survey of, 3rd Ed., 1981, 766 pages, by Ralph E. Boyer, Professor of Law, University of Miami.

Real Estate Finance Law, Osborne, Nelson and Whitman's Hornbook on, (successor to Hornbook on Mortgages), 1979, 885 pages, by George E. Osborne, Late Professor of Law, Stanford University, Grant S. Nelson, Professor of Law, University of Missouri, Columbia and Dale A. Whitman, Professor of Law, University of Washington.

Real Property, Burby's Hornbook on, 3rd Ed., 1965, 490 pages, by William E. Burby, Professor of Law Emeritus, University of Southern California.

Real Property, Moynihan's Introduction to, 1962, 254 pages, by Cornelius J. Moynihan, Professor of Law, Suffolk University.

Remedies, Dobbs' Hornbook on, 1973, 1067 pages, by Dan B. Dobbs, Professor of Law, University of Arizona.

Sales, Nordstrom's Hornbook on, 1970, 600 pages, by Robert J. Nordstrom, former Professor of Law, Ohio State University.

Secured Transactions under the U.C.C., Henson's Hornbook on, 2nd Ed., 1979, with 1979 Pocket Part, 504 pages, by Ray D. Henson, Professor of Law, University of California, Hastings College of the Law.

Torts, Prosser's Hornbook on, 4th Ed., 1971, 1208 pages, by William L. Prosser, Late Dean and Professor of Law, University of California, Berkeley.

Trial Advocacy, Jeans' Handbook on, Student Ed., Soft cover, 1975, by James W. Jeans, Professor of Law, University of Missouri, Kansas City.

HORNBOOKS & BASIC TEXTS

Trusts, Bogert's Hornbook on, 5th Ed., 1973, 726 pages, by George G. Bogert, Late Professor of Law, University of Chicago and George T. Bogert, Attorney, Chicago, Illinois.

Urban Planning and Land Development Control, Hagman's Hornbook on, 1971, 706 pages, by Donald G. Hagman, Professor of Law, University of California, Los Angeles.

Uniform Commercial Code, White and Summers' Hornbook on, 2nd Ed., 1980, 1250 pages, by James J. White, Professor of Law, University of Michigan and Robert S. Summers, Professor of Law, Cornell University.

Wills, Atkinson's Hornbook on, 2nd Ed., 1953, 975 pages, by Thomas E. Atkinson, Late Professor of Law, New York University.

Advisory Board

PRODUCTS LIABILITY

IN A

NUTSHELL

SECOND EDITION

By

DIX W. NOEL

Late Professor of Law, University of Tennessee

and

JERRY J. PHILLIPS

. P. Toms Professor of Law, University of Tennessee

ST. PAUL, MINN.

WEST PUBLISHING CO.

1981

Uniform Commercial Code. Copyright 1978. Portions reprinted herein with the permission of the American Law Institute and the National Conference of Commissioners on Uniform State Laws.

Restatement, Second, Torts. Copyright 1965. Portions reprinted herein with the permission of the American Law Institute.

Library of Congress Cataloging in Publication Data

Noel, Dix W
    Products liability in a nutshell.

    (Nutshell series)
    Includes index.
    1.   Products liability—United States.
I.   Phillips, Jerry J., 1935–   joint author.
II. Title.
KF1296.Z9N6   1981   346.7303'82   80-39726

ISBN 0-8299-2121-4

        N. & P.Prod.Liab. 2d Ed.
        1st Reprint—1982

To

Mary Noel

*

XVII

PREFACE

Since the first edition of this book was published in 1974, there has been considerable activity in the products field. Examples of this activity are: the publication of three products liability casebooks (including one by the authors of this book); passage of legislation affecting products litigation in approximately twenty states; a full-scale study and report about products liability by the United States Department of Commerce; and continued development of the common law in this area in such important matters as the scope of the products liability doctrine, the definition of defect and of unreasonable danger, the application of comparative fault, and the allocation of burden of proof. In addition, products liability has become one of the most extensive and important areas of private tort litigation in this country. It is for these reasons that a revision of the Nutshell is timely.

The revision, as the original, contains extensive case analysis based on the belief that the reader can obtain a better grasp of the principles involved by seeing their application to concrete factual situations. It is not expected of course that any student will remember many of the cases by name, but it is expected that he or she will remember a number of fact situations as vivid illustrations of the principles involved.

PREFACE

In the interests of economy, reference to outside authoritative support has been kept to a minimum. In a number of situations involving fairly self-evident or easily demonstrable principles, outside support is omitted. At the same time, the products liability field is sufficiently focused so that the subject can be given a reasonably detailed analysis within the scope of this book. The outline of the book follows that of the Noel and Phillips casebook on products liability, so their mutual use should be enhanced by students who study both.

Dix Noel died shortly after we began work on this revision. I deeply regret his death. I hope this book substantially reflects his views on the subject. His sister Mary Noel has been of invaluable assistance to us in the preparation of this book, as in our other professional work together.

Products liability has come of age. Although its future course is not clear in detail, its basic principles are now firmly ingrained in the law of this nation. I am gratified to be able to contribute to an understanding of the far-reaching social forces implicit in the development of the law in this field.

JERRY J. PHILLIPS

Knoxville, Tennessee
December, 1980

OUTLINE

CHAPTER I. DEFINITION AND SCOPE

CHAPTER II. THE CAUSES OF ACTION

CHAPTER III. THE PARTIES

CHAPTER IV. FACTORS AFFECTING THE CHOICE OF REMEDIES OR OF JURISDICTION

CHAPTER V. PRODUCTION AND DESIGN DEFECTS

CHAPTER VI. DEFECTIVE WARNINGS AND DIRECTIONS

CHAPTER VII. CAUSATION, FORE-SEEABILITY, AND THE AFFIRMATIVE DEFENSES

CHAPTER VIII. PROOF OF DEFECT AND OF NEGLIGENCE

TABLE OF CASES

References are to Pages

TABLE OF CASES

TABLE OF CASES

TABLE OF CASES

TABLE OF CASES

TABLE OF CASES

TABLE OF CASES

TABLE OF CASES

TABLE OF CASES

TABLE OF CASES

XXXVI

TABLE OF CASES

*

PRODUCTS LIABILITY

CHAPTER I

DEFINITION AND SCOPE

A. WHAT IS A PRODUCT?

Products liability is concerned with injuries caused by products that are defectively manufactured, processed, or distributed. The liability attaches to those who make a profit in the distributive chain, from the extractors of raw materials and the makers of component parts to the retailers. Usually they are sellers or lessors, but in some cases they may render supportive services, such as certifying, applying, or installing a product.

Originally a "product" was a chattel only; but increasingly the courts, for the purpose of allowing recovery under products liability doctrine, have regarded houses and rental apartments as products, and sometimes even a commercial unit or a lot "manufactured" by much earthmoving, or a condominium in Washington's luxurious Watergate. A product also includes its container, whether sold with the product, as in the case of an unreturned soft drink bottle that explodes, or not sold, as in Bainter v. Lamoine LP Gas Co., 321 N.E.2d 744 (Ill.App. 1974). Here the defendant furnished a tank as "an incident of the sale of the gas and the consideration for the sale included the use of the tank." In Shaffer v. Victoria Station, Inc., 588 P.2d 233 (Wash.1978), the defendant restauranteur was held strictly liable when a wine glass shattered, injuring the hand of the patron.

In Dubin v. Michael Reese Hosp. and Medical Center, 393 N.E.2d 588 (Ill.App.1979), where plaintiff allegedly contracted cancer because of excessive x-radiation administered by the hospital, the court held that x-rays were a product and "that the supply of x-radiation for absorption into a patient for treatment purposes by a hospital, for which a charge is made, places such hospital in the business of introducing such x-radiation in the stream of commerce." This opinion was reversed by the state supreme court, CCH Prod. Liab. Rptr. par. 8822 (Ill.1980). Although the supreme court decision is phrased in terms of whether an x-ray is a product, the actual holding appears to be that there was no showing of defect. "Plaintiff's argument does not center on any inherent defect in the x-radiation itself, but on the inappropriateness of the application of certain amounts of x-radiation to treat plaintiff's condition." In Ransome v. Wisconsin Elec. Power Co., 275 N.W.2d 641 (Wis.1979), it was held that electricity of 1,000 to 4,000 volts that entered a house, causing a fire, was "when it left the possession of the Wisconsin Electric Power Company . . . in such defective condition as to be unreasonably dangerous to a prospective customer." Courts differ, however, on this question, many of them holding that the supplying of electricity is a service only and, no matter how dangerous, not subject to a products liability action.

B. WHAT IS A DEFECT?

1. CONSUMER EXPECTATIONS

If the definition of a product has caused some difficulty, that of defect has caused even more. Regardless of the basic theory of products liability, whether negligence or some form of strict liability, absent a misrepresentation a defect must be proven, the defect must have existed at the time the product left the defendant's control, and the defect must have caused the injury. Thus every products liability case involves a definition of defect, with the result that the variety of approach presents one of the most difficult and challenging aspects of case law. The Second Restatement of Torts, § 402A, speaks of "a defective condition unreasonably dangerous to the user", and the majority of courts have regarded "unreasonably dangerous" as inseparable from the definition of defect. Some courts, however, have objected that the phrase is unsuitable in a strict liability context, since it "rings

[*3*]

of negligence." This question will be discussed in the chapter on design, after the reader has become familiar with the various causes of action in products cases. Another more strictly definitional objection to the phrase was raised in Hansen v. Cessna Aircraft Co., 578 F.2d 679 (7th Cir. 1978), where it was suggested that to a jury "unreasonably" might mean extraordinarily dangerous. In the Restatement the word carries no such meaning, and courts generally give an instruction which corresponds to comment i of § 402A which states: "The article sold must be dangerous to the extent beyond that which would be contemplated by the ordinary consumer who purchases it, with the knowledge common to the community as to its characteristics." Good whiskey and a sharp hunting knife are both dangerous, but not unreasonably so. Perhaps the semantic confusion might have been avoided if § 402A had read "unexpectedly dangerous."

The Restatement test of what constitutes a defect sufficient to fasten liability upon a defendant raises questions of law. Proof of the condition of a product at the time of injury and at the time when it left defendant's control obviously involves an investigation of facts with the finding to be made by the jury. But how is it possible to prove what an average consumer expects that condition to be, short of a census or a statistically valid sampling? The result of this uncertainty is that, once the actual condition of the product has been shown, whether this condition constitutes a defect will sometimes be decided by the court, sometimes by the jury. Thus in Webster v. Blue Ship Tea Room, Inc., 198 N.E.2d 309 (Mass.1964), where a fishbone lodged in plaintiff's throat as she was eating the defendant's fish chowder, the court held as a matter of law that the fishbone, so far from being a foreign substance that rendered the chowder unwholesome, was a natural hazard with which the consumer should be prepared to cope. The occasional presence of such bones "is, it seems to us, to be anticipated . . . in the light of a hallowed tradition." Without the use of whole chunks of fish, containing bones, the consumer would indeed be deprived of a "gustatory adventure" distinctive of New England. Consequently, ruled the court, fish chowder made with such whole chunks of fish, very likely with bones, meets ordinary consumer expectations. Less dramatically the court held in Coffer v. Standard Brands, Inc., 226 S.E.2d 534 (N.C.App.1976), where plaintiff injured his tooth on an unshelled nut from a glass jar of mixed shelled nuts, that the consumer should expect a few such unshelled nuts in the jar.

On the other hand, where the plaintiff broke a tooth on a pit in a cocktail olive, the question of defect was held for the jury in Hochberg v. O'Donnell's Restaurant, Inc., 272 A.2d 846 (D.C. App.1971). Plaintiff had assumed the olive was pitted because of a hole cut in its end. The court rejected the foreign-natural rule of *Webster*. Again, where plaintiff injured his teeth and gums on a rough pearl in a can of oyster soup, the court in Matthews v. Campbell Soup Co., 380 F.Supp. 1061 (S.D.Tex.1974), held the question of defect for the jury, no matter how natural pearls might be to some oysters.

Another "rule" which some courts have used to take the issue of defect from the jury is that of patent as against latent dangers. This question will be discussed more fully in connection with specific design and warning defects. But where products, such as darts for children to throw, B-B guns, and even baseball bats, are obviously dangerous and cannot be made less so by safety devices, courts have frequently held them to be nondefective as a matter of law.

Where a product has failed to meet a certain level of performance, the court may hold that a jury has "no experiential basis" for knowing "what reasonable consumers do expect from the product." In Heaton v. Ford Motor Co., 435 P.2d 806 (Or.1967), plaintiff was injured when a pickup truck of defendant's manufacture left the road and tipped over about 35 miles after hitting a rock which plaintiff described as about five or six inches in diameter. The truck was moving on a black-topped highway at normal speed. After the accident the rim of one of the wheels was found separated from the interior part. The truck had been driven only "some 7,000 miles" and without the driver "noticing

[6]

anything unusual about its performance." The court held that this situation furnished "no basis for a jury to do anything but speculate." "High-speed collisions with large rocks are not so common . . . that the average person would know from personal experience what to expect under the circumstances."

On the other hand, in Dunham v. Vaughan and Bushnell Mfg. Co., 247 N.E.2d 401 (Ill.1969), the expected performance of a claw hammer which chipped after eleven months' use was for the jury. The experts agreed that the hammer was flawlessly made, but disagreed as to whether a hammer made with steel of lower carbon content and therefore less hard would be less likely to chip. The hammer had not been put to any extraordinary use. "The jury could properly have concluded that, considering the length and type of its use, the hammer failed to perform in the manner that would reasonably have been expected, and this failure caused the plaintiff's injury."

A court's ruling on defect has often been influenced by the process in which the alleged defect developed. It may have occurred during the production process, such as an inadequate weld, a loose nut, or an insect in a bottle of soft drink. Here the condition was unintended by the manufacturer. It may have been the manufacturer's design decision, either one made with consciousness of a risk taken in order to secure a benefit, or one made inadvertently with no awareness of possible danger. Or it may have been a failure to warn or to warn adequately of a possible danger. Both the varying rules of law followed by courts in these differing situations and the wide variety of apparently ad hoc decisions will be discussed more fully in the chapters dealing with the specific varieties of defect.

The consumer expectation test has been subject to criticism, since often enough the consumer will have no way of knowing how safe the product could be made. Especially in design cases, as the court said in Barker v. Lull Engineering Co., Inc., 573 P.2d 443 (Cal.1978), "the manufacturer could frequently argue that its product satisfied ordinary consumer expectations since it was identical to other items of the same product line with which the consumer may well have been familiar." A manufacturer's test has been suggested as an alternative. In Phillips v. Kimwood Machine Co., 525 P.2d 1033 (Or.1974), the court said: "A dangerously defective article would be one which a reasonable person would not put into the stream of commerce *if he had knowledge of its harmful character.* The test, therefore, is whether the seller would be negligent if he sold the article *knowing of the risk involved.*" (Emphasis by the Court.) The court, however, saw no necessary inconsistency between this seller-oriented standard and a consumer-oriented standard, since " 'each turns on foreseeable risks.' " To the argument that the standard imposed an absolute liability on the manufacturer, since he could not "reasonably put into the stream of commerce an article which he realized might result in injury to a user," the court answered: "The manner of injury may be so fortuitous and the chances of injury occurring so remote that it is reasonable to sell the product despite the danger. In design cases the utility of the article may be so great, and the change of design necessary to alleviate the danger in question may so impair such utility, that it is reasonable to market the product as it is, even though the possibility of injury exists and was realized at the time of the sale. Again, the cost of change necessary to alleviate the danger in design may be so great that the article would be priced out of the market and no one would buy it even though it was of high utility. Such an article is not dangerously defective despite its having inflicted injury."

Although the court in *Phillips* considered that the jury could be instructed on both seller and consumer oriented tests, the two tests were considered "obviously inconsistent" in Stenberg v. Beatrice Foods Co., 576 P.2d 725 (Mont.1978). Here plaintiff tripped and fell into a moving grain auger, losing his left arm below the elbow. Given the two definitions, "a jury could conclude under the first test that the unshielded auger was not 'unreasonably dangerous' but under the second test that it was 'unreasonably dangerous.' What then was the jury to do?" The court's chief objection to the comment i test was that it seemed to rule out any recovery when the danger was obvious, one that could be clearly contemplated by the consumer. However, some recent decisions allow recovery for the thousands of accidents that occur in the operation of obviously dangerous machinery on the farm or in the factory, or even in the home or on the lawn.

As can be seen, the attempt to define defect in generalized terms or as a matter of law has not been particularly successful. Cases such as *Heaton* have been relatively rare. Today *Heaton* in some jurisdictions would go to the jury on the basis that the fact of the accident itself, with an almost new vehicle, might be proof of a defect originating with the defendant. The jury would be permitted to accept plaintiff's evidence that the speed of the vehicle was normal and that the rock was of a size that might frequently be on the road, thus excluding other causes. It is to be hoped that the large number of cases, involving a great variety of defects that have increasingly gone to the jury on the consumer-expectation issue, are building precedents which clarify the nature of defect. This problem of definition pervades the entire body of products liability law, as will be evident in the following chapters.

2. UNKNOWABLE DEFECTS

Special problems arise in connection with defects which are known to exist in a few batches of otherwise useful products but which are undetectable. That such cases should involve an issue will become clearer after strict liability has been explained in the next chapter. Suffice it to say here that if a retailer is to be held liable for botulism in a can of mushrooms, why should not a hospital be liable for a hepatitis virus in a blood transfusion, or a meat packer or butcher for trichinae in pork? Although cases are still brought, almost invariably in recent years recovery has been denied when plaintiff contracted trichinosis after purchasing avowedly fresh pork. In general, the courts have implied that such pork was simply not defective, since it is generally recognized by the consuming public that fresh pork is fit for eating only after thorough cooking. Where, as in Heubner v. Hunter Packing Co., 375 N.E.2d 873 (Ill.App.1978), plaintiffs alleged that they had "contracted trichinosis after consuming pork which had been 'properly cooked'", the court held that the complaint had been properly dismissed since the allegation was of a "factual impossibility." Moreover, as observed in Tavani v. Swift & Co., 105 A. 55 (Pa.1918), the policy of the federal government has been that any "attempt to inspect all pork for trichinae would result in more danger to the public than no inspection", since the procedure is far from fool-proof and might give the public an unjustified sense of security and cause a neglect of imperative cooking precautions. Although inspection by trichinoscope is now widely used in western Europe, the United States government still does not consider any such inspection feasible in this country. A common argument for liability—that it would promote research—is of little validity here since neither retailers nor packers are equipped to carry on such research, lacking not only the scientific staff necessary but also the electronic apparatus.

Blood or blood products infected with hepatitis virus are unquestionably defective. Here again, the deterrence argument fails, since neither hospitals nor blood banks have the scientific staff, let alone the requisite number of chimpanzees, to carry on such research. So far the efforts of the Bureau of Biologics of the FDA and of the large pharmaceutical houses have produced effective tests for detecting the presence of Hepatitis B virus in blood used for transfusions. Hepatitis A, though it *can* be transmitted through transfusion, is generally associated with inadequate sanitation facilities. A third type of viral hepatitis, unrelated to either A or B, and possibly produced by more than one agent, has been designated as "non-A, non-B hepatitis," and "is responsible," according to an article by FDA scientists, "for 89% of the cases of posttransfusion hepatitis in the United States, now that donor blood

[*12*]

positive for hepatitis B surface antigen   .   .   .
has been excluded." Since it has been determined
that blood from paid donors, with often unrevealed
histories of medical problems or of drug addiction, is
more likely to transmit hepatitis than is blood from
volunteer donors, the FDA now requires that all
blood for transfusion be labeled as to its source.
Blood from paid donors is still absolutely necessary;
and, with the prevailing shortage, a patient may have
little choice. FDA scientists are hopeful that an
effective test will soon be developed for the
remaining undiscovered type of viral infection.

Again, as with trichinosis, actions are still brought
by victims of transfusion-contracted hepatitis, but
with rare success. Actions for strict liability are
now virtually impossible, either because, as in Brody
v. Overlook Hosp., 317 A.2d 392 (N.J.Super.1974), a
court has declared such liability inapplicable to
either a hospital or a blood bank, or because, as in
the overwhelming majority of states (44 by 1975),
especially those where the courts had decided
otherwise, strict liability has been barred by
legislation. There remains an action for negligence,
one which is unlikely to succeed because of the
difficulty in proving, in such a closely regulated
industry, that the defendant has in fact been
negligent. However, in Hoder v. Sayet, 196 So.2d
205 (Fla.App.1967), where an action for negligence
was allowed, there was testimony that the defendant
blood bank had not asked donors the requisite

[*13*]

questions as to their medical histories. It was also found that the hospital might have been negligent in its selection of this particular bank, especially since the hospital pathologist was also the owner-operator of the bank.

3. UNAVOIDABLY UNSAFE PRODUCTS

In a number of hepatitis cases the courts cite comment k to § 402A of the Second Restatement of Torts on "unavoidably unsafe products." The comment would seem to be relevant to products of uniform quality which, because of their high utility in spite of a known risk, are nevertheless deemed free of defect if "properly prepared, and accompanied by proper directions and warnings." The example given is the Pasteur treatment for rabies, which may be the only alternative to death and therefore justified in spite of very common and severe side effects. It is likely that this ominous example will soon be removed, since recent research has developed a rabies vaccine with few side effects. Yet the doctrine may be applicable to a large number of prescription drugs where warnings to doctors include many possible side effects and contraindications. Comment k states that the exemption from strict liability may specifically apply to "many new or experimental drugs." In Gaston v. Hunter, 588 P.2d 326 (Ariz.App.1978), plaintiff alleged that she was injured rather than helped by the drug chymopapain designed to provide an

[14]

alternative to risky back surgery in cases of disk disease. The drug was then under investigation in accordance with the regulations of the FDA before it was to be marketed. It was distributed "to selected physicians [without charge] for use under carefully controlled conditions, with rigorous reporting of the results." The court affirmed a jury verdict for the defendant manufacturer.

The exemption has been extended to oral contraceptives where the danger of thromboembolic disorders has been well publicized and where the FDA, contrary to its usual requirement for prescription drugs, has, since 1970, required the issuance of a warning directly to the patient as well as to the physician. Successful cases have indeed been brought against drug manufacturers for their failure to give timely warning after the first authentic reports of the disorders had been circulated. But, except for a few delayed reactions where the plaintiff alleges injuries from the drug taken before a timely warning was given, these actions seem unlikely in the future.

Just as millions of Americans have decided that the benefit of oral contraceptives outweighs the risk, so have a similar number decided that tobacco belongs in much the same category. A few tobacco cases arose before the surgeon general's warning was required by law to be affixed to all cigarette packages and advertisements. The required warning, along with the present impossibility of removing the carcinogen, would seem to bring tobacco within the purview of comment k as nondefective; although assumption of the risk in defiance of the warning may also account for the lack of litigation today. A somewhat different issue was presented when the risk, unlike those covered by comment k, was unknown and presumably unknowable. The five significant cases involved various theories, with three denying recovery as a matter of law for "unknowable risks" and two allowing the action. In Green v. American Tobacco Co., 409 F.2d 1166 (5th Cir. 1969), after years of litigation including two rehearings with conflicting decisions, a jury verdict for the defendant was affirmed by the federal court of appeals. The jury had decided that the cigarettes used by Mr. Green were nondefective, that is, "reasonably fit and wholesome for human use." Would a jury decide differently today?

CHAPTER II

THE CAUSES OF ACTION

A. HISTORICAL EVOLUTION

Unlike most other areas of the common law, products liability law is almost entirely a 20th-century development. The delay was owing to the barring of actions by a consumer against a remote manufacturer through the doctrine of privity. Such actions now comprise the bulk of products litigation. Before the privity barrier was removed the need for products liability was fully as great as it is today. That was the time when factory machinery tended by little children was left totally unguarded, and government regulation of food products was unknown. Indeed, the very greatness of the need caused the English court in Winterbottom v. Wright, 152 Eng.Rep. 402 (1842), to impose the privity requirement lest the courts be faced with "an infinity of actions."

At least since the 15th century, a seller could be held liable for breach of an implied warranty that his product was merchantable, that is, fit for its ordinary purpose; but the warranty extended only to his immediate vendee. In *Winterbottom* the privity requirement was extended to the negligence action of an injured driver against the supplier of a defective mail coach. This holding left the driver remediless owing to the governmental immunity of the employing postmaster who had contracted for the coaches. *Winterbottom* was generally followed in 19th-century America, although a few exceptions were made for such "inherently dangerous" products as poisons not so labeled or defectively constructed scaffolds. The real departure came in 1916 with the landmark case of MacPherson v. Buick, which will be discussed in the section on the negligence cause of action.

The fifty years after *MacPherson* saw the erosion in many jurisdictions of the privity requirement not only in negligence actions but for breaches of warranty, both express and implied, at least in personal injury cases. Here the emphasis was upon the growth of large-scale manufacturers and their direct appeals to consumers through extensive advertising. Along with elimination of privity came expansive definitions of warranty, as well as a higher standard of care expected of the expert seller.

B. BREACH OF EXPRESS WARRANTY

For a long time an express warranty, besides extending only to an immediate vendee, had to be very explicit, using the word warranty as well as describing exactly what was warranted. Only in recent times has any affirmation of material fact on which a customer relies been considered an express warranty. Thus in Wat Henry Pontiac Co. v.

[18]

Bradley, 210 P.2d 348 (Okl.1949), the seller of a used car expressly warranted its condition when he assured the buyer that "this is a car we know; this is a car I can recommend—it is in A–1 shape." The buyer was "a trained nurse . . . ignorant of the facts", while the "seller was an expert in handling automobiles, having served for a long period of time as an automobile mechanic before becoming a salesman."

In Lane v. C. A. Swanson & Sons, 278 P.2d 723 (Cal.App.1955), a bone from a can of boned chicken processed by the defendant lodged in plaintiff's throat, necessitating surgical treatment. The court held that an express warranty ran from the processor to the consumer, not only because of the label "boned chicken" on the can, but also because of advertisements saying of the chicken: "*No bones*". Plaintiff had relied on both representations in purchasing the food. The court said: "The tendency of the modern cases is to construe liberally in favor of the buyer language used by the seller in making affirmations respecting the quality of his goods and to enlarge the responsibility of the seller to construe every affirmation by him to be a warranty when such construction is at all reasonable. . . . The representation in the newspaper advertisements may be considered a part of the contract of sale."

In the early landmark case of Baxter v. Ford Motor Co., 12 P.2d 409 (Wash.1932), a public

[*19*]

representation was held to be an express warranty made to the consumer. Here the plaintiff had purchased a new automobile in reliance on the manufacturer's advertisements that the windshield was "shatterproof." Soon afterwards a stone did in fact so shatter the windshield that small pieces of glass flew into the plaintiff's eye and destroyed it. Recovery was permitted against the remote manufacturer, not in privity with the plaintiff, without proof that the advertising misrepresentations were either fraudulently or negligently made.

The court observed that the automobile purchaser "was in a position similar to that of the consumer of a wrongly labeled drug, who has bought the same from a retailer, and who has relied upon the manufacturer's representation that the label correctly set forth the contents of the container." Furthermore, where modern methods of advertising by radio, billboards, and printing press have created a large demand for goods, it would "be unjust to recognize a rule that would permit manufacturers . . . to create a demand for their products by representing that they possess qualities which they, in fact, do not possess, and then, because there is no privity of contract existing between the consumer and the manufacturer, deny the consumer the right to recover if damages result from the absence of those qualities, when such absence is not readily noticeable."

The plaintiff also had an action in tort for public misrepresentation, a theory which has since been crystallized in the Second Restatement of Torts, § 402B, that will be discussed later in this chapter.

In Randy Knitwear, Inc. v. American Cyanamid Co., 181 N.E.2d 399 (N.Y.1962), labels attached to the product and "advertisements appearing in trade journals and in direct mail pieces" to potential purchasers were considered express warranties whose breach involved liability on the part of a remote seller. In Seely v. White Motor Co., 403 P.2d 145 (Cal.1965), the warranty consisted of a printed form in the plaintiff's purchase order passed on from the manufacturer to the purchaser through an intermediate dealer. In neither of these cases was any personal injury involved. In *Randy* the plaintiff manufacturer had purchased fabrics treated with defendant's "Cyana", warranted to protect against shrinkage. Children's wear made by the plaintiff from these fabrics shrank and lost shape under ordinary washing. In *Seely* a truck of the defendant's manufacture proved to have such serious "galloping" that it was unusable in plaintiff's work.

If the seller expressly warrants that the product performs in a superior manner, and the purchaser is injured because he relies on that warranty, the seller will be liable even if there is no defect. Thus in Huebert v. Federal Pac. Elec. Co., Inc., 494 P.2d 1210 (Kan.1972), the defendant company warranted

[21]

that the door to a panel containing an electrical switch would not open unless the switch was in the "off" position, with all current shut off. The company was held liable to a repairman who received a severe shock and burns when an interlock device was bypassed by lightning damage. Although plaintiff made no showing of a defect in manufacture, the court held that the "warranty was breached by the existence of electric current in the panel. . . . A manufacturer may by express warranty assume responsibility in connection with its products which extends beyond liability for defects."

In Collins v. Uniroyal, Inc., 315 A.2d 30 (N.J. Super.1973), a tire manufacturer was held liable for breach of its warranty that the tire would survive extraordinary road hazards. It was held that its advertisement, to the effect that one of its tires could safely pick up a nail, or hit a pothole at 70 miles an hour, explained the scope of the "road hazard" warranty. Similarly, in Hansen v. Firestone Tire & Rubber Co., 276 F.2d 254 (6th Cir. 1960), when the tires fell off the wheels, the court held that the company had breached its express warranty that the tires could round sharp curves at 80 miles an hour. No defect was shown—only the failure to perform as warranted. The buyer's negligent acts, "bringing about the revelation that the qualities do not exist, would not defeat recovery." This case is reminiscent of an early

[22]

express warranty case, Bahlman v. Hudson Motor Car Co., 288 N.W. 309 (Mich.1939), where plaintiff in an accident was injured by a jagged seam in a car roof that had been advertised as one of seamless metal. The court found that the "particular construction of the roof of defendant's cars was represented as protection against the consequences of just such careless driving as actually took place. Once the anticipated overturning did occur, it would be illogical to excuse defendant from responsibility for these very consequences."

C. BREACH OF IMPLIED WARRANTY

1. DEFINITION

Implied warranty, as distinct from express warranty, is not dependent upon words of the seller, either oral or written. Rather "a warranty that the goods shall be merchantable is implied in a contract for their sale if the seller is a merchant with respect to goods of that kind." This rule, which is embodied in § 2–314 of the Uniform Commercial Code, has been accepted by every state of the Union, including Louisiana, the only state that has not expressly adopted that Code. The occasional sale by a housewife of her home-baked cookies would not come under the rule; nor would a one-time sale by a factory owner of a piece of used machinery. The warranty long antedates the UCC, appearing in the former Sales Act which, like the UCC, represented a

codification of the case law on the subject. Even
the key part of the UCC definition, that goods "to
be merchantable must be at least such as .   .   .
are fit for the ordinary purposes for which such
goods are used", may have little meaning apart from
its interpretation in the case law. Thus, in the case
cited in the previous chapter, Coffer v. Standard
Brands, Inc., where plaintiff injured his teeth on an
unshelled nut, the court held that defendant had not
breached the implied warranty of merchantability.
Even though the glass bottle revealed only unshelled nuts, the court felt "that the goods were
impliedly warranted to be nuts, a natural incident of
which were the shells." The opinion cites federal
regulations permitting a small percentage of unshelled peanuts per unit of shelled peanuts and
considers that the standard is logically applicable to
unshelled filberts, even though no precise regulation
can be cited. Thus the nuts were "fit for ordinary
purposes and merchantable" under the UCC definition.

In McCabe v. L. K. Liggett Drug Co., 112 N.E.2d
254 (Mass.1953), plaintiff purchased from the defendant retailer a coffee maker in a sealed carton.
When the plaintiff was making coffee according to
instructions, the appliance blew up in her face. The
court reversed the trial court's directed verdict for
the defendant since a jury could find that "the area
of the notches of the filter was inadequate to

provide for the release of the pressure which developed from the boiling water."

A seller, whether merchant or not, may impliedly warrant that goods shall be fit for a particular purpose where he "at the time of contracting has reason to know any particular purpose for which the goods are required and that the buyer is relying on the seller's skill or judgment to select or furnish suitable goods." This U.C.C. § 2–315 was held applicable in Northern Plumbing Supply, Inc. v. Gates, 196 N.W.2d 70 (N.D.1972). There the seller knew that the buyer was purchasing pipe to be used in manufacturing harrow attachments requiring a certain minimal thickness, and the seller was held to have impliedly warranted the pipe to be of sufficient thickness for the attachments and to have breached the warranty in furnishing "standard" pipe of a lesser thickness. Similarly, in Lewis v. Mobil Oil Corp., 438 F.2d 500 (8th Cir. 1971), a buyer recovered for damages to his sawmill caused by the seller's furnishing the wrong kind of oil, where the buyer made it known that he was purchasing oil "specifically for his hydraulic system, not just for a hydraulic system in general," that "he didn't know what kind was necessary," and that he was relying on the seller to select the proper oil.

Although emphasis is placed upon the buyer's reliance upon the seller, such reliance is not precluded when an article is sold under its patent or trade name where the seller makes the selection.

[25]

2. THE EROSION OF THE PRIVITY RULE

In some states privity is still necessary in an action for breach of warranty, especially in a few of the many states where a strict tort action is available against the manufacturer for personal injury or property damage. Most jurisdictions, however, follow the landmark case of Henningsen v. Bloomfield Motors, Inc., 161 A.2d 69 (N.J.1960), where privity was not required. There the plaintiff was injured when an almost new car uncontrollably left the road. In a broadly based opinion the court said that "where the commodities sold are such that if defectively manufactured they will be dangerous to life or limb, then society's interests can only be protected by eliminating the requirement of privity between the maker and his dealers and the reasonably expected ultimate consumer. In that way the burden of losses consequent upon use of defective articles is borne by those who are in a position to either control the danger or make an equitable distribution of losses when they do occur."

The significance of the *Henningsen* principle, and of those cases in other jurisdictions which, up to that time, had been confined to food and products of intimate bodily use, was recognized in comment 3 to UCC § 2–318. That section extends warranties to designated third parties. The comment states that the section "is neutral and is not intended to enlarge or restrict the developing case law on whether the seller's warranties, given to his buyer who resells, extend to other persons in the distributive chain."

In *Henningsen*, however, the injured plaintiff was not the buyer of the car and not therefore "in the distributive chain." The court, then, in addition to eliminating the necessity of establishing privity between buyer and seller, also held that Mrs. Henningsen, whose husband had purchased the car as a present to her, could maintain an action against the remote manufacturer. It held that "an implied warranty of merchantability chargeable to either an automobile manufacturer or a dealer extends to the purchaser of the car, members of his family, and to other persons occupying or using it with his consent. It would be wholly opposed to reality to say that use by such persons is not within the anticipation of parties to such a warranty of reasonable suitability of an automobile for ordinary highway operation. Those persons must be considered within the distributive chain."

In response to this development, the UCC gives in § 2–318 three alternatives involving extensions of the seller's warranty, whether express or implied. The first two alternatives cover only personal injury. Alternative A specifies "any natural person who is in the family or household of his buyer or who is a guest in his home if it is reasonable to expect that such person may use, consume, or be affected by the goods and who is injured in person by breach of the warranty." Alternative B specifies "any natural person who may reasonably be expected to use, consume or be affected by the goods and who is injured in person by breach of the warranty." Alternative C covers all persons, and is not confined to personal injury. Under any of the alternatives a seller "may not exclude or limit the operation of this section with respect to injury to the person." Such warranties as the buyer has, the § 2–318 beneficiary also has.

The majority of the states have enacted Alternative A. This relatively restrictive requirement was bound to cause considerable dissatisfaction. In addition, the UCC specifically provides that implied warranties, either of merchantability or of fitness, can be excluded or modified in the contract of sale. *Henningsen* held that the particular disclaimer or limitation of remedy in the standard automobile contract was invalid partly because of the unequal bargaining position of the parties, with the buyer having no choice. The bearing of such disclaimers upon products liability cannot be fully understood without some consideration of strict tort liability. The discussion of disclaimers will therefore be postponed to Chapter 4.

D. NEGLIGENCE

Although one court eliminated the privity requirement in a food warranty case as early as 1913, the most significant case for the future development of products liability came three years later when Justice Cardozo opened the way for consumer actions against negligent manufacturers of any product. In MacPherson v. Buick Motor Co., 111 N.E. 1050 (N.Y.1916), it was held that an action in negligence could be maintained against a remote manufacturer of an automobile with a defectively made wheel that broke, causing injury to the plaintiff. The court found that the category of inherently dangerous products "is not limited to poisons, explosives, and things . . . which in their normal operation are implements of destruction." Rather, if "the nature of a thing is such that it is reasonably certain to place life and limb in peril when negligently made, it is then a thing of danger." *Winterbottom* was essentially overruled when the court further stated: "If to the element of danger there is added knowledge that the thing will be used by persons other than the purchaser, and used without new tests, then, irrespective of contract, the manufacturer of this thing of danger is under a duty to make it carefully." The presence of a sale does not control the duty. "We have put aside the notion that the duty to safeguard life and limb, when the consequences of negligence may be foreseen, grows out of contract and nothing else. We have put the source of the obligation where it ought to be. We have put its source in the law."

MacPherson has been so widely followed that the issue of privity is no longer raised in personal injury cases involving negligence allegations.

[*29*]

Negligence in products cases is most likely to involve a failure to warn or to warn adequately of foreseeable dangers, a failure to fully inspect or test, a failure in either design or production to comply with standards imposed by law or to live up to the customary standards of the industry. Liability for negligence, however, is not limited to such situations, but is determined the same way in products cases as in any other case where the defendant has failed to use due care. If defendant either foresaw or should have foreseen that the plaintiff might be injured by his negligent act or omission, then he is liable to the plaintiff who is in fact so injured.

Proof of negligence, however, has presented special difficulties in products cases. A manufacturer's entire process, from initial design to the final labeling and packaging of his product, is peculiarly within his control. At relatively little expense he can produce expert witnesses from among his own employees or consultants to show that his manufacturing and testing procedures are so thorough that no bottle from his soft drink plant could possibly explode unless misused by others, or that his washing and sterilizing procedures are such that no mouse could possibly survive in either a recognizable or an unhealthy form in the contents of the bottle. Yet the bottle *did* explode after normal handling, or there *was* a mouse in the bottle when it was first opened. Where plaintiff cannot, in fact, show any

[*30*]

specific acts of negligence, the court may consider an instruction on res ipsa loquitur appropriate. Thus in Escola v. Coca-Cola Bottling Co. of Fresno, 150 P.2d 436 (Cal.1944), where a waitress was severely injured when a bottle exploded in her hand, the court affirmed a judgment for the plaintiff in spite of defendant's evidence of due care. The jury had been instructed that res ipsa was applicable if "(1) defendant had exclusive control of the thing causing the injury and (2) the accident is of such a nature that it ordinarily would not occur in the absence of negligence by the defendant." To show exclusive control plaintiff had only to show proper handling since it left the defendant's hands. In a concurring opinion, Justice Traynor took the opportunity to state that in such a case the manufacturer's negligence should no longer be singled out as the basis of a plaintiff's right to recover. He then reviewed the basic policy reasons for imposing a strict liability in tort.

E. STRICT TORT

1. BASIC POLICY

In *Escola*, Justice Traynor stated that "public policy demands that responsibility be fixed wherever it will most effectively reduce the hazards to life and health inherent in defective products that reach the market. It is evident that the manufacturer can

[*31*]

anticipate some hazards and guard against the recurrence of others, as the public cannot. . . . The cost of an injury and the loss of time or health may be an overwhelming misfortune to the person injured, and a needless one, for the risk of injury can be insured by the manufacturer and distributed among the public as a cost of doing business." After pointing out the relative ease with which a manufacturer can dispel any inference of negligence, Justice Traynor observed that in leaving to a jury the decision as to "whether the inference has been dispelled, regardless of the evidence against it, the negligence rule approaches the rule of strict liability. It is needlessly circuitous to make negligence the basis of recovery and impose what is in reality liability without negligence." He observed that a state statute forbidding the adulteration of food imposed a criminal liability without fault; and that the retailer, again without fault, was absolutely liable to his customer for breach of implied warranty. Of course the retailer may "recoup any losses by means of the warranty of safety attending the wholesaler's or manufacturer's sale to him. Such a procedure, however, is needlessly circuitous and engenders wasteful litigation. Much would be gained if the injured person could base his action directly on the manufacturer's warranty." Such a warranty should be "severed from the contract of sale between the dealer and the consumer and based on the law of torts. Warranties are not necessarily rights arising under a contract. An action on the warranty was, in its origin, a pure action of tort."

The doctrine which Justice Traynor thus justified in so comprehensive a way was not adopted by the California court until almost twenty years later. In Greenman v. Yuba Power Products, Inc., 377 P.2d 897 (Cal.1963), Justice Traynor spoke for the court. There the plaintiff's wife purchased a combination power tool from the defendant retailer and gave it to her husband. Sometime later, when plaintiff was using the tool as a lathe for turning a large piece of wood to be made into a chalice, the wood flew out of the machine and struck him on the forehead inflicting serious injuries. He brought an action for damages against both the retailer and the manufacturer of the power tool, alleging negligence and breach of warranty in selling a product with inadequate set screws which, had they been properly designed, would have prevented the accident.

The appellate court sustained the trial court's judgment that the manufacturer had breached express warranties contained in a sales brochure. "Moreover," said the court, "to impose strict liability on the manufacturer under the circumstances of this case, it was not necessary for plaintiff to establish an express warranty. . . . A manufacturer is strictly liable in tort when an article he places on the market, knowing that it is to be used without inspection for defects, proves to have a defect that causes injury to a human being."

In reaching this result, the court reviewed cases where a manufacturer was held strictly liable to a remote purchaser for breach of implied warranty. It criticized the warranty basis for these decisions noting that: "the abandonment of the requirement of a contract between them, the recognition that the liability is not assumed by agreement but imposed by law . . . and the refusal to permit the manufacturer to define the scope of its own responsibility for defective products . . . make clear that the liability is not one governed by the law of contract warranties but by the law of strict liability in tort.

" . . . The purpose of such liability is to insure that the costs of injuries resulting from defective products are borne by the manufacturers that put such products on the market rather than by the injured persons who are powerless to protect themselves. Sales warranties serve this purpose fitfully at best."

In the interests of the injured consumer, the California court thus swept aside all of the impediments of a warranty action, including the requirement of notice of breach. By removing products liability from the confines of sales law, *Greenman* left other courts free to fashion the law in this area as justice might require. As a result, tort law has developed with steadily increasing emphasis on strict liability theory independent of warranty.

[*34*]

In 1965 the American Law Institute published the Second Restatement of Torts, § 402A, which has been widely adopted by the courts as a description of the rules of strict tort liability. The section provides as follows:

(1) One who sells any product in a defective condition unreasonably dangerous to the user or consumer or to his property is subject to liability for physical harm thereby caused to the ultimate user or consumer, or to his property, if

(a) the seller is engaged in the business of selling such a product, and

(b) it is expected to and does reach the user or consumer without substantial change in the condition in which it is sold.

(2) The rule stated in Subsection (1) applies although

(a) the seller has exercised all possible care in the preparation and sale of his product, and

(b) the user or consumer has not bought the product from or entered into any contractual relation with the seller.

The relationship of this rule to warranty theory is explained in comment m to § 402A of the Second Restatement of Torts: "There is nothing in this Section which would prevent any court from treating the rule stated as a matter of warranty to

[*35*]

the user or consumer. But if this is done, it should be recognized and understood that the warranty is a very different kind of warranty from those usually found in the sale of goods, and that it is not subject to the various contract rules which have grown up to surround such sales."

Comment f to § 402A defines the "seller" who may be liable. Such a seller may not be engaged primarily in the sale of the product involved: he may be a motion picture operator who sells popcorn or ice cream. On the other hand, the section is not intended to apply to the occasional seller of a product, such as the housewife who "sells to her neighbor a jar of jam or a pound of sugar." The section's scope is thus analogous to UCC § 2–314, limiting the implied warranty of merchantability to sellers who deal in such goods. The Restatement section is "also not intended to apply to sales of the stock of merchants out of the usual course of business, such as execution sales, bankruptcy sales, bulk sales, and the like." Such sellers do not have "the special responsibility for the safety of the public undertaken by one who enters into the business of supplying human beings with products which may endanger the safety of their persons and property."

Questions have been raised as to whether recovery under the Second Restatement § 402A conflicts with the UCC especially in view of the disallowance of disclaimers and of the notice requirement in comment m.   As will be seen in the next chapter, some courts have considered that this problem is avoided when they limit tort recovery to personal injury and property damage as opposed to economic loss.   Be that as it may, an overwhelming number of courts have adopted § 402A without eliciting an unfavorable response from their legislatures.   In recent years a number of states have indeed passed product liability statutes; but these generally do not quarrel with the fundamental doctrine of strict tort liability, although they may limit its application by barring any such action after a certain number of years, often from the date of sale, or by establishing certain presumptions in favor of the manufacturer. The statutes exempting hospitals and blood banks from strict liability for hepatitis-infected blood do not question the principle as applied to other defendants.   Many of the statutes provide that the furnishing of blood for transfusion is not the selling of a product at all but the provision of a service.

Massachusetts has adopted strict tort liability through amendments to its commercial code, thus deviating from the UCC.   These amendments include the abolition of the requirement of privity, and prohibition of any disclaimer of the implied warranty of merchantability.   In Back v. Wickes Corp., 378 N.E.2d 964 (Mass.1978), the court, after summarizing these amendments, states: "The Legislature has made the Massachusetts law of warranty congruent in nearly all respects with the principles

[*37*]

expressed in Restatement (Second) of Torts § 402A (1965). For this reason, we find the strict liability cases of other jurisdictions to be a useful supplement to our own warranty case law."

Alabama has also drastically amended its commercial code to conform with much of the wording of § 402A and its comments. Its supreme court, however, held in Atkins v. American Motors Corp., 335 So.2d 134 (Ala.1976), that Alabama had not adopted a no-fault concept but rather one of negligence per se, where "the practical distinction, then, between our holding and the Restatement is that our ●ding will allow certain affirmative defenses, not recognized by the Restatement's no-fault concept of liability." The court deemed it "appropriate to reemphasize that our retention of the fault concept is to be treated in the context of a defective condition, which renders the product unreasonably dangerous or unsafe when put to its intended use, rather than in the context of traditional notions of negligence law." Perhaps this interpretation of the Alabama statutory amendments does not differ greatly from that of Wisconsin's interpretation of § 402A where the court held the selling of an injury-causing product to be a form of negligence per se. In that state, the affirmative defenses, as modified by a comparative negligence statute, are allowed. This problem will be discussed further in Chapter 7.

2. PUBLIC MISREPRESENTATION

Sellers have been held liable in strict tort when their product has failed to conform with their public representations of its quality. Sec. 402B of the Second Restatement of Torts reads:

> One engaged in the business of selling chattels who, by advertising, labels, or otherwise, makes to the public a misrepresentation of a material fact concerning the character or quality of a chattel sold by him is subject to liability for physical harm to a consumer of the chattel caused by justifiable reliance upon the misrepresentation, even though
>
> (a) it is not made fraudulently or negligently, and
>
> (b) the consumer has not bought the chattel from or entered into any contractual relation with the seller.

As in the case of liability under § 402A, and liability for breach of the warranty of merchantability, a plaintiff must show that the defendant was "in the business of selling chattels" to establish liability under § 402B. Similarly, as indicated in comment e, the section covers not only manufacturers but also "wholesalers, retailers, and other distributors" of a product.

Comment h states that the rule of the section "is limited to misrepresentations which are made by the seller to the public at large. . . . The form of

[*39*]

the representation is not important. It may be made by public advertising in newspapers or television, by literature distributed to the public through dealers, by labels on the product sold, or leaflets accompanying it, or in any other manner, whether it be oral or written." On the other hand, according to a caveat to the section as a whole, the Institute "expresses no opinion as to whether the rule stated in this Section may apply (1) where the representation is not made to the public, but to an individual."

It seems clear that no sharp line can be drawn between strict liability in tort and that for breach of express warranty in cases of public misrepresentation.

The landmark case in this area, Baxter v. Ford Motor Co., discussed above, was so decided that it is unclear whether the chief grounds for liability was express warranty or the more generalized theory that was later stated in § 402B. Only a few courts have had occasion to adopt the section, although it would seem that plaintiff's recovery, generally favored by the courts in products cases, would thereby be facilitated. In these actions the misrepresentation is usually made before the product left the seller's hands, although a post-sale misrepresentation may also be a sufficient basis for liability. The difficulty has been in proving that plaintiff's injury was caused by his reliance upon the misrepresentation, especially where the plaintiff was not the buyer. Proof of reliance is not required in § 402A actions. Thus in Lonzrick v. Republic Steel Corp., 218 N.E.2d 185 (Ohio 1966), a § 402A action, where an iron worker was injured by a collapsing steel joint, the court said: "The fact that the plaintiff saw the advertisement is a sound basis for recovery; *but the fact that he did not read an advertisement is not a sound basis for denying recovery*" (emphasis by the court).

In Hauter v. Zogarts, 534 P.2d 377 (Cal.1975), the defendant manufacturer of a "Golfing Gizmo" was held liable on both § 402B and express warranty grounds when plaintiff was injured while he was using the device in the intended way for improving his game. After he hit a ball attached indirectly to an elastic cord, the ball sprang back, hitting the minor plaintiff in the temple and seriously injuring him. Defendant had advertised: "COMPLETELY SAFE BALL WILL NOT HIT PLAYER." Plaintiff's expert testified that the device was in fact a "major hazard."

In Crocker v. Winthrop Laboratories, Div. of Sterling Drug, Inc., 514 S.W.2d 429 (Tex.1974), plaintiff's decedent became fatally addicted to "Talwin", a pain-relieving drug "which has no adverse side effects on the great majority of people who use it." Since the company's representatives had assured doctors of the drug's nonaddictive qualities, defendant company could be liable under §

402B. "Whatever the danger and state of medical knowledge, and however rare the susceptibility of the user, when the drug company positively and specifically represents its product to be free and safe from all dangers of addiction, and when the treating physician relies upon that representation, the drug company is liable when the representation proves to be false and harm results."

In Klages v. General Ordnance Equipment Corp., 367 A.2d 304 (Pa.Super.1976), a mace weapon failed to operate as a motel's night auditor attempted to use it to protect himself against robbers who then attacked him. The court held the defendant manufacturer liable under § 402B. In its sales literature, which had induced the auditor to provide himself with the weapon, the defendant had advertised that it effected "*instantaneous incapacitation.* . . . It will *instantly stop and subdue* entire groups," and so on.

In Winkler v. American Safety Equipment Corp., 604 P.2d 693 (Colo.App.1979), a policeman had bought from his department a helmet which had been discarded because of its appearance. It had been bought by the Denver Police Department for use in riot control, but was "originally packaged in a carton which depicted a motorcyclist wearing the seller's helmet." In reliance upon this picture, Winkler used the helmet when riding his cycle. When he collided with a truck the helmet, which had been designed for quick release, came off his head with

[42]

resultant severe injuries. Citing § 402B, the court held that "a misrepresentation has been made to the public when a seller, as part of his merchandising program, communicates the misrepresentation to potential purchasers or users of his product, even when they constitute only a small or a select portion of the consuming public."

F. NEGLIGENT MISREPRESENTATION

Aside from the strict liability of § 402B, the long-recognized tort of negligent misrepresentation has been useful in some products cases. In Pabon v. Hackensack Auto Sales, Inc., 164 A.2d 773 (N.J. Super.1960), plaintiff was injured when, in spite of the dealer's assurances that no problem existed, the steering gear of his new car finally locked and caused a crash. In response to plaintiff's prior complaints because of a "chopping" or "clicking" in the gear, the dealer had told him he had no cause for worry—"It'll wear out." The court said: "Negligence may be inferred not only from Hackensack's failure or refusal to repair or even to examine the reported defect, but also from its representation to Alphonse that the steering deficiency was normal and should cause him no concern. A false statement negligently made, and on which justifiable reliance is placed, may be the basis for the recovery of damages for injury sustained as a consequence of such reliance. . . . There must be knowledge, or reason to know, on the part of the

[*43*]

speaker that the information is desired for a serious purpose, that the seeker of the information intends to rely upon it, and that if the information or opinion is false or erroneous, the relying party will be injured in person or property."

Successful actions for negligent misrepresentation have been brought against certifiers and testers of products, the latter when no semblance of privity existed between the consumer and a testing company employed by the manufacturer of a fire extinguisher. These cases will be discussed more fully in the next chapter.

G. RECKLESS AND WANTON MISCONDUCT

In some products actions, punitive damages have been allowed on the theory that little difference exists between those torts recognized as intentional and conduct that is in reckless disregard of the safety of others. Doubtless the most publicized of these cases was one of the many against Ford for its placement of the Pinto gas tank so that fires entering the passenger compartment were frequent after rear-end collisions. In Grimshaw v. Ford Motor Co., No. 19–77–61 (Super.Ct., Orange Cty., Cal.), plaintiff was awarded $3,500,000 in punitive damages even after a drastic remittitur of the jury award by the trial judge.

In Sturm, Ruger & Co., Inc. v. Day, 594 P.2d 38 (Alaska 1979), the court said: "The evidence presented at trial indicated that top officials at Sturm, Ruger knew that the safety and loading notches of their single action revolver presented a danger of accidental discharge because of the propensity of the engaging middle parts to fail or break. The evidence also reflects knowledge on the part of Sturm, Ruger management that serious injuries had resulted from this deficiency, coupled with procrastination in changing the basic design, at an increased cost of $1.93 per gun. Because we find that fair-minded jurors in the exercise of reasonable judgment could differ as to whether Sturm, Ruger's actions amounted to reckless indifference to the rights of others, and conscious action in deliberate disregard of them, thereby evidencing a state of mind which could justify the imposition of punitive damages, we will not upset the jury's conclusions that punitive damages were warranted."

In Gillham v. Admiral Corp., 523 F.2d 102 (6th Cir. 1975), plaintiff was severely injured when a fire broke out in her television set. The defendant manufacturer was fully aware at the time of manufacture that the transformers in all sets of the same model were partly made of paper and wax materials that were fire-hazardous. "Nevertheless, Admiral did not warn prospective purchasers or owners of the danger despite the steady flow of reported fires originating in Admiral color television sets. Nor did Admiral redesign this model or stop marketing it during the period in question." Under

[45]

these circumstances the court held that the jury could find the malice necessary for an award of punitive damages.

Damages for the intentional infliction of emotional distress were allowed in Lemaldi v. De Tomaso of America, Inc., 383 A.2d 1220 (N.J.Super.1978). Here plaintiff had paid $12,000 for a car made by one of Ford's foreign divisions. He experienced constant difficulties with the car, such as the air conditioning unit falling out in the street, the seat tearing under normal use, and severe mechanical failures. "There was unrebutted proof of two years in which plaintiff's $12,000 dream car became a nightmare of expense and breakdown. Against this background the jury reasonably could have determined that when Ford regional personnel, aware of plaintiff's problems with the Pantera's Ford-caused defects, failed to take or advise him of corrective action or to honor his claims, and responded to Lemaldi varyingly from open hostility to inattention; in the already exasperating circumstances such conduct would aggravate an ordinary man to the point of 'mental anguish.' "

CHAPTER III

THE PARTIES

A. SELLERS OF CHATTELS AS DEFENDANTS

1. ASSEMBLERS AND COMPONENT PART MANUFACTURERS

In Suvada v. White Motor Co., 210 N.E.2d 182 (Ill.1965), the court held that defendant Bendix-Westinghouse Automotive Air Brake Company could be strictly liable in tort for a defective brake system installed in a tractor by White Motor Company. White had made no change in the brake system. Plaintiffs also had a cause of action against White.

That the assembler is the more likely defendant is shown by numerous cases. For example, in Ford Motor Co. v. Mathis, 322 F.2d 267 (5th Cir. 1963), it was held that where a manufacturer assembles and sells a product as his own, he may be vicariously liable for the negligence of a component-part manufacturer, even when, in the case of a defective dimmer switch, it was established that Ford "could not have discovered [the defect by] reasonable inspection."

In Pabon v. Hackensack Auto Sales, Inc., 164 A.2d 773 (N.J.Super.1960), a 19-year-old driver was injured when a steering wheel of a Ford car locked, allegedly because of a defect in a ball-bearing assembly manufactured by the New Departure Company—a defect which could not have been discovered except by a destructive test. Therefore, neither Ford nor the dealer, Hackensack, was negligent. It was held, however, that plaintiffs had a cause of action against both Hackensack and Ford for breach of implied warranty.

Liability of the manufacturer has been extended to situations where the unassembled product may have left the manufacturer's hands in a nondefective condition, and a defect occurs as the result of improper assembly by the distributor. Thus in Vandermark v. Ford Motor Co., 391 P.2d 168 (Cal.1964), the plaintiff, Vandermark, was injured as a result of an accident caused by a defective master cylinder in his new automobile. The plaintiff sued both the distributor of the car, Maywood Bell, and the manufacturer, Ford Motor Company. Ford contended "that it should not be held liable for negligence in manufacturing the car or strictly liable in tort for placing it on the market without proof that the car was defective when Ford relinquished control over it." Ford pointed out that in this case "the car passed through two other authorized Ford dealers before it was sold to Maywood Bell and that Maywood Bell removed the power steering unit before selling the car to Vandermark." These circumstances were insufficient to release Ford from liability. The rules of strict liability "focus responsibility for defects, whether negligently or nonnegligently caused, on the manufacturer of the completed product, and they apply regardless of what part of the manufacturing process the manufacturer chooses to delegate to third parties. . . . Since Ford, as the manufacturer of the completed product, cannot delegate its duty to have its cars delivered to the ultimate purchaser free from dangerous defects, it cannot escape liability on the ground that the defect in Vandermark's car may have been caused by something one of its authorized dealers did or failed to do."

However, in Verge v. Ford Motor Co., 581 F.2d 384 (3d Cir. 1978), Ford was held not liable to the plaintiff worker who was pinned between a garbage can and a garbage truck which had no warning device when put into reverse gear. Ford had built the cab and chassis and then sold it to another manufacturer who converted it into a garbage truck. Any liability for failure to install a warning device in the cab was that of the converting manufacturer, since the evidence was "that it would not be feasible to install the safety device in question on all F-700 trucks. Furthermore, there was no evidence that it would be feasible for Ford to determine which trucks were to be converted for refuse collection use," where the truck was a multipurpose vehicle.

In Union Supply Co. v. Pust, 583 P.2d 276 (Colo.1978), two manufacturers were involved in the design and assembling of an elaborate conveyer

[*49*]

system. Plaintiff's arm and part of his shoulder had to be amputated after his arm had been caught in the "nip point" of the conveyor and pulled in. If the jury should find the product defective in the lack of safety guards and in having no provision for an automatic cleaning device, then the manufacturers of the parts lacking these safety devices, as well as the final assembler, could be found liable. "We follow the majority view that a manufacturer of component parts may be held strictly liable for injuries to a consumer caused by design defects in the component parts when they are expected to and do reach the consumer without substantial change in condition." The court did not mean that the component part must not undergo any change, since in this case the purchaser added many elements in its final assembly at the installation site. "The present case reaches further because it involves alleged design defects in parts that may have undergone *some change* before reaching the consumer."

2. SUCCESSOR CORPORATIONS

Problems arise in connection with successor corporations where the original manufacturer of a defective machine is no longer in existence at the time of plaintiff's injury, and where the buying corporation purchased the assets of the selling corporation for cash. In general, courts in products cases have held the successor liable only if it falls

under one of four exceptions in corporation law to
the usual nonliability. Two of these exceptions, that
the liability must have been expressly assumed, or
that the purchase of assets was for the purpose of
fraudulently evading such liabilities, have been of
little significance in products cases. The applicable
exceptions have been (1) where a de facto merger
took place, or (2) where the successor in reality
simply continues the business of the original
corporation, using the same staff, processes, customers, and so forth. However, in Ray v. Alad
Corp., 560 P.2d 3 (Cal.1977), the court dispensed
with any necessity to prove that the successor fell
within any of the four exceptions. Instead, it
announced a products liability rule to be applied in
that case where the corporation did not fall within
any of the exceptions. It explained: "Justification
for imposing strict liability upon a *successor* to a
manufacturer under the circumstances here presented rests upon (1) the virtual destruction of the
plaintiff's remedies against the original manufacturer caused by the successor's acquisition of the
business, (2) the successor's ability to assume the
original manufacturer's risk-spreading role, and (3)
the fairness of requiring the successor to assume a
responsibility for defective products that was a
burden necessarily attached to the original manufacturer's good will being enjoyed by the successor in
the continued operation of the business."

The Supreme Court of Michigan handed down a similar decision; but whether courts generally will permit an engrafting of a products liability exception on the corporation law remains uncertain. A California decision, however, cannot be ignored, in view of the part such decisions have played in the past in setting products liability precedents that have been widely followed.

3. DISTRIBUTORS AND WHOLESALERS

It should be clear from the very definitions of strict tort and warranty liability that these causes of action apply to all sellers in the chain of distribution once the defect has arisen. Sometimes, as in the case of nondelegable duties, a manufacturer may be liable even for a defect arising later in the chain. But a component part manufacturer would normally not be liable for a defect that arose in assembly. The assembler, the packer, the wholesaler or jobber, and the retailer will all be liable for a defective component part, with an action over against the one primarily responsible for the defect.

In Canifax v. Hercules Powder Co., 46 Cal.Rptr. 552 (Cal.App.1965), summary judgment for the defendant wholesaler was reversed. Although upon trial the issue would be the duty to warn, the court here decided that, under § 402A, Hercules was a seller of dynamite fuses and therefore subject to strict liability should they prove defective. Hercules did not manufacture fuses, not did it ship to the customer. Rather, it took orders for fuses which were then passed on to the manufacturer who shipped directly to the customer. Hercules then billed the customer and paid the manufacturer's invoice.

It has been generally held, as in Slavin v. Francis H. Leggett & Co., 177 A. 120 (N.J.1935), that where a distributor markets a product under its own name, omitting that of its supplier, such a distributor is marketing the product as its own and can be held "to have made itself responsible for the acts of the undisclosed" manufacturer or packer.

Actions against wholesalers, although unquestionably allowed either for negligence or for strict liability, are relatively rare except for numerous actions against distributors of foreign cars in the United States. Actions against distributors of other foreign products, such as fabrics that prove highly flammable, have also been brought.

4. RETAILERS OF NEW GOODS

As was shown in the previous chapter, actions have been brought against retailers for negligent misrepresentation. Actions have also been brought for negligent inspection, although courts have differed as to the extent of the retailer's duty in this regard. The majority rule, as expressed in § 402 of The Second Restatement of Torts, is that he is not liable for failure to discover a dangerous feature unless he knows or "has reason to know" of the danger. A minority holds the retailer to a duty to discover and disclose defects which can be found by inspection alone. In perhaps all jurisdictions, if the retailer is more than a mere conduit for the manufacturer—if he is, say, an automobile dealer or an installer as well as a seller of appliances—he is liable on negligence grounds for any reasonably discoverable defects. He is not required to dismantle the product to discover concealed defects, or to conduct scientific tests beyond those for ordinary functioning.

In Bower v. Corbell, 408 P.2d 307 (Okla.1965), the blade of a power saw which the defendant retailer had assembled and installed for plaintiff's husband came loose and struck plaintiff, causing her severe and permanent head and back injuries. Her husband was using the newly purchased saw in the usual fashion to cut logs. The saw was defective in that the setscrews for holding the blade in position had no recesses into which they could fit, thus making it impossible to tighten them adequately. The court affirmed a judgment for the plaintiff grounded upon negligent inspection, and supported the majority rule when it stated: "Where a vendor supplies a purchaser with a device or instrumentality, and in exercise of ordinary care knows or should know if same is defective it will be dangerous to all who come in contact therewith during use for the purpose for which intended, the vendor owes a duty to ascertain the condition of the instrumentality by exercising reasonable care to see that it is safe for the use for which intended."

In many, perhaps most, cases against retailers, the question of negligent inspection is academic, since the defendant will be liable either on strict tort grounds or for breach of warranty. His recourse will be an action over against the manufacturer or distributor responsible for the defect. Thus in Vlases v. Montgomery Ward & Co., 377 F.2d 846 (3d Cir. 1967), 2,000 one-day-old chicks sold to the plaintiff were infected with avian leukosis, a disease undetectable by the retailer. The court held that the undetectability was relevant only to a negligence action, not to an action for breach of warranty. It observed: "The entire purpose behind the implied warranty sections of the Code is to hold the seller responsible when inferior goods are passed along to the unsuspecting buyer. What the Code requires is not evidence that the defects should or could have been uncovered by the seller but only that the goods upon delivery were not of a merchantable quality or fit for their particular purpose."

In Pierce v. Liberty Furniture Co., 233 S.E.2d 33 (Ga.App.1977), plaintiff was injured when a porch swing set collapsed as she first sat upon it after assembling. The kit had been purchased in a sealed package, containing also an oak chair and hardware, from the defendant retailer Liberty. The hardware was bought by defendant Gore from another company and inserted in the kit in its own closed, plastic container. The court held that the retailer was not liable for negligence in failing to inspect the hardware for latent defects, but could be found liable for breach of the implied warranty of merchantability since with the adoption of the UCC Georgia no longer held to the doctrine of exempting retailers from liability for defective goods sold in sealed containers. As to Gore, it could be held liable as a manufacturer, since it "sold the defective hardware as a part of a kit under its own name and trademark."

Although the case involved a car dealer, the court in Vandermark v. Ford Motor Co., 391 P.2d 168 (Cal.1964), gave policy reasons for imposing strict tort liability upon all types of retailers. "Retailers . . . are an integral part of the overall producing and marketing enterprise that should bear the cost of injuries resulting from defective products. In some cases the retailer may be the only member of that enterprise reasonably available to the injured plaintiff. In other cases the retailer himself may play a substantial part in insuring that the product is safe or may be in a position to exert pressure on the manufacturer to that end; the retailer's strict liability thus serves as an added incentive to safety. Strict liability on the manufacturer and retailer alike affords maximum protection to the injured plaintiff and works no injustice to the defendants, for they can adjust the costs of such protection between them in the course of their continuing business relationship."

In Shoppers World v. Villarreal, 518 S.W.2d 913 (Tex.Civ.App.1975), plaintiff slipped on some liquid soap that leaked from a bottle just after she had placed it in her shopping cart. The fall necessitated back surgery. It was stipulated that the slit in the bottle existed at the time Mrs. Villarreal picked it off the shelf, which the court regarded as the time of sale. Although the defendant was not liable for negligence since it had no notice of the defect, it was liable under § 402A since the defect existed at the time of "sale" and caused injury to the plaintiff. In some other jurisdictions neither a strict tort nor a breach of warranty action would be allowed for injuries in self-service stores occurring before the customer pays for her selection. An increasing number of jurisdictions, however, are allowing recovery on warranty grounds. Many of the cases involve exploding bottles, often causing very serious injuries, such as the loss of an eye.

As indicated in *Pierce*, some jurisdictions, either by court decision or more frequently by recent products liability statutes, have exempted the retailer from strict liability when the product reaches it in a sealed container which is not to be disturbed before final sale. Not all courts have considered that the UCC prohibits this exception. The UCC also provides for the exclusion or modification of an implied warranty; but such disclaimers are hardly practicable in the sale of ordinary consumer goods for immediate consumption, as opposed to durable goods such as washing machines and cars.

Restauranteurs have generally been held liable on the same grounds as retailers—negligence, breach of warranty, or strict tort.

5. USED GOODS DEALERS

Dealers in used goods may generally be held liable on negligence grounds. This is true even for one not in the business of selling, as in Bevard v. Ajax Mfg. Co., 473 F.Supp. 35 (E.D.Mich.1979), where it was held that a one-time seller of a used machine had a duty of care. Here it was alleged that safety features were lacking on the press with resultant injury to the operator. The negligence issue was for the jury. As for those in the business of selling used goods, they will generally be liable for failure to make a reasonable inspection or for failure to test for defects affecting safety, or for negligent repair or servicing of a product, especially a vehicle, so as to endanger others. Courts have, however, differed on strict liability for defects. Cases attempting to impose such liability, either in tort or for breach of warranty, have differed both on their facts and in their holdings. In Realmuto v. Straub Motors, Inc., 322 A.2d 440 (N.J.1974), where an accelerator stuck owing to a carburetor defectively installed by the used car dealer, the court held strict liability in tort applicable. It observed that the policy reasons for strict tort might not be "fully applicable to the seller of a used chattel—for example, the buyer cannot be said to expect the same quality and durability in a used car as in a new one and so the used car dealer should not be held to the same strict liability as the seller of new automobiles. We need not reach that broad question here, for we are of the view that a used car dealer ought to be subject to strict liability in tort with respect to a mishap resulting from any defective work, repairs or replacements he has done or made on the vehicle before the sale and we so hold."

Where there was no allegation that the defects in the braking system were created by the used car dealer, the Illinois Supreme Court in Peterson v. Lou Bachrodt Chevrolet Co., 329 N.E.2d 785 (Ill. 1975), refused to impose strict liability, since the dealer would then "in effect become an insurer against defects which had come into existence after the chain of distribution was completed, and while the product was in the control of one or more consumers." Does the used car dealer undertake repairs before sale at his peril?

In Hovenden v. Tenbush, 529 S.W.2d 302 (Tex. Civ.App.1975), the walls of a building made with used bricks began to deteriorate soon after completion, with the "shedding" of the mortar. The court, in holding that the defendant seller of the bricks might be strictly liable, found "nothing in

Sec. 402A, or in the accompanying comments, which suggests that the rule there announced is not applicable to dealers in used products. The liability is imposed on the seller of 'any product.'"

In Ortiz v. Farrell Co., Div. of U. S. M. Corp., 407 A.2d 1290 (N.J.Super.1979), summary judgment was denied a broker, or intermediate handler, of used machinery who had sold a pelletizer without essential safety devices. Plaintiff, an employee of the ultimate purchaser, was injured when the pelletizer was "accidentally started while he was cleaning its chamber through an unprotected porthole." The court ruled that "vendors of used products may also be held to strict liability." The fact that defendant expected subsequent purchasers to correct the safety defects would not relieve it of liability. The court found "nothing in the moving papers to support defendant's basis for the expectation, other than the skill and knowledge of the subsequent purchasers, a subjective determination not compelled by this record on summary judgment motion. Perhaps such expectation might be justified in many cases if suitable warning is given upon sale or transfer."

In Worthey v. Specialty Foam Products, Inc., 591 S.W.2d 145 (Mo.App.1979), a dealer was held to have breached an implied warranty in the sale of a used truck. The court observed that the UCC makes no distinction between used and new goods. Consequential damages were also allowed when the truck broke down on the first long trip. The court said the "overwhelming weight of authority" supports application of implied warranties "to the sale of used or second-hand cars and trucks."

B. PLAINTIFFS OTHER THAN BUYERS

1. EMPLOYEES AND OTHER USERS

Even if a state has adopted the most restrictive of the three privity alternatives of the UCC, an action in strict tort, as defined in the Second Restatement § 402A, can be maintained by any person who might reasonably be expected to use or consume the product and who is injured thereby. Very frequent are actions against manufacturers of machines or equipment by employees of an industrial purchaser. These will be discussed in the chapters on design and warning defects.

2. RESCUERS

Recovery was allowed for breach of implied warranty to rescuers in Guarino v. Mine Safety Appliance Co., 255 N.E.2d 173 (N.Y.1969). Here an engineer died in a sewer 30 or 40 feet below ground when the protective mask manufactured by the defendant failed because of a defective plunger. When he and another member of his work team entered the tunnel after testing for gas and finding none, the engineer nevertheless soon slumped, while the other, having difficulty breathing, "ripped off his own mask and hollered for help." Two more men were killed and five others were injured as they attempted rescue without masks. Recovery was allowed to the injured and to the survivors of the killed. The court cited Judge Cardozo's classic statement: "Danger invites rescue. The cry of distress is the summons of relief. . . . The *wrong* that imperils life is a wrong to the imperilled victim; it is a wrong also to his rescuer." A concurring judge considered that the doctrine, previously restricted to negligence actions, should be rigorously confined when breach of implied warranty was involved. He would limit the application to the factual setting where "the plaintiffs rescuers [were] part of a team of workers all similarly situated in a common effort" and therefore the "great moral obligation present in the case at bar" was evidenced. He deplored the absence of limitations once liability was imposed without fault.

Court v. Grzelinski, 379 N.E.2d 281 (Ill.1978), involved an allegedly defective gas tank resulting in an explosion which injured the plaintiff fireman as he was fighting a fire in the car. In an action against the defendant General Motors, the court held that the "fireman's rule", that a landowner owed no duty of care to a fireman fighting a negligently started fire, was not applicable to strict liability products case.

3. BYSTANDERS AND ONLOOKERS

A number of jurisdictions have allowed warranty recovery by bystanders who have been injured by defective products; but on this point no uniformity exists. On the other hand, the trend toward allowing recovery in strict tort to bystanders now seems irreversible. It has even been argued that bystander recovery alone is recoverable under § 402A, since the UCC provides a legislatively mandated scheme of recovery for those in the distributive chain. This view, however, has not generally been accepted. The landmark case for bystander recovery is Elmore v. American Motors Corp., 451 P.2d 84 (Cal.1969). There one of the plaintiffs was the driver of an automobile involved in a head-on collision caused by a defect in another car sold by the defendants. This plaintiff was found to be a proper party to sue the defendants. Any restriction on plaintiff's right was attributable only to "the distorted shadow of a vanishing privity which is itself a reflection of the habit of viewing the problem as a commercial one between traders, rather than as part of the accident problem." If there is any difference, the court reasoned, "bystanders should be entitled to greater protection than the consumer or user where injury to bystanders from the defect is reasonably foreseeable." Users and consumers, unlike bystanders, have the opportunity of prior inspection and of using only products manufactured by reputable manufacturers.

Bystanders have been frequent victims in power lawn mower accidents. In recent years courts have tended toward imposing liability if a guard that would have prevented the accident is shown to have been feasible. This subject will be discussed further in the chapter on design defects. One case will suffice here. South Austin Drive-In Theatre v. Thomison, 421 S.W.2d 933 (Tex.Civ.App.1967), involved an unguarded drive chain and sprocket at the rear of a mower designed for both backward and forward movement. A six-year-old boy was struck as the mower backed into him. When his leg fell under the unguarded chain and sprocket it was pinned down until the rotary blades of the backing mower reached and severed it. Since testimony revealed the availability of an inexpensive guard to push objects backward or deflect them to one side of the chain and sprocket, the court sustained a finding that the injury was proximately caused by a defective design of the machine as well as by its careless operation.

In Shepard v. Superior Court, 142 Cal.Rptr. 612 (Cal.App.1977), it was held that the parents and brother of a small child had a cause of action against a car manufacturer for physical injuries resulting from emotional shock when they saw the child killed. Plaintiffs alleged that the child fell out of the Pinto wagon in which they were riding when, after a collision, the rear door opened because of a defective locking mechanism. The child was then run over by the same car that had struck the Pinto. Whether this strict liability decision against the manufacturer will be followed in other states remains doubtful, especially since a similar California decision in negligence cases outside the products field has met with a mixed reception.

C. DEFENDANTS OTHER THAN SELLERS OF CHATTELS

1. LESSORS OF CHATTELS

It has been generally held that long-term leases, lasting the useful life of the product, do not differ essentially from conditional sales and that the defendant lessor may therefore be held strictly liable. In fact this situation is an advantage for the lessee over the usual conditional sales situation where the holder in due course will usually be exempt from the original seller's liability. In addition, it is now widely held that a strict liability action may be maintained against a short-term lessor, in spite of the apparent restriction of the UCC and § 402A to sellers. In the landmark case of Cintrone v. Hertz Truck Leasing & Rental Serv., 212 A.2d 769 (N.J.1965), no sale was involved. Yet the court found that the reasons for holding the bailor to strict liability might be even more impelling, noting that "such a bailor puts the vehicle he buys and then rents to the public to more sustained use . . . than most ordinary car purchasers. . . . Such a rental must be regarded as accompanied by a representation that the vehicle is fit for operation on the public highways." More-

[*65*]

over, when the implied warranty or representation of fitness thus arises, it should continue for the agreed rental period: "The public interests involved are justly served only by treating an obligation of that nature as an incident of the business enterprise. The operator of the rental business must be regarded as possessing expertise with respect to the service life and fitness of his vehicles for use. That expertise ought to put him in a better position than the bailee to detect or to anticipate flaws or defects or fatigue in his vehicles. . . . And, with respect to failure of a rented vehicle from fatigue, since control of the length of the lease is in the lessor, such risk is one which, in the interest of the consuming public as well as of the members of the public traveling the highways, ought to be imposed on the rental business."

Price v. Shell Oil Co., 466 P.2d 722 (Cal.1970), was perhaps an even more significant case in the breadth of the rule applied, since the danger to many persons posed by defective cars leased for highway use was not involved. Plaintiff recovered against Shell in a strict liability action for his injury upon the breaking of a defective ladder attached to a gasoline tank truck leased by Shell. In response to Shell's contention that the strict liability of § 402A applied only to sellers, the court could "find no significant difference between a manufacturer or retailer who places an article on the market by means of a sale and a bailor or lessor who

accomplishes the same result by means of a lease."
Nor could the court "see how the risk of harm
associated with the use of the chattel can vary with
the legal form under which it is held. Having in
mind the market realities and the widespread use of
the lease of personalty in today's business world, we
think it makes good sense to impose on the lessors of
chattels the same liability for physical harm which
has been imposed on the manufacturers and retailers. The former, like the latter, are able to
bear the cost of compensating for injuries resulting
from defects by spreading the loss through an
adjustment of the rental."

2. PROVIDERS OF SERVICES

a. CERTIFIERS AND TESTERS

A wide variety of defendants not directly involved
in selling goods but rather in servicing such sellers
have been held liable on one basis or another. Thus
in Hanberry v. Hearst Corp., 81 Cal.Rptr. 519
(Cal.App.1969), the court held that an independent
certifying agency could be found liable in negligence
for placing its "Good Housekeeping" seal of approval on shoes sold by its advertiser, where the
soles of the shoes proved dangerously slippery
causing plaintiff to fall and sustain personal injuries.
The defendant contended that its seal amounted to
nothing more than a representation that the shoes
were "good ones," and that such representation
constituted a mere statement of opinion. The court

found that the defendant's certification was, in fact, a representation to the public that "it posessed superior knowledge and information concerning the product it endorsed. Under such circumstances, respondent may be liable for negligent representation of either fact or opinion." Such liability, however, should be restricted to negligence in representing "the general design and materials used to be satisfactory." Liability for "individually defective items should be limited to those directly involved in the manufacturing and supplying process, and should not be extended through warranty or strict liability to a general endorser who makes no representation it has examined or tested each item marketed."

In Hempstead v. General Fire Extinguisher Corp., 269 F.Supp. 109 (D.C.Del.1967), the court ignored the privity rule so widely observed in negligent misrepresentation cases. Here it was held that a nonprofit testing organization, serving at the request of the manufacturer, was liable to the remote user when a fire extinguisher tested and approved by the defendant exploded, injuring the plaintiff. The court held that the "alleged failure of Underwriters to exercise reasonable care in approving the design of the extinguisher has obviously increased the risk of harm to plaintiff over that which would have existed if reasonable care had been exercised."

b. COMMERCIAL AND PROFESSIONAL APPLIERS AND USERS

An applier of a defective product was held liable to a beauty parlor patron in Newmark v. Gimbel's, Inc., 258 A.2d 697 (N.J.1969), where plaintiff's hair and scalp were injured through the application of a permanent wave lotion. The court held that "the policy reasons for imposing warranty liability in the case of ordinary sales are equally applicable to a commercial transaction such as that existing in this case between a beauty parlor operator and a patron. Although the policy reasons which generate the responsibility are essentially the same, practical administration suggests that the principle of liability be expressed in terms of strict liability in tort thus enabling it to be applied in practice unconfined by the narrow conceptualism associated with the technical niceties of sales and implied warranties." The court also held, however, that use of a permanent wave solution on the plaintiff's hair constituted a sale with a resulting breach of the implied warranty. "If the permanent wave lotion were sold . . . for home consumption . . . unquestionably an implied warranty of fitness for that purpose would have been an integral incident of the sale." The court found "no just reason" in defendant's argument "that if, in addition to recommending the use of a lotion . . . and supplying it for use, they applied it, such fact (the application) would

[*69*]

have the effect of lessening their liability to the patron by eliminating warranty."

In this case the defendant sought to equate the services of a beauty parlor operator with those of a doctor or a dentist. The court drew a sharp line between commercial and professional services, even where both might involve use of defective products. As to a doctor or dentist, the "use of instruments, or the administration of medicines or the providing of medicines for the patient's home consumption cannot give the ministrations the cast of a commercial transaction."

The court thus distinguished Magrine v. Krasnica, 227 A.2d 539 (N.J.Super.1967), aff'd sub nom. Magrine v. Spector, 250 A.2d 129 (N.J.1969), a leading case in the area of professional services. In *Magrine* the plaintiff sought recovery from a dentist for personal injuries caused by the breaking of a hypodermic needle injected into plaintiff's jaw. The court held that the dentist was not liable in warranty, since he had not "put the needle in the stream of commerce." Furthermore, he "neither created the defect nor possessed any better capacity" than the plaintiff to discover it. The court reasoned that the dentist should scarcely be held strictly liable for latent defects over which he has no control, when he is "liable only for negligence in the performance of his professional services, which he does control." Plaintiff raised the question of equitable risk allocation; the court concluded that though this policy had

[70]

been recognized in previous cases involving large enterprises, it was of doubtful value in medical situations. If "the dentist or physician were to obtain insurance covering strict liability for equipment failure, the risk would be spread upon his patients by way of increased fees. Can anyone gainsay the fact that medical and dental costs, and insurance therefor, are already bearing hard there? Witness the constant cry over increasing medical-surgical insurance premiums in New Jersey."

In LaRossa v. Scientific Design Co., 402 F.2d 937 (3d Cir. 1968), the court held that a company which designed, engineered, and supervised the initial operation of a plant for the manufacture of phthalic anhydride was not liable under breach of express or implied warranty to an employee who died from breathing vanadium dust generated by pellets loaded as a catalyst into a reactor. The court considered that professional services "lack the elements which give rise to the doctrine. There is no mass production of goods or a large body of distant consumers whom it would be unfair to require to trace the article they used along the channels of trade to the original manufacturer and there to pinpoint an act of negligence remote from their knowledge and even their ability to inquire." The court observed that "even in those jurisdictions which have adopted a rule of strict products liability a majority of decisions have declined to extend it to professional services." From professional experts only "reasonable care and competence" could be required, not perfection.

On the other hand, in Grubb v. Albert Einstein Medical Center, 387 A.2d 480 (Pa.Super.1978), a hospital was held strictly liable in tort for a defective bone drill which injured plaintiff during surgery. Said the court: "The surgical patient is without control over the procedures and instruments used upon him. His health and future safety are at the mercy and skill of the treating physicians and the instruments he employs. It is elementary that if a hospital supplies equipment to an operating physician the hospital must appraise themselves of the risks involved and adopt every effort to insure the safety of the equipment chosen. Furthermore, there was testimony in this case to indicate that the defect could have been discovered by a preliminary test on animal bone. To require this minimal technique is not unreasonable and may very well have avoided the injuries to the plaintiff."

c. Repairers

Some courts in recent years have extended the implied warranty of fitness to the repair and reprocessing of goods already purchased by the plaintiff or by his employer. Thus in McCool v. Hoover Equipment Co., 415 P.2d 954 (Okl.1966), in a contract for rechroming of plaintiff's second-hand crankshafts, a job requiring the exercise of care, skill, and knowledge, the court found an implied warranty that chrome work which the defendant undertook should be "of proper workmanship and reasonable fitness for its intended use." When the shafts so rechromed for the plaintiff failed to last more than 280 hours, while the normal life expectancy of a rechromed crankshaft was from 3,000 to 10,000 hours, defendant was held to have breached the implied warranty.

In Texas Metal Fabricating Co. v. Northern Gas Products Corp., 404 F.2d 921 (10th Cir. 1968), the repairer of a heat exchanger manufactured by another was held liable for breach of implied warranty to an employee of the plant using the exchanger for injuries caused by an explosion. The repair job was defective in that it caused the exchanger to leak gas. Even though the repair was undertaken to remedy a situation which, if not corrected, might in itself have eventually caused the gas leak and the resultant explosion, the court found that the alteration "at least accelerated the tube wearing and can be said to have caused this particular explosion to occur when it did."

In Rager v. Superior Coach Sales and Serv., 526 P.2d 1056 (Ariz.1974), Superior Coach had warranted a bus to the school district and then referred a brake problem to defendant Automotive Sales Company. When an accident owing allegedly to defective brakes later occurred, the court held both defendants subject to liability. "Service to the bus was performed under warranty by Superior Coach. Because repair of brakes on heavy vehicles is an undertaking which creates a high degree of risk of serious bodily harm . . . we believe that this is a non-delegable duty and Superior Coach Sales having selected Automotive Sales to do this work, Superior Coach Sales must also respond in damages."

Where the repair service has had no connection with the sale, courts have frequently ruled that the repairer should be liable for negligence only. A small local supplier, unlike a manufacturer or large retailer, will often be unable to spread the risk of loss among the general public. Moreover, when the defect lies in services performed rather than in the product itself, the local supplier cannot, like the local retailer, shift the loss back to the manufacturer. Also, proof of negligence will be somewhat easier when the repairer, his employees, methods, and equipment are all under local observation. On the other hand, imposition of strict liability for breach of warranty in the sale of goods has rarely turned on the size of the enterprise involved. It therefore seems likely that courts will continue to expand the application of strict liability to contracts for the furnishing of services apart from sales.

In Young v. Aro Corp., 111 Cal.Rptr. 535 (Cal. App.1973), where the manufacturer of a grinding machine to which an abrasive wheel was attached also repaired it, the court held that the manufacturer could be held to strict liability should the jury find that wrongful death from the disintegrating wheel occurred as a result of defective repair. Similarly, in Winters v. Sears Roebuck & Co., 554 S.W.2d 565 (Mo.App.1977), defendant seller was held strictly liable in tort, when after an attempt by the seller at repair, a television set originally purchased from the seller caught fire and damaged plaintiff's home.

3. CONTRACTORS

The law as to the liability of independent contractors has varied so much in recent years, depending upon the jurisdiction, that generalization is impossible. In Worrell v. Barnes, 484 P.2d 573 (Nev. 1971), the court held defendant Barnes could be found strictly liable when a fire was caused by propane escaping from a leaky fitting he had used in the installation of a gas heater. The trial court had dismissed plaintiff's strict tort and breach of warranty counts and the jury had returned a defendant's verdict on negligence grounds. The court said: "As we hold that Barnes must be said to have manufactured and sold a product so as to bring into operation the doctrine of strict liability, so also must we deem this case to involve goods within the purview of the Uniform Commercial Code."

More typically, perhaps, in Milau Associates, Inc. v. North Ave. Development Corp., 368 N.E.2d 1247 (N.Y.1977), the court ruled that the builder of a

[75]

warehouse and the subcontractor of the sprinkler system were not liable for breach of warranty to tenants for damages to their stored textiles from the massive bursting of an underground pipe connecting the sprinkler system with the city water line. "Given the predominantly service-oriented character of the transaction, neither the code nor the common law of this State can be read to imply an undertaking to guard against economic loss stemming from the nonnegligent performance by a construction firm which has not contractually bound itself to provide perfect results."

In Totten v. Gruzen, 245 A.2d 1 (N.J.1968), the court ruled that the architect, the general contractor, and the heating contractor of an apartment house could be held liable in negligence after the work had been completed and accepted by the owner. A three-year-old child was severely burned by an exposed supply pipe coming out of the wall and joining the radiator after making two turns. This design resulted in a ladder-like arrangement that the child tried to climb. Liability was for the jury, in spite of the fact that the contractors had followed the specifications of the public housing authority owner. On the other hand, the completed and accepted rule was followed in Chapman v. Lily Cache Builders, Inc., 362 N.E.2d 811 (Ill.App.1977), with the court holding that no liability could be imposed on the contractor either in strict tort or for negligence.

In Air Heaters, Inc. v. Johnson Elec., Inc., 258 N.W.2d 649 (N.D.1977), the court held that the defendant designer, constructor, and installer of an electrical distribution system that caused fire damage was liable, not under the UCC, but for breach of a common law implied warranty of fitness. Such a warranty is implied when four conditions are met: "(1) the contractor holds himself out, expressly or by implication, as competent to undertake the contract; (2) the owner has no particular expertise in the kind of work contemplated; (3) the owner furnishes no plans, designs, specifications, details, or blueprints; (4) the owner tacitly or specifically indicates his reliance on the experience and skill of the contractor, after making known to him the specific purposes for which the building is intended."

4. LICENSERS AND FRANCHISERS

Licensers of both tangible personal property and of trade marks, business inviters, and franchisers have been held liable for defective products connected with their operations. Thus in Garcia v. Halsett, 82 Cal.Rptr. 420 (Cal.App.1970), a laundromat operator was held liable to a plaintiff injured when a movable part of a washing machine began to spin after it had previously come to a stop and while plaintiff was reaching into the machine to remove his laundry. Although the defendant was held negligent for failing to install an inexpensive micro switch to prevent the machine from operating while the door was open, he was also held liable in strict tort for a latent defect, that of the machine's timing mechanism. Said the court: "Licensors of personal property, like the manufacturers or retailers or lessors thereof, are an integral part of the overall . . . marketing enterprise that should bear the cost of injuries resulting from defective products."

On the other hand, in Shaw v. Fairyland at Harvey's, Inc., 271 N.Y.S.2d 70 (App.Div.1966), when plaintiff sought recovery on warranty grounds for death caused by a dangerously defective gondola on a ferris wheel, the court denied recovery on any strict liability theory. Owners and operators of public amusements were only under the legal duty to their invitees to "exercise due care" in the maintenance of their premises.

In City of Hartford v. Associated Constr. Co., 384 A.2d 390 (Conn.Super.1978), the court held that the plaintiff had a strict tort cause of action against a trademark owner both for damage to its school building from a leaking roof and for the cost of replacement. The use of the trademark "All-Weather Crete" was licensed by defendant Silbrico to Skyway who then sold the product as a roofing base which was used in plaintiff's roof. Under such a licensing agreement the trademark owner retains the "control, right and title to the product." In fact, he is required to retain enough control over the use of the product to guarantee to the public, including the plaintiff here, that the mark retains the meaning it had before the licensing. "This legal responsibility to the plaintiff imposed upon Silbrico as a result of its licensing agreement with Skyway, guaranteeing to the consumer that the roofing base insulation branded by the trademark All-Weather Crete was of the same nature and quality as was the product before its licensing to Skyway, meets the condition precedent for strict tort liability under § 402A that the defective product 'is expected to and does reach the user or consumer without substantial change in the condition in which it is sold.'"

Kosters v. Seven-Up Co., 595 F.2d 347 (6th Cir. 1979), held that a franchiser was liable for breach of warranty to an ultimate consumer who was injured by a defective product. Plaintiff was injured when a bottle of Seven-Up dropped from a carton and broke, and a fragment of the glass blinded her in one eye. The bottling company, franchised by the Seven-Up Company, had chosen the carton and purchased it from an outside supplier. Nevertheless, it was required under the terms of the franchise to submit the carton to the franchiser who retained the right of control—to approve, disapprove, or insist upon modification of the carton. The court held that when "a franchisor consents to the distribution of a defective product bearing its name, the obligation of the franchisor to compensate the injured consumer for breach of implied warranty

. . . arises from several factors in combination." Among these was "the consumer's reliance on the trade name which gives the intended impression that the franchisor is responsible for and stands behind the product."

5. GRATUITOUS TRANSFERERS

Where defendants have gratuitously transferred a product as a demonstrator with the purpose of ultimately securing its sale, or as equipment for the purpose of promoting the sale of another product, strict liability has been invoked. Thus in Delaney v. Towmotor Corp., 339 F.2d 4 (2d Cir. 1964), it was held that the liability of the manufacturer arises from "[h]aving invited and solicited the use" when a hilo was not sold, but delivered to a stevedore company as a demonstrator for the purpose of trying out newly designed equipment. Moreover, strict tort liability was "surely a more accurate phrase to identify this concept than breach of warranty."

The defendant in Fulbright v. Klamath Gas Co., 533 P.2d 316 (Or.1975), in order to promote the sale of its propane gas, furnished to farmers free of charge a device using the gas for the burning of potato vines to prevent their clogging the mechanical diggers used for harvesting potatoes. Plaintiff, a farm hand, was severely burned when heat from the burners increased the pressure in the propane tanks so that gas escaped into the air and was

[*80*]

ignited by the burners. Defendant had failed to warn of this possibility if the burner was used on a windy day. The issue of defect was held for the jury. On the application of § 402A to a nonsale transaction, the court, after citing the leasing cases, held that "the sale of the propane gas cannot logically be separated from the loan of the vine burner in which the gas was to be used."

6. REAL PROPERTY SELLERS

One of the most striking developments in the law has been the extension of strict liability to the sale of new homes by a builder-vendor. Until recently the ancient rule of caveat emptor proved strangely persistent in real property transactions. In the absence of fraud or misrepresentation, the vendor was liable for defects only to the extent of the express agreement. Moreover, any warranties or representations made prior to or contemporaneous with the deed were "merged" in the deed—that is, lost forever unless expressed in that deed.

In the landmark case of Schipper v. Levitt & Sons, Inc., 207 A.2d 314 (N.J.1965), the defendant's contention that these rules still prevailed was firmly rejected by the court. "We consider that there are no meaningful distinctions between Levitt's mass production and sale of homes and the mass production and sale of automobiles and that the pertinent overriding policy considerations are the

[*81*]

same. . . . *Caveat emptor* developed when the buyer and seller were in an equal bargaining position and they could readily be expected to protect themselves in the deed. Buyers of mass produced development homes are not on equal footing with the builder vendors and are no more able to protect themselves in the deed than are automobile purchasers in a position to protect themselves in the bill of sale." So it was held that, if the jury found the proximate cause of the infant plaintiff's severe burns was the dangerously defective hot-water system, defendant should be held liable for a breach of the implied warranty of habitability.

In spite of the emphasis in *Schipper* on mass production of houses comparable to that of automobiles, the New Jersey court has recently held that "[w]hether the builder be large or small, the purchaser relies upon his superior knowledge and skill, and he impliedly represents that he is qualified to erect a habitable dwelling." The court went on to say, in McDonald v. Mianecki, 398 A.2d 1283 (N.J.1979), "[W]hether or not engaged in mass production, builders utilize standard form contracts, and hence the opportunity to bargain for protective clauses is by and large nonexistent. Finally, it is the builder who has introduced the article into the stream of commerce. Should defects materialize, he—as opposed to the consumer purchaser—is the less innocent party." Here the vendor-builder was held liable for breach of the implied warranty of

[*82*]

habitability where the well water supplied to plaintiff's new house contained such high iron content as to make it not only undrinkable but unfit for cleaning and washing purposes.

Not all courts have extended products liability theory to real estate sales. For example, in Mitchem v. Johnson, 218 N.E.2d 594 (Ohio 1966), the court found that in fact "the purchase of real estate is invariably preceded by a lengthy period of inspection, consideration and negotiation", so that the buyer is by no means the helpless figure in the bargaining process described in *Schipper*. The court further reasoned that the paucity of reported decisions involving an implied warranty in real estate transactions may indicate that buyers "have been successful in recovering for latent defects arising from improper work materials in actions sounding in deceit or misrepresentation for nondisclosure of those defects." Therefore the court saw no good reason for a strict liability which "avoids the harsh truth that unfortunate problems arise on real estate and in real structures which no prudence can avoid and which defy every reasonable skill." The Virginia Supreme Court, in Bruce Farms, Inc. v. Coupe, 247 S.E.2d 400 (Va.1978), citing difficulties in application, held that any change in the caveat emptor rule as applied to real property was for the legislature.

7. REAL PROPERTY LESSORS

Just as the lessors of chattels have been held liable
on the same basis as sellers of chattels, the implied
warranty of habitability has been extended in many
jurisdictions to lessors of real estate, especially
dwelling units. The landmark case in this area is
Javins v. First Nat'l Realty Corp., 428 F.2d 1071
(D.C.Cir. 1970), involving a large number of defects
in an apartment complex in Washington, D.C. After
an extensive review of the feudal and agrarian
origin of the lease as conveying an interest in the
land, the court draws the conclusion that under
modern urban conditions, where the tenant is
concerned with a place to live rather than with
economic exploitation of the land, leases should be
treated simply as contracts. Moreover, "the old
no-repair rule cannot coexist with the obligations
imposed on the landlord by a typical modern housing
code, and must be abandoned in favor of an implied
warranty of habitability. In the District of
Columbia the standards of this warranty are set out
in the Housing Regulations." The court cited such
products liability cases as *Henningsen* and *Cintrone*,
where the consumer was dependent upon the seller's
or lessor's expert knowledge of automobiles, and
observed that the average tenant was equally
dependent upon the landlord's skill and good faith.
Also, as in the case of the lessor of automobiles, the
landlord was under a continuing obligation to "keep

[84]

the premises in their beginning condition during the lease term," since the tenant's rental obligation did not change. The court suggested that it was going "beyond the rationale of traditional products liability law" in considering certain policies which have, nevertheless, been essential considerations in the development of that law. These include "the inequality in bargaining power" and "the standardized form leases," the latter surely comparable to the standardized automobile disclaimer. Other reasons given by the court for tenant protection may indeed lie outside the province of products law. These were the severe housing shortage, limiting the tenant's choice, racial and class discrimination as impediments to competition, and the "social impact of bad housing."

Javins has been widely followed, in other jurisdictions, including such important states as Pennsylvania and California. Presumably, however, the courts that have not allowed a breach of warranty action in real property sale would also disallow it in lease situations.

Damages in the landlord-tenant cases have generally been limited to the difference in rental value between the housing as warranted and its value with the existing defects. A significant precedent may have been established, however, in Fair v. Negley, 390 A.2d 240 (Pa.Super.1978), where damages were allowed for the intentional infliction of emotional distress. Here the violations, such as a leaking roof, falling plaster, broken windows, and a malfunctioning water system, caused severe discomfort.

D. JOINT TORTFEASORS

1. INDEMNITY

Claims for indemnity are frequent in products cases, especially where the plaintiff chooses to sue a retailer for breach of warranty, perhaps because he is the most accessible defendant. Since the retailer's liability is usually derivative, with the damage caused by the manufacturer of the defective product, he can usually be fully indemnified. Moreover, should the manufacturer be insolvent, or beyond the reach of the court—say a canner of corned beef in Argentina—the retailer can take advantage of his right to sue a wholesaler or distributor, either for breach of warranty or in strict tort. Again, the full recovery known as indemnity will be at issue.

A manufacturer may have an indemnity action against another manufacturer. In Burbage v. Boiler Engineering & Supply Co., 249 A.2d 563 (Pa.1969), a negligence case, the boiler manufacturer obtained a judgment against the manufacturer of a defective replacement valve which had been the cause of an explosion killing the original plaintiff. The court said: "The right of indemnity rests upon a difference between the primary and secondary liability of two persons each of whom is made responsible by law to an injured party. The right to indemnity enures to a person who, without active fault on his own part, has been compelled by reason of some legal obligation to pay damages occasioned by the negligence of another. The difference between primary and secondary liability is not based on a difference in degrees of negligence or on any doctrine of comparative negligence but rather on a difference in the *character* or *kind* of the wrongs which cause the injury and in the nature of the legal obligation owed by each of the wrongdoers to the injured person."

In Tromza v. Tecumseh Products Co., 378 F.2d 601 (3d Cir. 1967), Tecumseh sold to Marquette a sealed compressor refrigeration unit which was then incorporated into a refrigerator manufactured by Marquette. Plaintiff Tromza, a repairman, was injured when the refrigerator exploded as he applied a pressure of 170 pounds to the unit in repairing a gas leak. The manufacturer had been negligent in not testing the unit for its ability to withstand at least 235 pounds of pressure, as was standard in the industry. The court held that Marquette was entitled to judgment against Tecumseh for the full amount of the judgment against Marquette for the injury to Tromza. Tecumseh "was primarily responsible for manufacturing a defective compressor unit and failing to detect the defect by a proper inspection. Since Marquette's liability arose because of a failure to discover or correct a defect or

remedy a dangerous condition caused by the act of
the one [Tecumseh] primarily responsible, its liability
is secondary."

2. CONTRIBUTION

a. ABROGATION OF THE NO–CONTRIBUTION RULE

Recently many, perhaps most, states have either
by statute or court decision abrogated the common
law rule that there can be no contribution among or
between wrongdoers. This change has often meant
some modification of the rule announced in *Tromza*,
at least where the defect could be discovered by a
reasonable inspection or testing. For example, in
Tolbert v. Gerber Indus., Inc., 255 N.W.2d 362
(Minn.1977), where the defendant in manufacturing
equipment for loading grain hopper cars included a
part which failed to conform to its own drawings,
the court reversed the trial court's award of full
indemnity to the installer. Since the latter might,
with due care, have discovered the defect, the court
held that both the manufacturer and the installer
were negligent, and that, on remand, the jury should
apportion the cost of compensating the injured
workman in proportion to their "relative culpability."

A landmark decision in which the court adopted
the principle of contribution is that of Dole v. Dow
Chem. Co., 282 N.E.2d 288 (N.Y.1972). Here it was

alleged that Dow had supplied to the employer of plaintiff's husband a "penetrating and poisonous fumigant" without adequate warning of the dangers attendant upon its use. The decedent died as a result of entering, for the purpose of cleaning as directed by the employer, a recently fumigated storage bin. Dow contended that its warnings had been adequate and that the death was caused by the employer's failure to relay its precautions, to employ adequately trained personnel, and to properly test and aerate the storage bin after fumigation. The court reversed an intermediate court's ruling that Dow would have no action over "if the plaintiff established that Dow's negligence in mislabeling and insufficient warning contributed to the accident . . . even though the user was also negligent." It held that the right to either apportionment of liability or to full indemnity, "as among parties involved together in causing damage by negligence, should rest on relative responsibility and [is] to be determined on the facts."

At least one court, in Barth v. B. F. Goodrich Tire Co., 92 Cal.Rptr. 809 (Cal.App.1971), allowed the manufacturer of defective tires to seek contribution from the dealer that sold them without a warning to the purchaser of the danger from overloading. While both defendants were held strictly liable, it seems clear that the court found the dealer to be negligent as well.

Not all jurisdictions have abrogated the "no contribution" rule. In Wenatchee Wenoka Growers

Ass'n v. Krack Corp., 576 P.2d 388 (Wash.1978), the court was "not persuaded to discard a simple, workable doctrine in favor of a complicated 'unknown'. But, we neither hold nor mean to suggest that we will reject further consideration of this matter in an appropriate case."

b.　WHERE GROUNDS OF LIABILITY DIFFER

Many product cases involve the negligence of two or more parties, say the manufacturer of equipment and either the installer or the purchaser when the equipment requires maintenance or changes for safe use by others. Special problems arise when the grounds of liability differ. Thus in Fenton v. McCrory Corp., 47 F.R.D. 260 (W.D.Pa.1969), the defendant retailer had been held liable because a small rubber suction cap attached to the leading end of an arrow shaft and intended as a safety device was nevertheless penetrated by the arrow. The court denied contribution from a playmate who negligently shot the arrow in the direction of the original plaintiff's eye. It held that a strictly liable tortfeasor had no right of contribution from a negligent one. Other courts have allowed contribution in similar situations. For example, in Safeway Stores, Inc. v. Nest-Kart, 579 P.2d 441 (Cal.1978), where plaintiff was seriously injured when a shopping cart broke and fell on her foot, the jury found Nest-Kart strictly liable for a defectively manufactured cart. But it found that "the primary fault for the accident lay with Safeway because of its negligent failure properly to maintain the cart in safe working condition." The court referred to the suggestion "that no logical basis can be found for comparing the relative 'fault' of a negligent defendant with that of a defendant whose liability rests on the 'no fault' concept of strict product liability." Its answer to this argument was the pragmatic one that juries found no difficulty in making such comparisons. In the instant case the jury "apparently had no difficulty in finding both the manufacturer and Safeway liable for the accident, and apportioning the lion's share (80 percent) of the fault for the accident to Safeway, rather than to the manufacturer. We see no reason to assume that a similar common sense determination of proportional fault or proportional responsibility will be beyond the ken of other juries in similar cases." Moreover, "to hold that the comparative indemnity doctrine could only be invoked by a negligent defendant" would permit the negligent manufacturer to shift "the bulk of liability to more negligent cotortfeasors, while the strictly liable defendant would be denied the benefit of such apportionment."

Perhaps the most difficult situation arises where the manufacturer of a defective machine or chemical claims contribution from an employer who has permitted or encouraged the negligent use of the product or its dangerous modification. Here the employer's liability to the employee is not only a strict one, but one limited by a workers' compensation statute; while the manufacturer's liability will be determined by the extent of the damage. To permit recovery from the employer in such cases would appear to defeat the purpose of the compensation statutes. Perhaps the most thorough discussion of this issue, on which courts have disagreed, is in Lambertson v. Cincinnati Corp., 257 N.W.2d 679 (Minn.1977). Here the operator of a press brake used to bend metal was severely injured when he reached through the jaws of the machine to retrieve a fallen piece of metal without knowing that a fellow worker had put his foot on a pedal causing the ram to descend. The employer who purchased the machine had refused to install safety devices which had been urgently recommended by the defendant manufacturer and which would have prevented this accident. The court followed the Pennyslvania Supreme Court in allowing "contribution from the employer up to the amount of the workers' compensation benefits. This approach allows the third party to obtain limited contribution, but substantially preserves the employer's interest in not paying more than workers' compensation liability. While this approach may not allow full contribution recovery to the third party in all cases, it is the solution we consider most consistent with fairness and the various statutory schemes before us. If further reform is to be accomplished, it must be effected by legislative changes in workers'-compensation-third-party law." It is perhaps of some significance that the Pennsylvania legislature amended its compensation law in 1975 to provide that a defendant may neither join nor seek contribution from the plaintiff's employer.

CHAPTER IV

FACTORS AFFECTING THE CHOICE OF REMEDIES OR OF JURISDICTION

A. IN GENERAL

It is clear that a defendant may be liable under any or all of the three basic theories of recovery: negligence, warranty, and strict tort. Fortunately, it is not often necessary to choose among them—all three may be pleaded. Strict tort, however, is usually the simplest remedy, requiring only that the product be defective; that the defect exist at the time the product leaves the defendant's hands; and that the defect be the cause of the plaintiff's harm. In a few jurisdictions, where strict tort is still not an available ground of recovery, implied warranty may be the best remedy since here, too, no proof of negligence is required. In a breach of warranty case, plaintiff may have to overcome such contract defenses as disclaimers, the requirement of notice of breach, limitation of remedies, and lack of privity. Moreover, under the UCC, the number of permissible plaintiffs beyond those in the "chain of distribution" may be limited; while in strict tort the plaintiff can be any person foreseeably affected by the goods. Such practical considerations as the availability or solvency or a particular defendant may also affect the cause of action.

Negligence is sometimes asserted as an additional ground of recovery. This is done not solely out of caution, but because of the belief that juries are likely to return more substantial verdicts where negligence is shown.

The trend toward strict tort, as by far the most important remedy in products liability cases, seems irreversible. The increasing emphasis on equitable allocation of the risk of loss to those best able to redistribute it provides a major thrust toward greater liberality in allowing recovery. The thrust continues despite objections raised in some quarters that the advantages of a law-controlled liability in a society of big business and mass production may not outweigh the disadvantages of further restrictions on freedom of contract and on the development of private sectors of the economy.

B. RELIANCE

Actions for public misrepresentation under § 402B of the Second Restatement of Torts have generally required proof of reliance; while in express warranty cases reliance may be presumed. In both actions, the representation must be material, influencing the decision to make the purchase or to use the product. As indicated by comment g to § 402B, it is assumed that plaintiff will not rely upon "the kind of loose general praise of wares sold which, on the part of the seller, is considered to be 'sales talk', and is commonly called 'puffing'—as, for example, a statement that an automobile is the best in the market for the price." However, in Ford Motor Co. v. Taylor, 446 S.W.2d 521 (Tenn.App. 1969), a purchaser of a defective tractor recovered

[*95*]

against the manufacturer for loss in value of the tractor and loss of profits on the basis of the manufacturer's representations that the tractor had "new strength" and "new toughness" and was designed to deliver "outstanding performance with remarkable economy."

On the other hand, even where a seller has made a specific representation in a brochure, as in Garbage Disposal Serv. v. City Tank Corp., CCH Prod. Liab. Rptr. par. 6539 (Tenn.App.1971), plaintiff may be denied recovery if he is unable to show "any statement in the brochure on which he relied."

Reliance must be shown to establish an implied warranty of fitness for a particular purpose, but not for an implied warranty of merchantability. However, in Erdman v. Johnson Bros. Radio & Television Co., Inc., 271 A.2d 744 (Md.1970), the court held that where plaintiffs demonstrated their lack of reliance upon any warranty, implied or express, by continuing to use a television set that emitted smoke and sparks, recovery was barred. Their constant complaints to the defendant retailer resulted in ineffectual attempts at repair, so that the set finally caught fire and their home was completely destroyed. The court held that "although there may have been a breach of the warranty . . . the breach is no longer considered the proximate cause of the loss."

Reliance is also lacking where the product is manufactured according to the plaintiff purchaser's specifications. Thus in Mohasco Indus., Inc. v. Anderson Halverson Corp., 520 P.2d 234 (Nev.1974), the plaintiff hotel ordered a rug which was manufactured according to the specifications of the hotel's decorator. The carpet developed excessive shading owing to the fact that "twist yarn" had not been used. The court held that the "manufacturer-seller was not at liberty to add 'twist yarn' and charge a higher price. . . . Buyer reliance is lacking in this case."

C. DISCLAIMERS AND LIMITATIONS OF REMEDIES

1. DEFINITION AND MINIMUM REQUIREMENTS

A disclaimer is a denial of all liability, while a limitation of remedies recognizes some liability but limits the remedy, often, as indicated by UCC § 2–719(1)(a), to "return of the goods and repayment of the price or to repair and replacement of non-conforming goods or parts." Since, for the most part, courts make little distinction between disclaimers and limitations of remedy, the two defenses will be considered together under the general description of disclaimers.

Even though disclaimers of implied warranties are generally permitted under the UCC, certain minimum requirements must be met. According to § 1–201(10), the language must be conspicuous, that is, in larger type or a different color. The question of whether particular language is conspicuous "is for decision by the court." Where, in Hunt v. Perkins Machinery Co., Inc., 226 N.E.2d 228 (Mass.1967), the disclaimer was placed on the back of a purchase order on a pad of blank forms, it was held to be inconspicuous within the meaning of the UCC. The purchaser had signed on the front of the order where no clear reference to the disclaimer on the back was made, and the seller did not call the disclaimer to the buyer's attention. Under these circumstances, the buyer's first reasonable opportunity to discover the disclaimer "was when the executed form was returned to him."

It may well be that the UCC will serve to call the manufacturer's bluff. The seller who advertises his product as well-nigh perfect may be willing to place a disclaimer of liability for its imperfections where no one will read it; but he may not be willing to bring it clearly to the attention of the hoped-for purchaser.

Clarity is also required, including the mention of the word "merchantability" in the disclaimer of that implied warranty, as required by UCC § 2–316(2). This requirement is presumably imposed as a safeguard against ambiguous disclaimers, but it may not effectively serve this purpose. The word "merchantability" may suggest to the ordinary buyer resalability rather than soundness of quality, and he may not think that a disclaimer which uses this term withdraws protection against latent defects in the goods. Mere mention of the word merchantability, therefore, even if in larger or contrasting type or color, may not be sufficiently clear to apprise the buyer that there is a disclaimer of general fitness of the product.

In Henningsen v. Bloomfield Motors, Inc., 161 A.2d 69 (N.J.1960), the landmark case emphasizing inequality of bargaining power, the court rejected the manufacturer's claim that a limitation of remedies in the standard automobile warranty relieved the manufacturer of any liability for personal injury. "It is not unreasonable to believe that the entire scheme being conveyed was a proposed remedy for physical deficiencies in the car. *In the context* of this warranty, only the abandonment of all sense of justice would permit us to hold that, as a matter of law, the phrase 'its obligation under this warranty being limited to making good at its factory any part or parts thereof' signifies to an ordinary reasonable person that he is relinquishing any personal injury claim that might flow from the use of a defective automobile. Such claims are nowhere mentioned."

Any disclaimer of warranties to be valid must generally be delivered to the buyer before consummation of the sales agreement. Moreover, remote parties, such as employees of the purchaser, are not barred from recovery by a disclaimer in a contract between the employer and the seller of a product that proves defective. For example, in Velez v. Craine & Clark Lumber Corp., 305 N.E.2d 750 (N.Y.1973), employees were injured because of a collapsing plank in a scaffold for which the defendant had provided the lumber. The court observed: "Plaintiffs were complete strangers to the contract. . . . We see no necessity to labor the point that, in the absence of special circumstances not present here, buyer and seller cannot contract to limit the seller's exposure under strict products liability to an innocent user or bystander."

Finally, UCC § 2–719(2) provides that where the "circumstances cause an exclusive or limited remedy to fail of its essential purpose," a party may resort to any remedy which he has at law. Champion Brick Co. v. Signode Corp., 263 F.Supp. 387 (D.C.Md.1967), involved losses owing to an irreparably defective machine for packaging bricks. Not only had many bricks been damaged, but plaintiff had been put to considerable expense in modifying his plant to accommodate the machine. The defendant relied on a contractual clause limiting the purchaser's remedy to recision of the contract. The court notes, in denying the motion for summary judgment, that such a clause "will be construed strictly against the seller," and that "a fuller development of the facts may disclose that the parties intended that the clause limiting liability would operate only upon the condition that the machine furnished by the defendant was substantially as warranted." It concluded: "Common sense would indicate the likelihood of such a condition."

Recently failure of essential purpose has been grounds for allowing recision or consequential damages or both in the typical "lemon" situation where frequent attempts to repair have been of no avail. In Goddard v. General Motors Corp., 396 N.E.2d 761 (Ohio 1979), a car's starter repeatedly failed after several replacements during the warranty period, the transmission failed so that after four attempts at repair it was replaced, and the fuel pump failed and was replaced. The car then developed vibrating and electrical problems. The new transmission failed and another replacement was made. The court held that, under these circumstances, with the plaintiff frequently deprived of the use of his car, or delayed on a journey, the limited remedy of repair and replacement of parts had failed of its essential purpose. Also, the court declined to enforce the disclaimer of consequential damages such as loss of use, inconvenience, and loss of time. It cited Adams v. J. I. Case Co., 261 N.E.2d 1 (Ill.App.1970), as follows: "The limitations of remedy and of liability are not separable from the obligations of the warranty. Repudiation of the obligations of the warranty destroys its benefits."

In Clark v. International Harvester Co., 581 P.2d 784 (Idaho 1978), plaintiff purchased from the defendant through a dealer a turbo-diesel tractor for use in his business of "custom farming," that is, plowing and fertilizing the farmland of others. Owing to frequent breakdowns of the machine and the failure of either defendant—the retailer or the manufacturer—to analyze the difficulty, plaintiff lost many days of work and also suffered a reduction of the acreage he could cover when the machine was indeed operating but inefficiently. The court held that plaintiff was entitled to recover for such consequential damages if, on retrial, it was found that the tractor's push rods were defective at the time of delivery to Clark and that "defendants had failed to cure the defect within a reasonable time, thereby causing the limited remedy to fail."

2.   AS WAIVERS OF VARIOUS LIABILITIES

a.   STRICT TORT

Granted that the disclaimer is in accord with the minimum requirements, courts differ as to what sources of liability other than warranty may be disclaimed and under what circumstances. Distinctions are made not only between personal injury and property damage, but between the latter as a direct result of an accident and consequential economic loss, such as loss of working time.

Comment m to § 402A of the Second Restatement of Torts states that the strict liability for harm to person or property arising from a defective and dangerous product "is not affected by limitations on the scope and content of warranties," or "by any disclaimer or other agreement, whether it is between the seller and his immediate buyer, or attached to and accompanying the product into the consumer's hands." Comment d to § 402B, dealing with strict tort liability based on public misrepresentation, states that the above comment m is equally applicable to that section.

The leading case holding disclaimers inapplicable to actions in strict tort is Vandermark v. Ford Motor Co., 391 P.2d 168 (Cal.1964). The plaintiffs brought an action against the manufacturer and the retailer of a car for damages resulting from a defect in the brakes. The retailer, Maywood Bell, contended that it had validly disclaimed warranty liability for personal injuries in its contract with plaintiff Vandermark, the purchaser. In denying this defense, the California court said: "Since Maywood Bell is strictly liable in tort, the fact that it restricted its contractual liability to Vandermark is immaterial. Regardless of the obligations it assumed by contract, it is subject to strict liability in tort because it is in the business of selling automobiles, one of which proved to be defective and caused injury to human beings." The emphasis in *Vandermark* on personal injury reveals the court's special concern for the consumer who suffers unduly because of a defective product.

Under the terms of § 402A, comment m, strict tort liability for direct damage to property can also not be disclaimed. However, in Keystone Aeronautics Corp. v. R. J. Enstrom Corp., 499 F.2d

146 (3d Cir. 1974), the plaintiff purchased three used helicopters from the defendant which had also originally manufactured them. After one of the helicopters crash-landed with substantial damage to the aircraft but no personal injury, the FAA ordered the two others grounded until the cause of the crash was determined. The court held that a limitation of liability to the replacement of defective parts and the exclusion of all other warranties in the purchase contract could be construed as a release from § 402A liability for property damage. It held "that Pennsylvania law does permit a freely negotiated and clearly expressed waiver of § 402A between business entities of relatively equal bargaining strength."

Again, in K-Lines, Inc. v. Roberts Motor Co., 541 P.2d 1378 (Or.1975), the warranty accompanying the sale of five truck-tractors contained the standard limitation to repair and replacement of defective parts and stated furthermore that this "shall be Buyer's sole and exclusive remedy whether in contract, tort or otherwise, and Kenworth shall not be liable for injuries to persons or property." After one of the trucks had gone about 113,000 miles during a year and a half, it went off the freeway on a curve and was heavily damaged owing, it was alleged, to a defective assembly connecting the fifth wheel to the truck. The court said that comment m to § 402A meant only that "such garden variety disclaimers were not sufficient to disclaim the strict liability established by 402A because 402A was not based on warranty. It means simply that a disclaimer of '*warranties*' is not sufficient to affect strict liability in tort. We do not take it to mean that an agreement to bar all tort remedies is treated the same, regardless of whether such agreement is denominated a disclaimer, exclusion or limitation." But suppose the driver had been injured? Or a pedestrian on a path by the road had been killed? It is difficult to see how two commercial entities, negotiating through desk personnel with little exposure to occupational injury, could contract away the remedies that others might have under § 402A.

b. NEGLIGENCE

In Blanchard v. Monical Machinery Co., 269 N.W.2d 564 (Mich.App.1978), plaintiff was injured when a foot treadle on an air-operated clamp, sold as a used machine, was accidentally tripped. The court held that the issue of defendant's negligence in selling the clamp without a guard was for the jury. "Further, the designation of the sale in the within case as being on an 'as is' basis, does not relieve defendant seller of his duty of care. While disclaimers are generally not favored, the Uniform Commercial Code, recognizing that they have some utility in promoting free commerce, provides for such disclaimers in limited circumstances. However, whatever the impact of the UCC warranties and disclaimer attempted by defendant seller in the within case, it does not result in relieving defendant

[*105*]

seller of his duty of care to plaintiff under the common law. Common law tort liability in Michigan is distinct from the warranty liabilities imposed by the Uniform Commercial Code, and may not be abrogated by the disclaimers permitted under the code."

A less sweeping approach has been to invalidate a disclaimer of liability for negligence where it is not made perfectly clear that negligence is being disclaimed. In Willard Van Dyke Productions, Inc. v. Eastman Kodak Co., 189 N.E.2d 693 (N.Y.1963), the disclaimer merely provided for replacement of the product if defective. Even though it was conceded that the plaintiff was aware of the words of the disclaimer, the court held it ineffective to exclude liability for negligence since it was not "absolutely clear that such was the understanding of the parties." This understanding must "plainly and precisely" appear from the disclaimer.

While some courts have held that the word negligence must be included in the disclaimer, others have rejected this view that negligence must be so specifically disclaimed. Thus in Gates Rubber Co. v. USM Corp., 351 F.Supp. 329 (S.D.Ill.1972), reversed on other grounds, 508 F.2d 603 (7th Cir. 1975), the trial court, applying Illinois law, held that negligence liability was effectively disclaimed by the following: "We shall have no liability for any special, indirect or consequential damages arising from loss of production or other losses owing to failure of machinery or equipment." Emphasis was placed upon the equal bargaining positions of the "two large corporations and a claim of wholly commercial loss."

In general, the two factors thus emphasized in *Gates* have been present where courts have recognized a disclaimer of negligence. In Delta Air Lines, Inc. v. McDonnell Douglas Corp., 503 F.2d 239 (5th Cir. 1974), the nose gear of a plane manufactured by the defendant collapsed during a landing because of an incorrectly installed component part. Considerable damage resulted. The purchase agreement expressly excluded seller's liability for any negligence on its part, Delta understanding that, for a price, the exculpatory clause could be removed. The court concluded that under the applicable California law such a "contract between two industrial giants fixing the dollar responsibility for McDonnell's alleged negligence" was valid.

c. STATUTORY DUTY

Courts tend to invalidate disclaimers whose effect is to relieve the seller of an obligation imposed by statute. Thus, an "as is" sale of a used car, in Mulder v. Casho, 394 P.2d 545 (Cal.1964), was ineffective to exclude a seller's liability for breach of a statutory duty to inspect the brake system. In Hunter v. American Rentals, Inc., 371 P.2d 131 (Kan.1962), a disclaimer in the rental agreement of

[*107*]

all liability and claims "including those resulting from defects, latent or apparent" was held invalid. Plaintiff's car overturned when the rented trailer attached to it came loose at the hitch but remained attached with a safety chain so that it swung from one side of the highway to the other. A statute laid down rigid requirements for such a hitch.

3. THE UNCONSCIONABILITY ISSUE

The Uniform Commercial Code has given to the courts some latitude even in breach of warranty actions to declare disclaimers unconscionable. The first paragraph of the UCC § 2–302 reads as follows: "If the court as a matter of law finds the contract or any clause of the contract to have been unconscionable at the time it was made the court may refuse to enforce the contract, or it may enforce the remainder of the contract without the unconscionable clause, or it may so limit the application of any unconscionable clause as to avoid any unconscionable result." Comment 1 to this section recognizes the long-exercised policing powers of the courts, even when exerted by indirect means such as "determinations that the clause is contrary to public policy or to the dominant purpose of the contract." Moreover the "section is intended to allow the court to pass directly on the unconscionability of the contract."

On the other hand, comment 1 to the section disparages the very reason—the superior bargaining power of the seller—why many courts have considered disclaimers unconscionable. *Henningsen*, cited in the previous section, is the landmark case for the invalidation of a disclaimer not only for its failure to meet the minimum requirement of clarity but for broad reasons of policy where the consumer is injured after presumably agreeing to a disclaimer of liability. The court stated: "The warranty before us is a standardized form designed for mass use. It is imposed upon the automobile consumer. He takes it or leaves it, and he must take it to buy an automobile. No bargaining is engaged in with respect to it. In fact, the dealer through whom it comes to the buyer is without authority to alter it; his function is ministerial—simply to deliver it. The form warranty is not only standard with Chrysler but . . . it is the uniform warranty of the Automobile Manufacturers Association. . . .

"The gross inequality of bargaining position occupied by the consumer in the automobile industry is thus apparent. There is no competition among the car makers in the area of the express warranty. Where can the buyer go to negotiate for better protection? Such control and limitation of his remedies are inimical to the public welfare and, at the very least, call for great care by the courts to avoid injustice through application of strict common-law principles of freedom of contract." This decision has led to widespread invalidation by the courts of such "contracts of adhesion," not only in

[*109*]

the automobile industry but also as to other mass-produced consumer goods.

UCC § 2–719(3) provides: "Consequential damages may be limited or excluded unless the limitation or exclusion is unconscionable. Limitation of consequential damages for injury to the person in the case of consumer goods is prima facie unconscionable but limitation of damages where the loss is commercial is not."

In Collins v. Uniroyal, Inc., 315 A.2d 30 (N.J.Super.1973), plaintiff's decedent was killed in an auto accident following the sudden failure of one of defendant's tires. The appellate court affirmed the trial judge's decision to excise from the warranty, before it was submitted to the jury, the following paragraph: "This Guarantee does not cover consequential damage, and the liability of the manufacturer is limited to repairing or replacing the tire in accordance with the stipulations contained in this guarantee. No other guarantee or warranty, express or implied, is made." The court held that there was "no evidence in the record to overcome the clear unconscionability of limiting consequential damages in this case to the repair or replacement of the tire."

In Tuttle v. Kelly-Springfield Tire Co., 585 P.2d 1116 (Okla.1978), plaintiff was severely injured when she lost control of her car and crashed into a bridge abutment, allegedly as a result of a tire blowout. The defendant manufacturer, Phillips Petroleum

Company, had guaranteed the tire "for the life of the original tread" and "against failure from blowouts." At the same time it limited the company's liability to repair or replacement of the tire. It was held that the trial court had erroneously refused to admit the written guarantee into evidence in support of plaintiff's contention that, because of the guarantee, defendant's limitation of liability was unconscionable. "Under § 2–719(3) . . . the presumption of unconscionability arises from the simultaneous presence of three facts: (1) a contract clause excluding consequential damages, (2) an accident caused by a consumer product and (3) resulting personal injuries. The absence of a defect, as argued by Phillips, is irrelevant to the question of liability in an action for breach of warranty under the code. . . . This does not mean all limitations of remedies under this provision are per se unconscionable. The explanation lies in the problem of proof. The seller has the burden of establishing the validity of any limitation." The court also made an illuminating comment: "It may appear illogical that the code permits a disclaimer of warranties altogether if § 2–316 requirements are met but makes it very difficult to create a warranty and then limit the remedy.

"This illusive inconsistency may be clarified in the framework of public policy concerning consumer protection. In the case of consumer goods to give what looks like relief in the form of an express warranty, but is not, is unconscionable as a surprise limitation and therefore against public policy."

In Steele v. J. I. Case Co., 419 P.2d 902 (Kan.1966), the court invalidated a disclaimer of consequential damages in an action for breach of an express warranty where three combines failed to work properly, causing plaintiff to lose much of his harvest. It held "the principles espoused in *Henningsen* are applicable in this case" where a consumer with little or no bargaining power signed "a printed form dictated by a corporate seller. . . . In this case, also, the seller knew the combines were purchased for use in the 1960 harvest and must be deemed to have known, through its representatives, the urgency of harvest on the High Plains and the dangers consequent upon any stoppage in operations after the grain has ripened and is ready to cut. And in this case, despite such knowledge, the seller wasted thirty crucial days in attempting to remedy defects and to get the machines working, refusing during this critical time either to replace the machines with others which would operate or to repay the purchase price, even though such was demanded."

D. ECONOMIC LOSS

1. NEGLIGENCE

If a plaintiff suffers economic or pecuniary loss along with physical damage to person or property, he can recover under any theory for all losses and harms. Thus in Hales v. Green Colonial, Inc., 490 F.2d 1015 (8th Cir. 1974), where a defective gas heater caused a fire in plaintiffs' business property, the court deemed "the cost of repairs and clean-up . . . an integral part of the direct property damage incurred. We are, however, somewhat troubled by the $8,000.00 awarded for loss of profits." The court held that the situation was not analagous to one where the heater caused loss of business because it was inadequate. "Here the defective heater burned plaintiffs' building and disrupted their business for eight months. Loss of profits by reason of the tortious destruction of the plaintiffs' business was a foreseeable damage ordinarily cognizable in tort liability and therefore we find it to be compensable under Missouri law."

If, on the other hand, plaintiff suffers only an economic or pecuniary loss, with no direct damage to property, one theory of recovery may have a distinct advantage over another. In negligence law, a difference is made between physical harm to property and economic loss. Thus, in Dunn v. Ralston Purina Co., 272 S.W.2d 479 (Tenn.App.1954), a defendant that negligently manufactured livestock feed was held liable for the loss of plaintiff's horse, which died from eating the feed. Where only economic loss is involved a privity requirement has sometimes been imposed, thus denying plaintiff the right to sue the manufacturer. In Trans World

[*113*]

Airlines v. Curtiss-Wright Corp., 148 N.Y.S.2d 284 (N.Y.Sup.Ct.1955), decided by the court of original jurisdiction, the court said: "The damage asserted by TWA is for replacement cost of allegedly inferior engines—a matter of qualitative inadequacy in a product purchased from Lockheed, a proper subject for a claim of breach of warranty, pure and simple. It is true that when the planes 'failed to operate', the planes became 'imminently dangerous'; but the danger was 'averted.' There was no accident."

It is possible that *Trans World* would not be followed today, since its effect is to penalize the plaintiff for diligence in preventing accidents. The court in Berg v. General Motors Corp., 555 P.2d 818 (Wash.1976), allowed a negligence action by a commercial fisherman against a remote manufacturer for lost profits resulting from an allegedly defective diesel engine and clutch. Similarly, in Jones v. Bender Welding & Machine Works, Inc., 581 F.2d 1331 (9th Cir. 1978), where an oil cooler supply line cracked, immobilizing a fishing vessel, recovery was allowed against the manufacturer in admiralty for negligence causing lost profits.

2. STRICT LIABILITY: TORT AND IMPLIED WARRANTY

To avoid the penalizing effect of *Trans World,* a court might apply the criterion used in the strict tort case of Russell v. Ford Motor Co., 575 P.2d 1383 (Or.1978). Here plaintiff remained uninjured after his axle housing fractured owing to a defective weld, causing the car to leave the road, hit a rock pile, upend, and finally come to rest on its wheels. In allowing recovery for damage to the car, the court stressed that the defect was in fact a "man-endangering one" of the sort for which strict liability was imposed upon a manufacturer.

Courts have differed on the question whether damage only to the defective product itself, as in *Russell*, should be treated as property damage coming under § 402A or as economic loss recoverable only under the warranty provisions of the UCC. In Mid Continent Aircraft Corp. v. Curry County Spraying Serv., Inc., 572 S.W.2d 308 (Tex.1978), defendant Mid Continent had sold a reconditioned aircraft to the plaintiff crop spraying service for use in its business. When the plane was destroyed in a crash that admittedly was caused by a defect, the court held: "In transactions between a commercial seller and commercial buyer, when no physical injury has occurred to persons or other property, injury to the defective product itself is an economic loss governed by the Uniform Commercial Code. Curry County's cause of action for the damage of the airplane lies in breach of warranty as provided by the Code." Mid Continent, however, had effectively eliminated all warranties by an "as is" disclaimer in the contract of sale.

In Brown v. Western Farmers Ass'n, Inc., 521 P.2d 537 (Or.1974), strict tort recovery was denied where plaintiffs' chickens, allegedly as a result of being given defendants' feed, produced bad-tasting eggs and so became valueless. Plaintiffs sought recovery for lost profits as well as for the cost of the defective feed. The court's emphasis, however, was not so much on the economic loss issue but on its belief that the feed was "not unreasonably dangerous."

In Mead Corp. v. Allendale Mut. Ins. Co., 465 F.Supp. 355 (N.D.Ohio 1979), the court held that under Ohio law recovery could be had under either a strict tort theory or for negligence when a defective steam turbine broke down causing business losses as well as expenses connected with putting the turbine back in working condition.

Perhaps a majority of jurisdictions have denied recovery for economic loss in strict tort cases. A widespread feeling exists, among both judges and commentators, that while a tort recovery can be justified for physical injury, recovery for economic losses alone must be guided by the UCC. Even if no unconstitutional conflict exists, it may be contended that the rules of warranty function better than those of negligence or strict tort in the commercial setting of economic loss. In Seely v. White Motor Co., 403 P.2d 145 (Cal.1965), where the plaintiff purchased a truck which was defective in that it "galloped" or bounced violently, recovery from the manufacturer was allowed for loss of profits as well as for money paid on the purchase price of the truck. The court held, however, that this liability stemmed entirely from the manufacturer's breach of express warranty, made directly to the plaintiff. While it was reasonable, the court stated, to hold the manufacturer liable for physical injuries caused by his sale of a defective product, even where the manufacturer has not expressly agreed to such liability, he should not be liable "for the level of performance of his products in the consumer's business unless he agrees" that the product will meet such level of performance. If this distinction is not drawn, the manufacturer would be liable for business losses caused by the failure of its trucks to meet "the specific needs" of a consumer's business "even though those needs were communicated only to the dealer." Such liability "could not be disclaimed, for one purpose of strict liability in tort is to prevent a manufacturer from defining the scope of his responsibility." Moreover, the "manufacturer would be liable for damages of unknown and unlimited scope."

The dissenting judge in *Seely* found no essential difference between damages resulting from physical harm to person or property and other types of damages, and saw no reason why recovery in strict tort should turn on the type of damage involved. He argued that the crucial test should be whether the claimant can be classed as an ordinary consumer, as opposed to a sophisticated merchant or businessman. On the facts of this case he concluded that the plaintiff more nearly resembled an ordinary user than a businessman. Also he pointed out that a consumer may suffer "overwhelming misfortune" from economic loss as well as from physical injury to person or property. Moreover, the lay consumer usually lacks the seller's expertness with regard to the goods, and also lacks the seller's ability equitably to spread the risk of loss. These considerations indicate the desirability of invalidating disclaimers where consumer losses are involved, regardless of the kind of damages suffered.

A leading case which does permit recovery of economic loss against a remote seller is Santor v. A and M Karagheusian, Inc., 207 A.2d 305 (N.J.1965). There the plaintiff bought carpeting from a local dealer. The carpeting was sold as grade No. 1, but it turned out to be defective in developing an "unusual line" that would not "walk out" in use. Unable to receive satisfaction from the local dealer, plaintiff brought suit against the remote seller and manufacturer for breach of implied warranty, and sought damages for loss of value owing to the defect. The New Jersey Supreme Court upheld a judgment for the plaintiff, but said it was more appropriate to describe such liability as one in strict tort. The court rested its holding on the policy judgment that "the great mass of the purchasing public has neither adequate knowledge nor sufficient opportunity to determine if articles bought or used are defective." A fair measure of the manufacturer's obligation in such a case "must be the price at which the manufacturer reasonably contemplated that the article might be sold."

In Ford Motor Co. v. Lonon, 398 S.W.2d 240 (Tenn.1966), a strong case was presented for holding a manufacturer not in privity strictly liable in tort for economic loss when plaintiff purchased a tractor which was widely advertised as possessing live-power takeoff and other features needed on plaintiff's farm. In consequence of the machine's lacking such features, and possessing such a serious defect as a continuous leakage of oil from the crankshaft, plaintiff and his employees lost many days of work during the planting season. In adopting strict tort liability "by expansion of the concept of misrepresentation rather than by expansion of warranty concepts," the court cited comment a to the Second Restatement of Torts § 402B which refers to a parallel rule that is to be contained in a proposed § 552D. The tentative draft (No. 17) for this proposed section reads as follows: "One engaged in the business of selling chattels who, by advertising, labels or otherwise, makes to the public a misrepresentation of a material fact concerning the character or quality of a chattel sold by him is subject to liability for pecuniary loss caused to another by his purchase of the chattel in justifiable reliance upon the misrepresentation, even though it is not made fraudulently or negligently."

This draft, referring especially to sellers of chattels, was not incorporated in the Restatement, although a more restrictive provision is embodied in § 552C allowing recovery for out-of-pocket losses alone resulting from an innocent misrepresentation occurring "in a sale, rental or exchange transaction."

Plaintiffs in Morrow v. New Moon Homes, Inc., 548 P.2d 279 (Alaska 1976), had bought a mobile home only to find it falling apart shortly after the retailer went out of business. Although Alaska had adopted strict tort in personal injury cases, the court here followed *Seely* in considering the doctrine inapplicable where only economic loss was involved. It held, however, that even without privity of contract the manufacturer could be liable for breach of his implied warranties to the ultimate purchaser. The court said that "there is no satisfactory justification for a remedial scheme which extends the warranty action to a consumer suffering personal injury or property damage but denies similar relief to the consumer 'fortunate' enough to suffer only direct economic loss. . . . Our decision today preserves the statutory rights of the manufacturer to define his potential liability to the ultimate consumer, by means of express disclaimers and limitations, while protecting the legitimate expectation of the consumer that goods distributed on a wide scale by the use of conduit retailers are fit for their intended use." In Cloud v. Kit Mfg. Co., 563 P.2d 248 (Alaska 1977), the court made clear that *Morrow* did not preclude strict tort recovery for direct physical injury to property. Here "the damage to the product, the trailer package, was the result of a sudden and calamitous occurrence, the fire. Accordingly, we hold that the damage to the product in this case was direct property damage. The damage alleged in the complaint to the Clouds' personal belongings, furniture, apparel and jewelry is direct damage to their personal property and thus is compensable if proven to be attributable to a defect in the product as manufactured by Kit Manufacturing. We note that the harm alleged in this case is much different from that alleged by the Morrows in *New Moon*", where the defects "resulted in a deprivation of the value of the Morrows' bargain."

E. NOTICE OF BREACH

The *Morrow* court observed that among the statutory obligations of the injured purchaser is that of giving notice of breach to the defendant seller. As stated in U.C.C. § 2–607(3)(c), he must do this "within a reasonable time after he discovers or should have discovered any breach." In products cases where the buyer is seeking damages, the notice enables the seller to inspect the goods, investigate the claim, or seek to minimize damages by settlement. Also, the seller can better protect himself against fraudulent claims if time is allowed him for an investigation.

In Mattos, Inc. v. Hash, 368 A.2d 993 (Md.1977), it was held that an employee of the buyer was not required to give notice of his injury to the defendant seller of a defective product. Where a bystander is injured, as in Piercefield v. Remington Arms Co., 133 N.W.2d 129 (Mich.1965), when the barrel of a shotgun exploded, notice of breach was not required.

Notice of breach to all defendants in the distributive chain may be required. However, in Prutch v. Ford Motor Co., CCH Prod. Liab. Rptr. par. 8540 (Colo.1979), it was held that a prompt notice to the dealer of malfunctioning farm machinery satisfied the UCC requirement that the *seller* be notified of a breach of warranty. The dealer in this case had "promptly advised Ford of the problem, and Ford dispatched a service representative who arrived to work on the equipment within a few days after it had been delivered. Surely formal notice communicated directly from the buyers to Ford could have accomplished no more."

In Pollard v. Saxe & Yolles Development Co., 525 P.2d 88 (Cal.1974), where an action was brought against vendors for breach of warranty for defective apartment buildings purchased by the plaintiffs, it was held that the notice requirement of the UCC was applicable to real property as well as to chattels.

In most jurisdictions today the notice need not formally assert a claim for damages or even describe in detail the nature and cause of the injury. Thus in Wojciuk v. United States Rubber Co., 122 N.W.2d

737 (Wis.1963), it was held the question of sufficiency of notice was for the jury where the buyer
called the seller and stated: "Herb, what kind of
tires did you sell me? . . . We had a blowout
and a terrible accident resulted from it."

In general, no exceptions are allowed even in
personal injury actions for breach of warranty, in
spite of Prosser's description of the requirement as a
"booby trap for the unwary." The harshness of the
rule has been somewhat mitigated by applying comment 4 to UCC § 2–607 which states that the time of
notice "is to be determined by applying commercial
standards to a merchant buyer," but that a reasonable time for notice "from a retail consumer is to be
judged by different standards so that in his case it
will be extended." The rule requiring notice "is
designed to defeat commercial bad faith, not to
deprive a good faith consumer of his remedy."

The notice requirement in products liability generally has been restricted to cases based on breach
of warranty. No such requirement is imposed where
the plaintiff seeks recovery in negligence.

The landmark case dispensing with the notice
requirement in strict tort is Greenman v. Yuba
Power Products, Inc., 377 P.2d 897 (Cal.1962), discussed in chapter 2 in connection with the recognition of a strict tort action against a remote manufacturer. The court held that the notice requirement
"is not an appropriate one for the court to adopt in
actions by injured consumers against manufacturers

with whom they have not dealt." What is appropriate for businessmen, the court said, is inappropriate
for injured consumers to whom it will not normally
occur to give such notice until they have secured
legal advice.

Although *Greenman* confines itself to the situation
where privity is lacking between plaintiff and defendant, subsequent decisions have not so restricted
the holding. In Vandermark v. Ford Motor Co., 391
P.2d 168 (Cal.1964), the court held that notice was
not required in an action for personal injuries by a
purchaser against a retail seller of a defective automobile, since the seller was subject to strict liability
in tort and the "requirement of timely notice of
breach of warranty . . . is not applicable to
such tort liability just as it is not applicable to tort
liability based on negligence."

The rule dispensing with notice of breach apparently extends to all strict tort actions, including
those involving property damage or economic loss,
and actions based on § 402B as well as § 402A. It is
possible, however, that those courts which uphold
between equal bargainors disclaimers of strict tort
claims for physical property damage would also
require reasonable notice of such a claim.

F. WRONGFUL DEATH

A number of courts, as in Schnabl v. Ford Motor
Co., 195 N.W.2d 602 (Wis.1972), allow a breach of
warranty action for wrongful death, thus permitting

the plaintiff to take advantage of a favorable statute of limitations. On the other hand, such an action was held not maintainable in Necktas v. General Motors Corp., 259 N.E.2d 234 (Mass.1970). The issue usually turns on a construction of the language of the applicable wrongful death statute.

G. JURISDICTION

In products cases where the defendant is often in a state different from plaintiff's place of residence, the plaintiff may have a choice of jurisdictions. Under the "long-arm" statutes of most states a defendant may be brought within the jurisdiction of states outside his principal place of business. Generally a defendant has been shown to carry on some business activity within the state. In Pennsalt Chem. Corp. v. Crown Cork & Seal Co., 426 S.W.2d 417 (Ark. 1968), necessary "minimum contacts" were established by the shipment of twelve valves to Arkansas within a five-year period for a total revenue of $11.60. Some states have held that where a product causes injury within the state, the defendant seller is subject to the state's jurisdiction even though he did no business within the state. Such a holding, however, was reversed by the Supreme Court in World-Wide Volkswagen Corp. v. Woodson, 444 U.S. 286 (1980). The original plaintiffs were severely injured while traveling in Oklahoma by a fire caused by the rupture of a gas tank when their Audi was struck in the rear by another car. Alleging defective design of the tank and fuel system, they joined as defendants not only the manufacturer and importer but also the regional distributor and the retailer from whom they bought the car. The court held that the latter two were not subject to the jurisdiction of Oklahoma, when their "only connection with Oklahoma is the fact that an automobile sold in New York to New York residents became involved in an accident in Oklahoma."

H. CONFLICT OF LAWS

Where a plaintiff may have a choice of jurisdiction, he will be influenced by the state's conflicts rules. Deciding what state law is applicable, especially in cases involving multiple plaintiffs or multiple defendants or both, residing or doing business in different states, with perhaps the place of injury in still another state, may be very complicated. The decision will be made in accordance with the forum's conflicts rules. Such rules were at one time relatively simple when, in tort actions, the law of the place of injury generally controlled, or in warranty actions, the law of the place of contract or sale. Although these rules have not altogether disappeared, they have been replaced in many jurisdictions by rules that involve the determination of what state had "the most significant relationship with the occurrence and with the parties to the occurrence," especially in motor vehicle cases such as Williams v. Texas Kenworth Co., 307 F.Supp. 748 (W.D.Okl.

1969). There the collision, allegedly caused by a tire blowout, took place in Missouri where the action for wrongful death would be barred by Missouri's one-year limitation statute. The court held the law of Oklahoma applicable, since the vehicle was purchased either in Oklahoma or Texas by a leasing company located in Oklahoma, the truck with the allegedly defective wheel and tire was tagged and garaged in Oklahoma, and the plaintiffs and each of their decedents were all residents of Oklahoma where the action was not time-barred.

Another rule is that of "state interest analysis," applied in Turcotte v. Ford Motor Co., 494 F.2d 173 (1st Cir. 1974). Here plaintiff, a Rhode Island citizen, sought recovery for the wrongful death of her son as a passenger in Massachusetts because of a fire allegedly caused by a defectively positioned gas tank. Defendant, a Delaware corporation, would have Massachusetts law controlling. Applying the conflicts rules of the forum state, Rhode Island, the court held that the trial court had properly decided that Rhode Island's wrongful death statute and its law on strict liability governed the case. Rhode Island, unlike Massachusetts, had no ceiling on wrongful death recoveries. Its interest here was in securing adequate compensation for its citizens who might otherwise become a burden on the state. As to strict liability, not at that time expressly adopted by Massachusetts, the court held that Rhode Island had an interest in protecting its citizens from defective products, a protection less assured under Massachusetts law.

In some jurisdictions an even more flexible and less predictable conflicts rule has been applied. For example, in Decker v. Fox River Tractor Co., 324 F.Supp. 1089 (E.D.Wis.1971), plaintiff was injured by the allegedly defective moving parts of a forage harvester manufactured in Wisconsin by defendant. Plaintiff, a resident of Pennsylvania, purchased the harvester from a Pennsylvania dealer. The court found that a true conflict existed in that Wisconsin applied comparative negligence principles while Pennsylvania held that contributory negligence was a complete bar to recovery. In applying Wisconsin law, the court found that among the various "choice-influencing" factors was the "application of the better rule of law."

I. STATUTES OF LIMITATIONS

1. THE APPLICABLE STATUTE

Occasionally a plaintiff may be able to choose a jurisdiction where his case is not barred by a limitations statute as opposed to one where it is so barred. However, as observed in Heavner v. Uniroyal, Inc., 305 A.2d 412 (N.J.1973), "about three-quarters of the states" have borrowing statutes, enacted for the very purpose of preventing forum-shopping. "Generally these statutes either bar the action if it is barred by the state where the defendant, or both of the parties, resided or of the place where the cause of action arose." Absent such a statute in New Jersey, the court adopted the rule that "when the cause of action arises in another state, the parties are all present in and amenable to the jurisdiction of that state, New Jersey has no substantial interest in the matter, the substantive law of the foreign state is to be applied, and its limitation period has expired at the time suit is commenced here, New Jersey will hold the suit barred."

Many cases involving statutes of limitations involve a choice of remedies rather than of jurisdiction. One case involved both choices. This was Schnabl v. Ford Motor Co., 195 N.W.2d 602 (Wis. 1972), in which plaintiff's decedent was killed in a roll-over accident in Indiana where the action was barred by a two-year statute of limitations. Plaintiff alleged that the seat belts, manufactured and installed in Minnesota, were defective. The car, with the seat belts, was purchased in Wisconsin where a three-year statute applied to breach of warranty actions. The defendant contended that such warranty actions sounded in contract, whereas the wrongful death statute applied to tort actions only. The court cited various cases in other jurisdictions which allowed a contract action for wrongful death. Then, without a clear holding on the contract issue, the court emphasized the essentially tort nature of breach of implied warranty and held that plaintiff's action for such breach was maintainable under the Wisconsin wrongful death statute.

Until recently, statutes of limitations were not adopted with products liability in mind; and the recent products statutes may create more problems than they solve. A plaintiff injured by a product ten years after its sale by the defendant may be barred by a statute which sets a limit of ten years from the date of sale. The statutes usually vary from five to twelve years. Very few of the statutes have been tested in the courts. Possibly they will be ruled unconstitutional, as denying equal protection of the laws. Unless a state has a general statute of ultimate repose, a classification seems unjust if it allows recovery for a negligent burial of chemical wastes that years later seep into the town's water supply, but denies recovery when a storage drum deteriorates in as many years with the result that useful but dangerous chemicals are released into the workplace. Moreover, to apply the same outer limitations period to a child's toy and to an apparently solid steel drum does not seem to make much sense. Unfortunately, such outer cutoff periods have now been adopted by statutes in a substantial number of state legislatures. It remains to be seen what exceptions the courts may be able to develop without contravening the statutes.

The older statutes also create problems in the field of products liability. The action may be considered as one of contract or of tort, as coming under the

UCC or under the Second Restatement of Torts, § 402A, or as a negligence action resembling other such actions. If personal injury is involved, it may fall under a limitation period specifically assigned to personal injury actions; or it may come under the UCC limitation of four years from the date of sale regardless of the nature of the injury, especially if the action is for breach of warranty. If, as in most cases, several causes of action are included in the complaint, the problem of what statute is applicable becomes still more complicated.

The solution to these problems and many others is given by a particular court's interpretation of a statute in its own jurisdiction which was not designed to cover the products situation. The solutions therefore may vary among the different jurisdictions. The only generalization that may safely be made is that a tendency exists to use some discretion in interpreting statutes that would deprive a plaintiff of his cause of action before he ever had one. A leading case in this regard is Victorson v. Bock Laundry Machine Co., 335 N.E.2d 275 (N.Y.1975). The suit in fact involved three cases, one where the defendant's extractor was sold in 1948 with the injury in 1969, another where the sale was in 1959 and the injury in 1967, and the third with a sale in 1955 and the injury in 1965. The New York court in *Victorson* overruled its previous decisions by refusing to apply the UCC limitation of four years from the date of sale, and instead applied the

[*131*]

three-year personal injury limitation which began to run on the date of injury. Such a ruling might, however, work to plaintiff's disadvantage. In Salvador v. Atl. Steel Boiler Co., 389 A.2d 1148 (Pa.Super.1978), where plaintiff's tort action was barred by a two-year personal injury statute, the court held that he could not bring an implied warranty action against the remote manufacturer under the UCC four-year statute of limitations.

On the other hand, a court may allow plaintiff a choice of remedies in order to bring him under a favorable limitation statute. In Redfield v. Meade, Johnson & Co., 512 P.2d 776 (Or.1973), plaintiff's action for personal injury from taking an oral contraceptive of defendant's manufacture was barred by the two-year tort statute of limitations. To allow the action, the court applied the four-year statute of the UCC for breach of implied warranties.

2. THE DATE OF ACCRUAL

Even where the applicable statute of limitation is reasonably certain under the law of a particular jurisdiction, the date of accrual may remain uncertain. The statute may begin to run from the date of injury or from the date when the injury is discovered. Even where the injury is immediately known, plaintiff's temporary ignorance of his cause of action may justify the application of the "discovery" rule. In Ohler v. Tacoma Gen. Hosp., 598 P.2d 1358 (Wash.1979), plaintiff, now 22 years old, had been blinded as a result of being given too much oxygen after a premature birth. Although she had known for some time the cause of her blindness, it was not until she was 21 years old that she had learned that the hospital and the incubator manufacturer might have breached a duty owed to her. The court held that appellant's claim against both defendants "did not accrue until after she discovered or reasonably should have discovered all the essential elements of her possible cause of action. This ruling accords with rulings in products liability cases in other jurisdictions."

In Raymond v. Eli Lilly & Co., 371 A.2d 170 (N.H.1977), plaintiff suffered legal blindness caused by hemorrhages in her optic nerves. But "she did not know, nor had any reason to know of her potential claim against the defendant [manufacturer of an oral contraceptive] until sometime in 1970 or 1971." The court, in holding the discovery rule made plaintiff's action timely, said that "the proper formulation of the rule and the one that will cause the least confusion is the one adopted by the majority of the courts: A cause of action will not accrue under the discovery rule until the plaintiff discovers or in the exercise of reasonable diligence should have discovered not only that he has been injured but also that his injury may have been caused by the defendant's conduct."

Courts have differed on the accrual date for indemnity and contribution actions. For some it is the date of sale from the indemnitor to the indemnitee, for others the date of the judgment against the indemnitee. If a date before judgment or payment is adopted as the accrual date, the applicable period may run before the indemnitee knows either his liability or its extent.

Some courts, as in Boains v. Lasar Mfg. Co., 330 F.Supp. 1134 (D.C.Conn.1971), have held that where there is a continuing duty to warn, the statute of limitations does not run as long as that duty exists.

UCC § 2–725(2) provides that when a warranty "explicitly extends to future performance", the statute of limitations does not accrue until a breach of warranty is or should have been discovered. Such warranties cannot readily be distinguished from the usual warranties, and it has been suggested that all warranties can be construed as extending to future performance if the breach is not reasonably discoverable at the time of delivery. In Mittasch v. Seal Lock Burial Vault, Inc., 344 N.Y.S.2d 101 (App. Div.1973), the defendant manufacturer had expressly certified that the vault would "give satisfactory service at all times." It was held that since this was a warranty extending to future performance, the cause of action accrued when the plaintiff, twelve years later, exhumed the body of her deceased husband for transfer to another cemetery. A leak in the casket had caused damage to the casket and the body from "water, vermin, and other matter."

In Perry v. Augustine, 37 D. & C.2d 416 (Pa.1965), a warranty that a heating system would heat well in sub-zero weather was held a warranty of future performance, since discovery of the breach "would necessarily have to await winter weather." On the other hand, in Binkley Co. v. Teledyne Mid-America Corp., 460 F.2d 276 (8th Cir. 1972), it was held that an express warranty that a "welder could perform a precise number of welds per minute" was a warranty of present performance which did not extend to the future, despite the fact that the breach could not be discovered until the welder was used and failed to perform. Any distinction between the performance of the heating system and that of the welder seems unjustified if considered merely one of semantics. If, on the other hand, the distinction turns on the degree of discoverability of the defect, the issue should normally be a question of fact for the jury and not one of law for the court.

CHAPTER V

PRODUCTION AND DESIGN DEFECTS

A. DEFECTS AS A RESULT OF PRODUCTION OR HANDLING

In recent years cases reported from the higher courts involving production or handling defects have been relatively few in number, perhaps because few of them involve difficult points of law that might be appealed. These defects are not those designed into the product, but rather a deviation from the defendant's own standard that has occurred during manufacture, processing, servicing or simply storing. Defect in such cases is easily defined. Proving that the cause of the injury was the defect will not differ substantially from other cases and will be dealt with in the chapter on causation. Proving that the defect existed when it left the defendant's control will probably be more difficult than in the design and warning cases where the same defect will occur in the entire product line. For example, a burr in a dish of peas might have been brought in from the plaintiff's own yard. In Athens Canning Co. v. Ballard, 365 S.W.2d 369 (Tex.Civ.App.1963), where plaintiff's mouth was cut by such a burr, a most meticulous account was given of the opening, heating, and serving of the offending peas. The numerous cases involving mice or other foreign matter in bottles of soft drink generally demand a tracing of the bottle's history from the bottling plant to the time it is opened by the plaintiff, in the effort to exclude any possibility of tampering. Exploding bottles remain a serious problem which may become even more serious if the drive to require returnable bottles is successful. Internal scratches caused by pebbly earth or other foreign matter that might easily enter a used bottle are practically undetectable by inspection. But whether the defendant is the manufacturer of the bottles or the bottling company, such cases are rarely successful for the plaintiff except on a strict liability basis. Invariably the defendant can produce evidence of the impeccable methods used in his plant.

Mechanical defects are often difficult to trace to the production process because of the likelihood that the accident itself might have caused the defect. For example, in Jenkins v. General Motors Corp., 446 F.2d 377 (5th Cir. 1971), the minor plaintiff was paralyzed over a major portion of her body when her friend, driving a two-months-old Corvair, lost control of the steering and landed in a culvert. Plaintiff brought a negligence action against the defendant, tracing the accident to a failure "to properly tighten and inspect a nut on a bolt in the left rear suspension system." Experts disagreed as to whether the "missing" bolt was lost before or as a result of the accident. The court affirmed a jury verdict for the plaintiff, since it was the province of the jury to determine the facts in such a "battle of the experts," especially where the "jury was allowed to inspect and even handle the various components of the rear suspension assembly involved," in addition to viewing "hundreds of photographs, exhibits and the movies that were shown."

B. DEFECTIVE DESIGN

1. LEGAL BASIS OF LIABILITY

Some courts have suggested that in design cases little difference exists between negligence and strict liability.   This contention, however, is firmly rejected in Gonzales v. Caterpillar Tractor Co., 571 S.W.2d 867 (Tex.1978).   Here the plaintiff, operator of a machine mounted on treads or tracks similar to those used on military tanks and equipped with a shovel for lifting dirt from the ground, slipped on a step used for dismounting with resultant back injuries from his fall.   The court held that where the operator could not see the step in dismounting, where he had to lean away from the machine to reach the step, where mud collecting on one of the treads was deposited on the step as the tread revolved, and where no adhesive or antiskid material was placed on the step, the defendant was liable for a defective and unreasonably dangerous design.   It also affirmed a jury verdict of negligence in design since there was evidence that "the primary consideration in the use by Caterpillar of the step in question was its availability from production of like steps for tractors other than the Model 941. There was evidence that no particular instructions regarding the safety of the step were given to the design engineer on the Model 941 project, and that no tests as to the safety of the step were made after it was incorporated in the Model 941 Traxcavator." Furthermore, the company had violated its own "design reference" guidelines for such a machine, requiring that "[a]ll steps, ladders, and walkways into platform area shall be designed to minimize accumulation of debris from the vehicle wheels and tracks," and they "shall be made of or coated with an 'antiskid' material."

In Roach v. Kononen, 525 P.2d 125 (Or.1974), the hood on Mrs. Hinen's Ford suddenly flew up, causing her to cross the center line and collide with plaintiff's vehicle. Shortly before the accident, a service station attendant had opened and closed the hood. Plaintiff alleged "that Ford was negligent in failing to design a hood that would provide 'sufficient visibility for a driver to safely guide the automobile should the hood fly up.' Alternatively, the plaintiff also alleged that Ford was strictly liable for such a defect in the design of the hood. Whether plaintiff is entitled to prevail as a matter of law on either of these two theories is the issue presented in this appeal." The court found that the conflicting evidence of a defect presented a question of fact for the court so that the trial court's judgment for the defendant must be affirmed. In its discussion of plaintiff's two theories of recovery the court observed that "it is generally recognized that the basic difference between negligence on the one hand and strict liability for a design defect on the other, is that in strict liability we are talking about the condition (dangerousness) of an article which is designed in a particular way, while in negligence we are talking about the reasonableness of the manufacturer's actions in designing and selling the article as he did. The article can have a degree of dangerousness which the law of strict liability will not tolerate even though the actions of the designer were entirely reasonable in view of what he knew at the time he planned and sold the manufactured article."

A strict liability action may be useful to the plaintiff in those jurisdictions which hold that contributory negligence is not a defense to such an action. The manufacturer almost invariably contends that the plaintiff has used the product negligently.

Although ordinarily, as in *Gonzales*, any unreasonably dangerous design is apt to involve negligence on the part of the maker of the product, that is not always the case. Furthermore, a retailer, wholesaler, or other supplier who takes no part in the design of the product is clearly not likely to be negligent; yet he may still be strictly liable for a dangerously designed article. The emphasis in this chapter will be on the nature of design defects, with only incidental reference to the basis of liability, whether negligent or strict.

2. DETERMINATION OF DEFECT IN DESIGN

a. SOME GENERAL CONSIDERATIONS

It is of course impossible to discuss all design issues in this chapter. Design problems are closely related to warnings, causation, foreseeability, affirmative defenses, and proof. They will therefore frequently appear in later chapters. A clear warning may justify a certain danger in design if the danger cannot be avoided without lessening the utility of a product.

Tracing the accident to some other cause may tend to show that the design was free from the alleged defect. Foreseeability of use, although generally determinative of negligence, may also be determinative of defect in a strict liability case. If feasible the design must be safe not only for an intended use but for any foreseeable use, whether intended by the defendant or not.

Design, of course, includes the materials used in a product as well as the way they are put together. The same principles apply to both an unsafe hair dye formula and a dangerous punch press.

In a design case, unlike a production case where the product has failed to meet the manufacturer's own standards, either court or jury may be reluctant to define as defective some feature of the product even though it has caused injury to the plaintiff. It is one thing to hold the manufacturer liable for an occasional mistake; it is quite another matter to find him potentially liable for a dangerous defect in an entire product line. Yet the deterrence value of products liability law is obviously more important to the public in the second situation than in the first. Presumably the greater and more widespread the danger, the greater the need for imposing liability. However, liability will in all probability be limited, since the defect will not generally result in injury. Yet the inquiry as to what constitutes a defect is apt to be far more searching in a design case than in one involving production error. Is the obvious lack of a safety feature a defect? Would it be feasible to provide the safety device without pricing a useful product out of the market or without rendering the product so inefficient that it would scarcely be marketable? Or is the danger so great that the product should be withdrawn from the market? Should the benefit of a product not absolutely safe be weighed against the degree of risk involved?

Some courts have deplored any distinction between a production and a design defect. Thus in Cronin v. J. B. E. Olson Corp., 501 P.2d 1153 (Cal.1972), the court said: "Although it is easier to see the 'defect' in a single imperfectly fashioned product than in an entire line badly conceived, a distinction between manufacture and design defects is not tenable. . . . The most obvious problem we perceive in creating any such distinction is that thereafter it would be advantageous to characterize a defect in one rather than the other category. It is difficult to prove that a widget was poorly welded —a defect in manufacture—rather than because it was made of inexpensive metal difficult to weld, chosen by a designer concerned with economy—a defect in design. The proof problem would, of course, be magnified when the article in question was either old or unique, with no easily available basis for comparison. We wish to avoid providing such a battleground for clever counsel. Furthermore, we find no reason why a different standard, and one harder to meet, should apply to defects which plague entire product lines. We recognize that it is more damaging to a manufacturer to have an entire line condemned, so to speak, for a defect in design, than a single product for a defect in manufacture. But the potential economic loss to a manufacturer should not be reflected in a different standard of proof for an injured consumer."

b. PRODUCTS MANUFACTURED TO SPECIFICATIONS

It is possible that a manufacturer or a contractor who, in making the product, follows the specifications of the prospective purchaser will be held liable in strict tort for a dangerous defect. In Castaldo v.

Pittsburgh-Des Moines Steel Co., 376 A.2d 88
(Del.1977), however, the court referred to the
"generally accepted rule that the manufacturer of a
product, built in accordance with plans and specifications of an employer, will not be liable for damage
occasioned by a defect in those specifications, unless
the plans are so obviously dangerous that no
reasonable person would follow them." Here an
employee attempted to replace a broken thermometer in a tank manufactured according to the
specifications of the employer of plaintiff's decedent
and used for storing liquid phenol. Having difficulty in reaching the broken pieces and believing
that the thermowell in which the thermometer was
enclosed was "backwelded" so as to prevent any
disturbance of the unit as a whole, the decedent
detached the thermowell and was sprayed with the
toxic contents of the tank, with resulting death. On
plaintiff's strict liability count for wrongful death
the court concluded that she had failed to show a
"defective condition."

In Garrison v. Rohm & Haas Co., 492 F.2d 346
(6th Cir. 1974), an allegedly defective dolly was
manufactured by Orangeville in accordance with the
purchaser's specifications. The court said: "To hold
Orangeville liable for defective design would amount
to holding a non-designer liable for design defect."
In Hunt v. Blasius, 384 N.E.2d 368 (Ill.1978), the
court denied a cause of action on negligence grounds
unless the specifications were "glaringly dangerous"

and simply found no defect on which strict tort liability could be based. Here defendant had met the requirements of the State of Illinois for a highway exit sign post with which a car collided. Two of the occupants were killed and three seriously injured. The court held that the failure to use a "break-away" design, the use of steel and concrete to anchor the post, and its installation within three feet of the surface of the highway did not constitute "a defect which subjects those exposed to the product to an *unreasonable* risk of harm." There was no ruling on the issue of strict liability had a defect been shown.

c.   EFFECT OF STATUTES

Although compliance with specifications generally relieves a manufacturer of liability, compliance with statutes or government regulations quite often does not. In Howard v. McCrory Corp., 601 F.2d 133 (4th Cir. 1979), pajamas sold at retail by a subsidiary of the defendant corporation and worn by a three-year-old child burst into flames when they were ignited in some unknown fashion. The flames, when first seen, were shooting a foot from the child's head and he received burns so severe as to cause his death. This fact, together with evidence that an available test, recommended but not required by federal regulations, had not been made, led the court to hold that "the reliability of this additional test and the weight to be given its results

[*145*]

were properly questions for jury determination. Compliance with federal standards, while plainly relevant, is not conclusive on the issue of McCrory's liability and the jury is entitled to consider any other reasonable evidence on the issue."

The court in Buccery v. General Motors Corp., 132 Cal.Rptr. 605 (Cal.App.1976), held that the issue of defect was for the jury where there was testimony that plaintiff's injury in a rear-end collision was greatly increased because of the lack of head restraints in his Light Utility Vehicle, allowing his head to strike the window in the back of the cab. Federal law at the time required headrests on passenger cars but was silent on the subject of utility vehicles. The court cited the specific provision of the National Traffic and Motor Vehicle Safety Act to the effect that compliance with the act "does not exempt any person from any liability under common law." Plaintiff's expert had testified not only as to the adaptability of headrests for use in plaintiff's vehicle, but also as to their low cost in proportion to the total cost of the vehicle.

In LaGorga v. Kroger Co., 275 F.Supp. 373 (W.D.Pa.1967), cited under retailers in chapter 3, the defendant retailer was held strictly liable for an "unreasonably dangerous" jacket, resulting in a child's severe burns, although it was "stipulated by all parties that the jacket conformed to or was not in violation of the Federal Flammable Fabrics Act, 15

U.S.C.A. §§ 1191 et seq., which stipulation was some evidence that the design was not unreasonably dangerous."

Under some recent product liability statutes, such as that of Tenn.Code Annot. sec. 23–3704 (1979), compliance with federal or state statutes or regulations shall raise "a rebuttable presumption that the product is not in an unreasonably dangerous condition in regard to matters covered by these standards."

d. FEASIBILITY

Courts generally agree that a useful design, even though dangerous, is not defective if no feasible way of eliminating the danger is possible. A warning may be required, but not a design change. Courts differ, however, as to what constitutes feasibility. In grain auger cases, for instance, courts have differed on the feasibility of screens. It is possible, of course, that these differences depend upon differences in the purpose and situation of the individual machines; but this is by no means clear from the cases. In Jones v. Hutchinson Mfg., Inc., 502 S.W.2d 66 (Ky.1973), the court agreed with defendant's experts that "shielding or guarding more than was done by the design of this auger, impairs the efficiency of the machine and makes it undesirable for the purposes intended." The fact that it was "common knowledge . . . that injuries frequently occur in the operation of farm machinery of the type here involved" did not impose a duty upon the manufacturer to put out a less dangerous but also less efficient machine. On the other hand, in Davis v. Fox River Tractor Co., 518 F.2d 481 (10th Cir. 1975), the court observed that after plaintiff's feet and legs were seriously injured as he slipped and fell into a grain auger, his employer "borrowed a machine which was similar to that which injured the plaintiff-appellee. A grid was welded across the top which was so spaced as to prevent a man's foot from entering into the dangerous area. The purpose of this was to refute the defendant-appellant's contention that the machine could not perform the work which it was designed to perform if grids of this dimension covered it. It would have been impossible for the grain to penetrate these grids, according to the defendant's witnesses. But plaintiff-appellee's evidence sought to demonstrate the contrary. Indeed, the employer was shown to have loaded more than a million pounds of grain into the silo with the use of the borrowed machine." Plaintiff's expert had also testified that defects in the grid spacing and protective shield "could have been remedied without substantial expenditure and without diminishing efficiency." A verdict for the plaintiff was affirmed.

In Turner v. General Motors Corp., 514 S.W.2d 497 (Tex.Civ.App.1974), plaintiff's hands and legs were paralyzed when the car roof collapsed upon his head in a roll-over accident. Plaintiff's expert testified that a roll bar or roll cage would have prevented the collapse, although he admitted "that no mass-produced automobile in the United States had ever come equipped with a roll bar or roll cage and conceded that the Impala's roof was no more dangerous than the roof in any other car produced at that time. He frankly stated that he considered the roof on all American cars defectively designed, including those currently manufactured." According to this witness the defendant had decided against roll bars for reasons of cost along with the fact that the buyer could not see what he was paying for. The court held: "We think the expert's condemnation of the industry for its failure to install roll bars constitutes a sufficient showing that the custom itself was unreasonably dangerous. General Motors' evidence points are overruled." Other issues were involved in the case; but after lengthy litigation the Supreme Court of Texas, at 584 S.W.2d 844, 851–2 (1979), affirmed the intermediate court's ruling as to the sufficiency of the evidence to support the jury's finding that the roof was unreasonably dangerous in its design.

Perhaps few courts would go as far as the *Turner* court as to the feasibility of a design change. In Olson v. Arctic Enterprise, Inc., 349 F.Supp. 761 (D.N.D.1972), the minor plaintiff's foot was injured when it was caught in an unguarded metal track and sprocket drive mechanism of a snowmobile. The court dismissed the case after hearing testimony on the lack of feasibility of the suggested safety features. Rubber tracks were subject to breakdowns, perhaps leaving the operator and passenger stranded in the snow. A guard on a running board in the rear would make the machine inoperable in deep snow. Handholds, footholds, or seatbelts would interfere with the necessary prompt ejection of the occupants from the machine in the event of a tipover.

The court in Garst v. General Motors Corp., 484 P.2d 47 (Kan.1971), in spite of a dissent indicating that such a procedure was improper, weighed the conflicting evidence and reversed a jury verdict for the plaintiffs. Garst had been severely injured when, as he was working on a job site, he was run into by a 40-ton earth mover. When the operator saw the plaintiff fifteen feet ahead of him, he was unable at the speed of 10–12 miles an hour, with the brakes filled with mud, to stop the vehicle in time to avoid the accident, or to turn the machine quickly. The dissent cited the testimony of General Motors' own witness that he had recommended in a 1957 written report that the steering control system could be improved, since the "torque is not great enough in some situations." The majority opinion reviewed at great length the evidence presented, and concluded that plaintiff's witness had failed to show the feasibility of shielding the braking system from mud. It concluded that General Motors was "not required to expend exorbitant sums of money in research to devise a sophisticated braking system which would price its product completely out of the market." As to the steering system, its performance "was reliable and durable. It was the standard steering system used in the heavy construction industry and no better turning device available was disclosed by the evidence."

e. STATE OF THE ART

Closely connected with the feasibility issue is the state of the art at the time of manufacture. As said in Cantu v. John Deere Co., 603 P.2d 839 (Wash. App.1979), " 'state of the art' . . . is sometimes confused with 'standards of the industry.' We believe the two phrases are not synonymous, and we limit our discussion to standards of the industry, customarily self-imposed by the manufacturer. This does not involve state of the art, which could be the same or conceivably a more demanding feasibility, but unrelated to other facts such as cost, gravity of harm, etc." The fact that a safety device is feasible would not necessarily mean its adoption by the industry. If the state of the art at the time of manufacture was such that the suggested device was unknown or unavailable, obviously such a device would not be a part of the product. Such a situation will generally relieve the manufacturer of liability in negligence cases.

In Ward v. Hobart Mfg. Co., 450 F.2d 1176 (5th Cir. 1971), plaintiff's hand was drawn into the auger of a meat grinder from which the original guard had been removed. The grinder had been manufactured about twenty years before by the defendant which was then in advance of the industry in providing any guard at all. The fact that in later models the defendant either permanently attached the guards or made the machine inoperable without the guard did not make the standard it followed in 1948 unreasonable. Here no proof was offered that the safety later provided was absolutely unavailable to the defendant. Rather, there was "evidence to the effect that in 1948 the public preferred a meat grinder without a guard—in order to speed up the grinding process. Nevertheless Hobart did provide a guard, pan and stomper for the model grinder under consideration."

In Pontifex v. Sears, Roebuck & Co., 226 F.2d 909 (4th Cir. 1955), plaintiff was struck in the eye by a rope pulled to start the engine of a lawn mower. Later models had a rope permanently attached by a spring coil mechanism, avoiding the danger present in this case. The court held that it was not negligent "to sell an old model machine not equipped with a safety device of later models."

In strict liability actions no uniformity exists as to the defense. In Bruce v. Martin-Marietta Corp., 544 F.2d 442 (10th Cir. 1976), the defendant was held not strictly liable for the failure, in 1952, to firmly fasten airplane seats to the floor as was done for planes made in 1970. A crash many years later caused them to break loose and to be thrown forward, blocking the means of exit before a fire developed. In Cryts v. Ford Motor Co., 571 S.W.2d 683 (Mo.App.1978), the plaintiff's back was broken when, in a collision, he was thrown against an armrest made of hard plastic and of pointed shape. In answer to Ford's contention that "it built the safest armrest possible under the technology existing in 1957," the court said: "Such a contention has no bearing on the outcome of the strict liability claim, where the sole object of inquiry is the defective condition of the product and not the manufacturer's knowledge, negligence, or fault."

A large manufacturer with extensive research and development departments may be held liable for a decision not to further develop safety elements but instead to devote attention to more profitable improvements. Thus in Spurlin v. General Motors Corp., 528 F.2d 612 (5th Cir. 1976), a school bus crashed when the fluid leaked out of the single hydraulic braking system. Reversing a judgment n. o. v. for the defendant, the court held that the jury could have found on the basis of plaintiff's expert testimony that safety required a dual system on such a school bus. There was evidence that such a braking system with air brakes that were "fail-safe" were in use in passenger cars and in some large buses at the time the bus was manufactured some four years before the accident, and that

General Motors had delayed work on a dual system for large vehicles "in order to give precedence to further development work on passenger car engines."

Courts hitherto holding that the "state of the art" defense is not available in a strict liability action may now be restricted by a state product liability statute. These statutes are summarized in the 1979 case of *Cantu*, cited at the beginning of this section. Colorado, Kentucky, Arizona, Indiana, Nebraska, New Hampshire and Tennessee have all enacted statutes creating an affirmative defense. Tenn. Code Annot. sec. 23–3705(a) (1979) declares that in making a determination of a product's defective condition at the time it left the control of a manufacturer or seller the "state of scientific and technological knowledge available to the manufacturer or seller at the time the product was placed on the market, rather than at the time of injury, is applicable." Other statutes, such as Colo.Rev.Stat. sec. 13–21–403(1)(a) (1979), simply provide that compliance with the state of the art creates a "rebuttable presumption" that the product is not defective.

f. RISK–BENEFIT ANALYSIS

Some courts, like the intermediate court in *Turner*, have considered feasibility to be little different from possibility. Others have allowed a full risk-benefit analysis to be considered in deciding feasibility. This would include the cost, degree of efficiency rather than mere workability, and sometimes, for consumer products, attractiveness. Thus in Metal Window Products Co. v. Magnusen, 485 S.W.2d 355 (Tex.Civ.App.1972), plaintiff was injured when she bumped into a glass door in the apartment of her host. The door itself did not shatter, break, or fracture. The court concluded that the lack of a decal or bar on the glass door was not a defect in that it did not constitute any unreasonable danger or condition uncontemplated by the consumer. Emphasizing the popularity of glass doors in spite of the risk of collision, the court observed: "The virtual invisibility now complained of is the very quality which gives desirability and value to glass doors," creating as they do "the illusion of space." In the *Turner* case itself, an opinion ultimately handed down by the Texas Supreme Court, 584 S.W.2d 844 (1979), held that evidence "upon the factors of risk and utility . . . as well as upon the expectations of the ordinary consumer may be admissible" at trial but that the jury is not to be instructed "to balance specifically enumerated factors." As one basis for eliminating such factors from the instructions, the court cited various opinions and articles where four, five, or seven factors were listed, and one article listing thirteen, and another listing fifteen. It stands to reason that the opinions written with the risk-benefit appraisal in mind tend to be lengthy.

One court, evidently sympathetic to a risk-benefit approach, considers that its effect is to limit the capacity of courts to make decisions in design cases. In Owens v. Allis-Chalmers Corp., 268 N.W.2d 291 (Mich.App.1978), the plaintiff's husband was killed in a forklift truck he was operating for his employer. The truck overturned after apparently striking a concrete-filled post off the roadway. The skull of plaintiff's decedent was crushed against the overhead protective guard. Plaintiff alleged defective design in the absence of driver restraints such as a protective enclosure or seat belts which, it was contended, were especially necessary in view of a forklift's inherent instability. In affirming the trial court's directed verdict for the defendant, the court said: "Considering the nature of the design process, we find that adjudication must necessarily play a limited role in setting design standards. Without some extrajudicially established guidelines, the adjudicatory standard-setting process would resort to an assessment of conflicting expert testimony by those not possessed of the requisite expertise to adequately evaluate the interrelated and interdependent design choice criteria. Additionally, this evaluation would be made within an atmosphere susceptible to influence by sympathy for an injured plaintiff, instead of an abstract concern for the desirable effect that public policy should play in governing a manufacturer's design choices. Inevitably, this would lead to varying standards from jury to jury or trial court to trial court. . . . This is not to say that plaintiffs have no means by which they can seek recovery for injuries resulting from the conscious design choices of manufacturers where extrajudicial design guidlines are absent." The means available is for plaintiff to show that a manufacturer has failed in his duty adequately to warn potential users of his product of any latent dangers because of design. Plaintiff must present, as evidence of a manufacturer's breach of a duty in product design, the following: "(1) That the particular design was not in conformity with industry design standards, design guidelines established by an authoritative voluntary association, or design criteria set by legislative or other governmental regulation; *or*

"(2) That the design choice of the manufacturer carries with it a *latent* risk of injury *and* the manufacturer has *not* adequately communicated the nature of that risk to potential users of the product."

In Dreisonstok v. Volkswagenwerk, 489 F.2d 1066 (4th Cir. 1974), the court was less diffident to outside authority in denying recovery. Here the plaintiff, a passenger in a Volkswagen microbus, sued for increased injuries when, under the impact of a collision with a telephone pole, her right leg was caught between the back of the seat and the dashboard and she was apparently thrown forward with resultant injuries in her ankle and femur. The court held that "there was no violation by the defendant of its duty of ordinary care in the design of its vehicle. The defendant's vehicle, described as 'a van type multipurpose vehicle', was of a special type and particular design. This design was uniquely developed in order to provide the owner with the maximum amount of either cargo or passenger space in a vehicle inexpensively priced and of such dimensions as to make possible easy maneuverability. To achieve this, it advanced the driver's seat forward, bringing such seat in close proximity to the front of the vehicle, thereby adding to the cargo or passenger space. . . . All of this was readily discernible to any one using the vehicle; in fact, it was, as we have said, the unique feature of the vehicle. . . . There was no evidence in the record that there was any practical way of improving the 'crashability' of the vehicle that would have been consistent with the peculiar purposes of its design." The court evidently felt its opinion corroborated when the father of the driver involved in the accident immediately purchased a new microbus of the same type.

In Seattle-First Nat'l Bank v. Volkswagen of America, Inc., 525 P.2d 286 (Wash.App.1974), the court distinguished *Dreisonstok* where the collision was at the rate of 40 m.p.h. while here the speed of the Volkswagen bus in relationship to the speed of the truck that struck it in the rear was 20 m.p.h. or less. The issue of defect in the design of the vehicle front without reinforcing members was for the jury.

In Bowman v. General Motors Corp., 427 F.Supp. 234 (E.D.Pa.1977), the court made a distinction between inadvertent design errors which could be treated in the same way as production or manufacturing flaws, and deliberate design choices. Here the fuel tank of a Toronado had exploded after a rear-end collision, causing a fire that invaded the passenger compartment with consequent disfiguring burns for plaintiff's wife. In deciding whether a product is "unreasonably dangerous" to an extent not contemplated by the ordinary consumer, the court held that, when a manufacturer has deliberately adopted a design which is less safe than another possible one, the jury should consider such factors as utility and lower price that entered into the manufacturer's choice. Also the jury can consider the manufacturer's conclusion that "the public, in inflationary times, is concerned about 'saving a dollar' and about a more useful product, and would prefer the slightly less safe product in return for the price and utility advantage."

Although the advocates of risk-benefit analysis have generally been defendants, the advantage may sometimes go to the plaintiff. In Dorsey v. Yoder Co., 331 F.Supp. 753 (E.D.Pa.1971), aff'd 474 F.2d 1339 (3d Cir. 1973), the obviousness to the injured plaintiff of the absence of a guard on the machine she was operating was only one factor to be considered in weighing defective design. Other factors were the availability of such a guard without eliminating the machine's usefulness and its relatively low cost of $200 to $500 for an $8,000 machine. A jury verdict for the plaintiff, based on the weighing of such factors, was affirmed.

Relatively few courts have as yet accepted risk-benefit analysis as determinative of defect. Perhaps other courts have realized that such analysis is at odds with one of the original policy reasons for products liability, the risk distribution policy. The analysis may place all the risk on the injured plaintiff, with the benefits going to other users and to the manufacturer. In Mitchell v. Fruehauf Corp., 568 F.2d 1139 (5th Cir. 1978), the court clearly rejected such analysis. Here defendant's driver was passing plaintiff when the trailer containing hanging meat overturned, severely injuring plaintiff in his pickup. The court held such a trailer unreasonably dangerous in design in view of expert testimony as to the imbalance caused by swinging meat. Plaintiff offered several alternatives, including tying the meat to the floor and installing partitions to restrict the swinging motion of the meat. The court rejected the defendant's contention that "specific proof of the economic and technical feasibility of alternative designs" should be considered.

Perhaps the recent losses by such major manufacturers as Ford and the near-bankruptcy of Chrysler will strengthen the risk-benefit approach, both in fixing legislative standards and in deciding cases. It was reported in the New York Times toward the end of 1978 that a study made by the National Highway Traffic Safety Administration found federal regulation so expensive to the auto industry that another recession might bring disaster to Chrysler and to American Motors.

Possibly risk-benefit analysis could be utilized without too much damage to the plaintiff's interest by following a rule laid down recently by the California Supreme Court. In Barker v. Lull Engineering Co., Inc., 573 P.2d 443 (Cal.1978), the plaintiff was operating a Lull High-Lift loader at a sharply sloping construction site. Although forks had been leveled to compensate for the slope, the machine nevertheless began to tip when lifting a load of lumber. Upon the advice of co-workers, plaintiff jumped from the lift but was then seriously injured by a piece of falling lumber. The court stated: "Because most of the evidentiary matters which may be relevant to the determination of the adequacy of a product's design under the 'risk-benefit' standard—e.g., the feasibility and cost of alternative designs—are similar to issues typically presented in a negligent design case and involve technical matters peculiarly within the knowledge of the manufacturer, we conclude that once the plaintiff makes a prima facie showing that the injury was proximately caused by the product's design, the burden should appropriately shift to the defendant to prove, in light of the relevant factors, that the product is not defective."

Barker has attracted considerable notice, much of it unfavorable. Yet California decisions have been conspicuous trend-setters in the past; and it is too early to decide what the effect of this decision upon other jurisdictions will be.

g. "UNREASONABLY DANGEROUS"

Another issue in product design cases is whether an instruction that a product must be "unreasonably dangerous" as defined in comment i to § 402A of the Second Restatement of Torts should be given to the jury. In Cronin v. J.B.E. Olson Corp., 501 P.2d 1153 (Cal.1972), an aluminum safety hasp, which was designed to hold in place the bread trays of the truck plaintiff was driving, broke upon collision with another truck and a roadside ditch. The loaded trays, driven forward, hurled plaintiff through the windshield with resulting severe injuries. Experts testified that the hasp was defective in that it was extremely porous. The court upheld the trial judge's refusal to instruct the jury that they must find the defect to be an "unreasonably dangerous" one. It held that such a limitation "has burdened the injured plaintiff with proof of an element which rings of negligence. As a result, if, in the view of the trier of fact, the 'ordinary consumer' would have expected the defective condition of a product, the seller is not strictly liable regardless of the expectations of the injured plaintiff. . . . Yet the very purpose of our pioneering efforts in this field was to relieve the plaintiff from problems of proof inherent in pursuing negligence . . . and warranty."

This decision has been rarely followed. Perhaps if a court gave a full explanation of unreasonably dangerous—that the term is meant to exclude products like whiskey and knives that are expected by the ordinary consumer to be dangerous if misused or overused—the instruction is at least harmless and perhaps useful. The results in jurisdictions permitting the instruction do not seem to be much different from the results where *Cronin* has been followed.

3. PARTICULAR TYPES OF DESIGN DEFECTS

a. CONCEALED DANGERS

Concealed dangers have received little or no tolerance from the law. Even if it was not feasible, or even possible, to remove the danger, it has always been possible to warn against it, thus rendering it unconcealed. If the manufacturer was unaware of the danger he would still be held strictly liable, or even liable for negligence for his failure as an expert to adequately test his product under the varied conditions in which it might be used. As with a professional, a manufacturer is held to the knowledge of an expert, even if he cuts corners by failing to employ the needed expert chemists or engineers.

Among the few concealed danger cases that have reached the higher courts in recent years are those involving automobile fuel tanks which burst into flames after a rear-end collision of moderate impact. The tank position may of course be obvious, but not the danger of that position. These cases will be discussed further in the section below on increased injuries.

In McCormack v. Hankscraft Co., 154 N.W.2d 488 (Minn.1967), a child of three bumped into a vaporizer with a loose top and suffered third-degree burns from hot water spilling on her when the lid fell off. Testimony revealed that if small holes had been made in the cap to prevent any dangerous buildup of steam, the cap could then have been attached to the vaporizer by use of threads or the like. The decision was based on negligence and breach of express warranty, but there was a clear dictum that liability for this design could also be imposed under strict liability in tort.

In d'Hedouville v. Pioneer Hotel Co., 552 F.2d 886 (9th Cir. 1977), the Monsanto Company was held strictly liable for both compensatory and punitive damages to the widow of a man who was burned to death in a hotel fire. Without sufficient testing, the company had sold a highly flammable fibre to the carpet manufacturer whose carpets were then sold to the hotel. To Monsanto's contention that it was under no duty to warn the immediate purchaser who presumably was aware of the danger, the court answered that the liability was not imposed for failure to warn but rather because of the product's inherent flammability. "Where, as here, the claim of liability rests upon the sale of a product unreasonably dangerous to the ultimate user or consumer because of its inherent unsuitability for the reasonably foreseeable use, the seller is not immunized from liability to the user or consumer because an intermediate link in the chain of distribution was aware of the risk. Such knowledge is a defense only when failure to warn is properly the basis for the claim."

A product may be found so dangerously defective that neither an alteration in design nor an emphatic warning would justify its marketing. Thus in Ruggeri v. Minnesota Mining & Mfg. Co., 380 N.E.2d 445 (Ill.App.1978), where plaintiff's intestate died from burns when an adhesive caught fire from the pilot light of a furnace fourteen feet away, the court held that "the defendant is under a duty to manufacture a product which is 'reasonably safe.'" Defendant had available a nonflammable adhesive which was equally effective. Yet the court held that this availability was irrelevant "inasmuch as the state of the art is no defense in strict products liability actions." Similarly, in Drayton v. Jiffee Chem. Corp., 395 F.Supp. 1081 (N.D.Ohio 1975), the court strongly implied that a liquid drain cleaner containing sodium hydroxide was so destructive of human tissue that it should not have been marketed at all. Through accidental spillage, a small child was burned so severely that her face was a "mass of grotesque scar tissue" even after undergoing eleven operations.

b. OBVIOUS DANGERS

In a number of cases the courts have found as a matter of law that a design is not unreasonably dangerous when the risk is one that anyone should recognize and avoid. It is clear, for example, that a sharp ax or knife involves no design defect, since the user will realize the danger. This obviousness factor applies to both negligence and strict liability situations.

Since 1976, however, when New York overruled a much cited case, relatively few courts have adhered to the older "patent danger" rule barring recovery regardless of other factors. Even before then, many courts had departed from this emphasis on obviousness. As was said in Luque v. McLean, 501 P.2d 1163 (Cal.1972), the unfortunate result of such a rule "would be to immunize from strict liability manufacturers who callously ignore patent dangers in their products while subjecting to such liability those who innocently market products with latent defects." In *Luque* the minor plaintiff had left a power mower running while he removed a carton from the grass. He slipped and his left hand went through an unguarded hole, with consequent mangling and laceration. Plaintiff's expert testified that the unguarded hole was "very hazardous," and that even at the time of marketing an effective guard costing less than one dollar per machine was available. A jury verdict for the defendant was reversed, largely on the ground of an erroneous instruction that plaintiff must prove that he was unaware of the defect. Other lawnmower cases, discussed under bystanders, have increasingly in recent years resulted in plaintiffs' verdicts.

Palmer v. Massey-Ferguson, Inc., 476 P.2d 713 (Wash.App.1970), involved a hay baler, where the court said that a rule "which excludes the manufacturer from liability if the defect in the design of his product is patent but applies the duty if such a defect is latent is somewhat anomalous. . . . The law, we think, ought to discourage misdesign rather than encouraging it in its obvious form."

Pike v. Frank G. Hough Co., 467 P.2d 229 (Cal.1970), involved an earth-moving machine designed to move backward as well as forward. On account of a large engine box at the rear, there was a sizeable blind area where the operator of the machine could not see even though he looked to the rear. A workman in a luminous jacket was killed while standing in the blind spot. The court, reversing an intermediate appellate court decision, held that the defendant manufacturer's motion for a nonsuit should not have been granted. The court found that even though the absence of a rear view mirror was apparent, an unreasonable danger was created. It rejected any definite requirement that the defect be latent, and adopted the modern rule that "even though the absence of a particular safety precaution is obvious, there ordinarily would be a question for the jury as to whether or not a failure to install the device creates an unreasonable risk." The design in the earth-moving machine case was regarded as defective under both negligence and strict tort principles.

In Micallef v. Miehle Co., Div. of Miehle-Goss Dexter, Inc., 348 N.E.2d 571 (N.Y.1976), plaintiff, the operator of a photo-offset press, removed a foreign object from the plate of the unit with a piece of plastic. His hand was drawn, along with the plastic, into the roller. Plaintiff was aware of the danger and also aware that the only safe method of removing an object which would otherwise mar the printed page was to stop the machine altogether with a resultant delay of three hours. It was therefore the common practice among operators to "chase the hickie" while the machine was in motion. Witnesses testified that guards could have prevented the accident and that at least three different types of guards were available. The court observed favorably the contention that finding a product free from defect because the danger was obvious amounted to allowing "an assumption of the risk defense as a matter of law." Plaintiff would thus be denied the opportunity of going to the jury on a defense which involved his subjective appreciation of the risk. The manufacturer was required to use reasonable care to avoid danger from an unintended but foreseeable use. On the issue of feasibility, evidence as to cost, workability and recent scientific developments in design would all be relevant upon remand.

In *Micallef* the court makes clear that upon trial to a jury defendant might still be found not liable if he could successfully raise the defense either of contributory negligence or of assumption of the risk. These defenses will be discussed in the chapter dealing with causation, including plaintiff's conduct. Suffice it to say here that the assumption of the risk defense is applicable only where plaintiff has voluntarily and unreasonably encountered a risk of which he was fully aware. Since the defense is subjective in nature and therefore a jury issue, it is less restrictive to the plaintiff's claim than a determination by the court that the danger is objectively obvious.

Some courts still adhere to the obvious danger rule. Thus in Vineyard v. Empire Machinery Co., 581 P.2d 1152 (Ariz.App.1978), the absence of a roll bar on an earth-moving machine manufactured by defendant Euclid was considered open and obvious and therefore not unreasonably dangerous. The earth-mover's tractor overturned when the trailer slipped down an incline with the result that the driver's leg was crushed and later amputated. Euclid was acquired by General Motors which was named as a defendant. This case might be

compared with Garst v. General Motors, given in the
section on feasibility and involving, apparently, the
same type of machine. In Skyhook Corp. v. Jasper,
560 P.2d 934 (N.M.1977), plaintiff's decedent was
electrocuted when he positioned the crane he was
operating too near high voltage lines. A clear
warning advised against bringing the lift cable
within ten feet of such lines; but decedent made no
measurements even though a tape measure was kept
in the rig's cab for that purpose. Plaintiff
contended that the crane was defective in that
Skyhook had failed to equip it with an "insulated
link" available as optional equipment for $300 or
$400, or with a "proximity warning device" available
at a cost of about $700. No crane manufacturer at
the time equipped its machines with either of these
two devices. Since the accident could have been
avoided had the decedent heeded the warning, the
court held that the machine was not defectively
designed, although the lack of safety features might,
in some products, constitute a defect.

c. UNCRASHWORTHINESS AND INCREASED INJURY

A manufacturer must design his product so that it
is safe not only for its intended use but for any
reasonably foreseeable use. This problem will be
discussed more fully in the chapter on causation and
foreseeability. In one large group of cases, however, the foreseeability issue has been generally
decided. These involve the extent to which automo-

biles shall be made crashworthy, over and above the requirements of federal statute and regulation. Automobiles, as defendants repeatedly have said, are not intended for use in collisions. But plaintiffs have, in most jurisdictions, successfully answered that accident statistics reveal that such "use" is plainly foreseeable. The landmark case in this area is Larsen v. General Motors Corp., 391 F.2d 495 (8th Cir. 1968), where plaintiff, as a result of a head-on collision, was injured by the rearward thrust of the steering mechanism. The court, in reversing a summary judgment for the defendant and remanding the case for trial, said: "We . . . do not think the automotive industry is being singled out for any special adverse treatment by applying to it general negligence principles in (1) imposing a duty on the manufacturer to use reasonable care in the design of its products to protect against an unreasonable risk of injury or enhancement of injury to a user of the product, and (2) holding that the intended use of an automotive product contemplates its travel on crowded and high speed roads and highways that inevitably subject it to the foreseeable hazards of collisions and impacts. Neither reason, logic, nor controlling precedents compel the courts to make a distinction between negligent design and negligent construction."

For a time the courts seemed to be about evenly divided on the issue of liability for uncrashworthy design. Now the plaintiff is generally allowed to recover, once a feasibly avoidable design feature increasing the injury has been shown. Conclusive in this regard is Huff v. White Motor Corp., 565 F.2d 104 (7th Cir. 1977), where the court overruled its own earlier opinion, based on Indiana law, barring recovery in accidents *caused* by a negligent driver, not by a defect in the car. Since that earlier opinion, Evans v. General Motors Corp., 359 F.2d 822 (7th Cir. 1966), no Indiana court had ruled expressly in a crashworthy case; but its Supreme Court had adopted strict liability as defined in § 402A of the Second Restatement of Torts. The federal court found it probable that Indiana would follow the trend toward rejecting *Evans* in favor of *Larsen.* It observed: "Currently a clear majority of jurisdictions follow *Larsen.* Only three jurisdictions continue to adhere to *Evans.* Moreover, no court has followed *Evans* since 1969 when the Mississippi Supreme Court decided Ford Motor Co. v. Simpson, 233 So.2d 797 (Miss.1970). Also noteworthy is the fact that commentators have been uniformly critical of the *Evans* rule."

Huff involved the rupture of a fuel tank with consequent fire after a collision. Whether the fuel tank was in fact defective was considered a jury question. Not all fuel tank cases have been held for the jury. Although in Self v. General Motors Corp., 116 Cal.Rptr. 575 (Cal.App.1974), the court held that the issue of defect was indeed for the jury, it nevertheless found difficulties in holding that any particular position of a fuel tank constituted a defect. It said: "We are also well aware that prosecution of a lawsuit is a poor way to design a motor vehicle, for the suit will almost invariably emphasize a single aspect of design to the total exclusion of all others. For example, defective design is claimed here because the vehicle was not sufficiently crashworthy from the rear." The court observed that in *Evans* the claim was lack of crashworthiness from the side, in *Dreisonstok* (cited above under risk-benefit analysis) from the front, and in *Larsen* lack of crashworthiness in a head-on collision. "Protection gained against a head-on collision may be at the expense of protection against one that is broadside, for like an army in battle the vehicle can't be uniformly strong at all points and under all conditions. We also appreciate that consensus design may tend to freeze innovation and inhibit manufacturers from making products that have not been made before." The dissent observed that the "retrial may well degenerate into a debate over the probabilities as to which type of impact is most likely to occur or which kind of accident is the 'most foreseeable', i.e., front, rear, side, etc."

On the other hand, in Buehler v. Whalen, 374 N.E.2d 460 (Ill.1978), statistics to the effect that 50% of all automobile collisions were rear-end were considered relevant on the positioning issue.

In at least two cases recovery has been allowed for sharp-edged exterior features that caused injuries to colliding motorcyclists. In Knippen v. Ford Motor Co., 546 F.2d 993 (D.C.Cir. 1976), the lower muscles and soft tissue of plaintiff's left leg were injured when his motorbike was struck by a station wagon attempting a left turn across his lane. The severity of the injury was "due in large part to contact with a sharply pointed triangular metal projection behind the plastic lens hood of the 1968 Mercury's turning signal and parking light assembly." There was evidence that "alternative yielding materials" had been available at the time of manufacture and that they were not only safer but less costly. Also, the "danger of enhanced injuries from protrusions of this same general character was well known throughout the industry in the 1960's and had been specifically brought to Ford's attention by a letter from the head of the National Highway Safety Board."

In Bolm v. Triumph Corp., 305 N.E.2d 769 (N.Y.1973), a jury trial was ordered where plaintiff sustained severe genital and pelvic injuries in a collision when he was thrown against a metal luggage rack of his own motorcycle. On the other hand, in Hunt v. Harley-Davidson Motor Co., Inc., 248 S.E.2d 15 (Ga.App.1978), the court upheld the trial judge's summary judgment for the defendant where plaintiff motorcyclist alleged that his injuries in a collision with the rear end of a car were increased by the absence of crash bars. The court, in addition to an ambiguous reference to plaintiff's assumption of risk as a matter of law, found that the product was hardly "in a condition not contemplated by the ultimate consumer."

In crashworthiness cases the most serious disagreement has been on the question of plaintiff's burden of proof as to relative damages: just how much did the uncrashworthy feature increase the injury. In Huddell v. Levin, 537 F.2d 726 (3d Cir. 1976), Judge Aldisert held plaintiff should be denied any recovery if he was unable to prove the extent to which a headrest, found defective by a jury, had increased the injury to the decedent. Decendent's car had been stopped on a bridge when it ran out of gasoline. Another driver, negligently colliding with the stopped car, suffered only superficial injuries. Huddell at first seemed to have sustained only superficial injuries, but he died a day later from an extensive fracture of the frontal portions of his brain. The jury had found that this fracture was caused by a sharp, unyielding metal edge in the headrest, covered by two inches of soft material. Medical experts testified that the accident would have been survivable if the restraint had been designed differently. No evidence was offered as to what injuries might have occurred "if the great forces of the collision had been more widely distributed over the head and body by an alternate head restraint design." Because of this lack of evidence as to what injuries might have occurred with the alternative safer design, plaintiff was denied recovery unless such proof should be offered upon a new trial. As to the argument that death, which occurred only because of the defect, was an indivisible injury for which a concurrent tortfeasor is jointly and severally liable, the court said: "Plaintiff may not argue that the ultimate fact of death is divisible for the purposes of establishing G.M.'s liability and then assert that it is indivisible in order to deny to G.M. the opportunity of limiting damages."

Some courts have accepted the *Huddell* view of plaintiff's burden of proof as to apportionment in most cases, but denied any such apportionment in wrongful death cases. Others have rejected the whole approach, citing § 433B of the Second Restatement of Torts to the effect that where two or more actors have tortiously harmed the plaintiff, the burden of proof as to apportionment is upon each actor.

In Chrysler Corp. v. Todorovich, 580 P.2d 1123 (Wyo.1978), the plaintiff sought recovery against defendant Chrysler for increased injuries suffered in an auto collision as the result of a defective seat bracket. Although judgment for the plaintiff was reversed on other grounds, the court sustained the trial judge's refusal to require plaintiff to apportion damages between Chrysler and the negligent driver who caused the accident. Where the injuries are "incapable of any logical, reasonable, or practical division," the defendants are "jointly and severally liable." To require apportionment would cause the jury "to speculate," since apportionment "in a factual instance such as this cannot be achieved on any rational basis."

Although most crashworthiness cases involve vehicles on the highways, they are not necessarily so limited. In McGee v. Cessna Aircraft Co., 147 Cal.Rptr. 694 (Cal.App.1978), it was held that the defendant, manufacturer of a small private aircraft, could be found strictly liable in a crashworthiness case. The amount of increased injury was not at issue, since it was conceded that plaintiff's serious injuries, involving amputation of both legs, were caused entirely by a fire which broke out in the plane after the crash. Occupants of the plane who escaped before the fire began were unharmed. Plaintiff asserted that the fire was owing to a defective fuel system, part of which—the nosewheel strut—collapsed as a result of the crash. The strut "telescoped upon impact and ruptured the accumulator tank, permitting fuel to escape in an area where combustion would and did occur."

In Harrison v. McDonough Power Equipment, Inc., 381 F.Supp. 926 (S.D.Fla.1974), the minor plaintiff suffered the loss of a foot when a power mower ran over him as it was being operated by a fifteen-year-old. Plaintiff's expert testified that a safety shield underneath the mower would have lessened the injury. The plaintiff settled with the minor operator and her grandfather-guardian, and the court held the manufacturer of the mower liable. It observed that in view of "the frequency of lawnmower-related accidents and the consequent number of injuries which result in the victim's loss of limbs, the imposition on the manufacturer of the duty of reasonable care in design to minimize or lessen the injurious effects of an accident is not unduly burdensome and is in line with the expansive trend of Florida negligence law."

CHAPTER VI

DEFECTIVE WARNINGS AND DIRECTIONS

A. GENERAL CONSIDERATIONS

Clearly related to the supplier's duty to furnish a safe design for his product is the duty to provide adequate warnings and directions. Where a design can feasibly be made safe, a warning of the danger will rarely relieve the defendant of liability. As said in Schell v. AMF, Inc., 567 F.2d 1259 (3d Cir. 1977), "as a matter of policy, it is questionable whether a manufacturer which produces a machine without minimal available safeguards is entitled to escape liability by warning of a dangerous condition which could reasonably have been avoided by a better design." Nor will a warning avail him if the product is incorrigibly unsafe and of doubtful value. In Stromsodt v. Parke-Davis & Co., 257 F.Supp. 991 (D.N.D.1966), a small child was afflicted with idiocy by a quadruple vaccine, one adding a poliomyelitis component to a triple vaccine previously developed. Since the vaccine had little value as against the two vaccines separately and safely administered, the court held the warning given by the manufacturer that the reaction the child suffered was "extremely rare" was inadequate. Later, In Tinnerholm v. Parke, Davis & Co., 411

F.2d 48 (2d Cir. 1969), the court held the defendant liable for breach of implied warranty in marketing at all so dangerous a product. Even before *Stromsodt* had come to trial, the drug had been withdrawn. In Sturm, Ruger & Co., Inc. v. Day, 594 P.2d ˙38˙ (Alaska 1979), plaintiff was severely injured when, as he was unloading his revolver, the gun slipped out of his hands and fired as he grabbed for it, the bullet striking his leg. The warning stated that the "revolver can be fired by excessive pull on the trigger from either the safety notch position . . . or the loading notch position." The court said that where "the most stringent warning does not protect the public, the defect itself must be eliminated if the manufacturer is to avoid liability."

If the dangerous feature cannot feasibly be removed, bearing in mind the various definitions of feasibility, the design is adequate when accompanied by adequate directions for use or warnings. An increasing number of warning cases have arisen as the complexity of modern chemical and mechanical products leads to increased possibilities of harm to unsophisticated users. Placing an adequate warning on the product or on its container rarely involves a serious burden to the defendant, with the result that courts and juries have more readily found liability for defective warnings than for design. A defendant may of course be reluctant to adopt a sufficiently strong warning for fear of scaring away his customers. The simple statement "safe for normal skin" on a deodorant jar for example may be an inadequate warning to allergic users. But defendant may prefer to incur occasional liability rather than jeopardize his vast market of normal users.

Plaintiff's problem of proof is often considerably less than in manufacturing or handling cases where the product is frequently destroyed in the accident. Whatever warning defect exists will be the same on many samples of the product. Nor will the plaintiff normally be faced with the necessity for expert witnesses, as is required in most design cases. Plaintiff's own testimony as to why a warning was needed, or why the one given did not fully advise him of the danger or of the precautions needed to avoid the danger, will often be sufficient to get the case to the jury. An exception may be a requirement of expert witnesses in drug cases, a rule laid down in Hill v. Squibb & Sons, E. R., 592 P.2d 1383 (Mont.1979). On the other hand, if plaintiff has put the product to some unforeseeable use, he will be denied recovery. As with design cases, this problem will be discussed in the chapter on causation and foreseeability. However, foreseeability will be discussed in this chapter in connection with allergies, where the users' only protection is a proper warning.

As stated in comment j, § 402A of the Second Restatement of Torts, "[w]here warning is given, the seller may reasonably assume it will be read and heeded; and a product bearing such a warning, which is safe for use if it is followed, is not in defective condition, nor is it unreasonably dangerous." In Douglas v. Bussabarger, 438 P.2d 829 (Wash.1968), plaintiff's doctor testified that, relying on his own knowledge, he had not read the instructions on the container of anesthetic supplied by the defendant. The court held that regardless of any negligent inadequacy of the warning, "this negligence was not a proximate cause of plaintiff's disability." Other courts have allowed the fact-finder to infer that an adequate warning would have been read, even when the evidence indicates that the plaintiff did not read the inadequate warning given.

A distinction should be drawn between the duty to give adequate directions for use and the duty to warn. Directions are calculated primarily to secure the efficient use of a product. Where, however, a departure from directions may create a serious hazard, a separate duty to warn arises. Thus in McLaughlin v. Mine Safety Appliances Co., 181 N.E.2d 430 (N.Y.1962), heat blocks were used to help revive injured persons. Instructions to wrap the blocks in insulating material before using were given, but there was no statement that if used without insulation the blocks would cause serious burns—as they did to the plaintiff. The court, in a dictum as to the need for a warning, observed with emphasis that "*instructions,* not particularly stressed, do not amount to *a warning of the risk at all.*"

In Midgley v. S. S. Kresge Co., 127 Cal.Rptr. 217 (Cal.App.1976), defendant retailer sold to a thirteen-year-old plaintiff a refracting telescope for sun-viewing. A warning clearly indicated that the sun should be viewed only through the sun filter. The instructional booklet, however, contained no diagrammatic or pictorial illustration of the proper way to install the filter. Plaintiff misunderstood such instructions as were given and removed the eye piece, replacing it with the sun filter. Instead, the eye piece should have been left in place, since it flanged so as to project beyond the circumference of the cylinder, and the sun filter should have been placed at the opposite end of the cylinder. With the eye piece removed, sunlight leaked across the filter, damaging the eyes of the plaintiff. The court emphasized the fact that the defendant was marketing "a technically complex product intended for use by technically unsophisticated consumers, to be assembled and used by them in accordance with instructions prepared and supplied by the technically knowledgeable supplier. . . . Therefore, the supplier is strictly liable for injury proximately resulting from composing and furnishing a set of instructions for assembly and use which does not adequately avoid the danger of injury." In McCully v. Fuller Brush Co., 415 P.2d 7 (Wash.1966), plaintiff immersed her hands for 4½ hours in a mixture of defendant's cleaner and water she was using and consequently contracted dermatitis. On a label which said "It's Kind to Your Hands," the defendant had issued instructions as to the proper mixture of water and cleaner which plaintiff had ignored. The court held the defendant liable, since the instructions were "directory only" and did not reveal any danger from their violation.

B. LEGAL BASIS

1. NEGLIGENCE

Most warning cases involve negligence, since courts reason that it is difficult to see how a manufacturer or seller can warn of a danger of which he neither knows nor should have known. A generalized warning by, say, a drug manufacturer that the product might be a danger at some time to some persons would be of little practical value. It might serve only to deter the use of a beneficial product. Yet a drug manufacturer rarely knows that his new product will prove absolutely safe over time to all of many users.

The liability of a supplier of a chattel for a negligent failure to warn was set forth long ago in the first Restatement of Torts and is reaffirmed with minor changes in the Second Restatement, § 388. The liability attaches if the supplier "knows or has reason to know that the chattel is or is likely to be dangerous for the use for which it is supplied" and "has no reason to believe" that the user "will realize its dangerous condition." The case law has extended the duty to warn to include danger not only from the use intended by the supplier but for any foreseeable use, whether intended or not. Other factors generally used to determine the existence of a duty are the probable seriousness of the injury if an accident does occur, and the feasibility of an effective warning.

In Pease v. Sinclair Refining Co., 104 F.2d 183 (2d Cir. 1939), the balancing of these factors was involved. Here the oil company furnished science teachers with a display of oil samples. To make the display mailable, the company placed water in a bottle marked kerosene. When the teacher, misinformed by the label, poured the water onto sodium, an explosion occurred causing serious injury. In finding a duty to warn, despite the small likelihood of the accident, the court considered the gravity of the plaintiff's injury and the fact that it "would have been so easy to have warned" of the inaccurate labeling.

2. STRICT LIABILITY

Strict liability for failure to warn is now conceded in a number of jurisdictions. Under § 402A of the Second Restatement of Torts such liability may arise when the product is "defective and unreasonably dangerous;" comment j states that "to prevent the product from being unreasonably dangerous, the seller may be required to give directions or warning, on the container, as to its use."

The various applications of strict liability in warning cases do not shed much light upon how this form of strict liability differs from negligence. In Borel v. Fibreboard Paper Products Corp., 493 F.2d 1076 (5th Cir. 1973), the court relied upon comment k to § 402A imposing a strict liability to warn of "unavoidably unsafe" products. Here eleven manufacturers of asbestos were sued for their failure to warn plaintiff's decedent of the danger of contracting the two forms of cancer from which he died. He had worked in asbestos plants at various times from 1936 to 1969 when the slowly cumulative disease became diagnosed. The court found that scientific literature was available to the defendants "at least as early as the 1930's" and that, although asbestos might be an "unavoidably unsafe" product whose benefit outweighed the risk, defendants were strictly liable for their failure to warn Borel and other insulation workers of the danger. The court observed that "the user or consumer is entitled to make his own choice as to whether the product's utility or benefits justify exposing himself to the risk of harm." Although referring to defendants' strict liability under § 402A, the court throughout the opinion speaks in terms of foreseeability of harm and defendants' knowledge as experts, concluding that "when a failure to give adequate warning is alleged to have made a product unreasonably dangerous, the standard for strict liability is essentially similar to the standard for establishing negligence: the seller or manufacturer has a duty to warn of foreseeable dangers."

Even when courts impose strict liability on manufacturers more widely than called for in comment k, they seem to define the liability in terms which differ little from negligence terms. Thus in Hamilton v. Hardy, 549 P.2d 1099 (Colo. App.1976), where plaintiff suffered a stroke allegedly as a result of taking oral contraceptives, the court reversed and remanded because the trial judge had failed to give an instruction on the manufacturer's strict liability. The court states that "the question to be posed to the jury with regard to the strict liability issue is whether the manufacturer's failure to adequately warn rendered the product unreasonably dangerous without regard to the reasonableness of the failure to warn judged by negligence standards. On remand, the jury should be so instructed." It adds that "we would also point out that, under a strict liability theory, a manufacturer must warn of dangers and risks, whether or not a causal relationship between use of the product and the various injuries has been definitively established at the time of the warning." Plaintiff's evidence of timely reports to defendant Searle of the danger of thrombotic disease from taking the drug is then given, followed by the observation that "the adequacy of the warning, which the parties agreed was to be measured by what was known or should have been known at the time of the warning, does not depend on knowledge of a definitive cause and effect relationship."

Perhaps in warning cases the courts are sometimes making a distinction without a difference as far as plaintiff's practical problem of proof is concerned. Thus in Smith v. E. R. Squibb & Sons, Inc., 273 N.W.2d 476 (Mich.1979), where plaintiff's decedent, owing to a rare hypersensitivity, died approximately two hours after injection of defendant's drug, the court said: "Although plaintiff is correct when he argues that negligence and implied warranty are separate and distinct theories, it is clear that Renografin–60 could not be defective unless Squibb was negligent. The test for determining whether a legal duty has been breached is whether defendant exercised reasonable care under the circumstances. Determination of whether a product defect exists because of an inadequate warning requires the use of an identical standard. Consequently, when liability turns on the adequacy of the warning, the issue is one of reasonable care, regardless of whether the theory pled is negligence, implied warranty or strict liability in tort."   Again, in Torsiello v. Whitehall Laboratories, Div. of Home Products Corp., 398 A.2d 132 (N.J.Super.1979), plaintiff suffered gastrointestinal hemorrhaging after prolonged use of an over-the-counter aspirin product. It was held for the jury to determine the adequacy of defendant's warning that the user should consult his physician if pain persisted over more than ten days or if redness developed. In discussing the legal basis for liability, the court noted: "We are satisfied that where the 'defect' of a product is in the failure of an appropriate accompanying warning as to use rather than in a design or manufacturer defect, the action is equally sustainable under § 388 of the Restatement, Torts 2d and under § 402A. See, e. g., Sterling Drug, Inc. v. Yarrow, 408 F.2d 978, 992 (8th Cir. 1969), a prescription drug case, holding that the gist of the cause of action based on an alleged inadequate warning is the same under both § 388 and § 402A."

It is difficult to see why, if the gist of the two actions is the same in warning cases, they should nevertheless be distinguished. When the courts insist, as they generally do, that a defendant must know or have reason to know of the danger of his product before he can be held liable for failure to warn, how can they at the same time say this is strict liability? Surely one who *should* know of danger and fails to discover it is negligent. If he *does* know he may be worse than negligent, committing an intentional wrong. On the other hand—as in design cases—when the action is against a wholesaler or retailer for failure to warn, the liability may truly be a strict one since such defendants usually lack the manufacturer's expert knowledge and may therefore have no reason to know of the duty to warn.

C. OBVIOUS DANGERS

It would serve no purpose to warn that knives, axes, or even golfballs might be dangerous. Some courts have extended this principle to borderline situations. Thus in Jamieson v. Woodward & Lothrop, 247 F.2d 23 (D.C.Cir. 1957), plaintiff had purchased from the defendant retailer a "Lithe-Line," or simple rubber rope with loops on the ends and intended for use as an exerciser. The product was described as "easily the best turn done to the body beautiful since the curve was invented." While the plaintiff was lying on the floor, doing an exercise termed the "Tummy Flattener," the rope slipped off her feet and struck her across the eyes, detaching a retina.

A summary judgment for the defendant manufacturer was sustained by a five-to-four decision. The majority, in finding no duty to warn, said that everyone knows rubber contracts violently when released, just as everyone knows that a dumbbell will hurt if dropped on one's foot. The dissenters pointed out that while it is obvious that rubber is elastic, a jury might find that when this exerciser was used as directed it was not apparent that the strap might slip and strike the user in the face.

More in accord with the modern trend, in warning as in design cases, is Shuput v. Heublein, Inc., 511 F.2d 1104 (10th Cir. 1975). Here the plaintiff sustained a serious eye injury when a polyethylene stopper ejected from a champagne bottle. The court held that "the propensities of bubbly wine may be well known to many but are not a matter of such common knowledge as to be established as a matter of law and imposed as a matter of judicial knowledge." Defendant's negligence in failing to give any warning at all on the bottle was for the jury. Again, in Jonescue v. Jewel Home Shopping Serv., 306 N.E.2d 312 (Ill.App.1973), where a household cleaner considered nontoxic under a federal labeling act was involved, it was held for the jury to decide whether the manufacturer was under a duty to warn that consumption of the product by a baby might make him sick.

D. PERSONS TO BE REACHED

1. EMPLOYERS OR EMPLOYEES

To be effective, a warning must be calculated to reach, directly or indirectly, those persons whom the supplier should expect to use his product. This does not mean that every potential user must be warned by the supplier himself. Where it can be shown that the supplier has good reason to suppose that the purchaser is able and likely to transmit the warnings he has received to probable users of the product, such as his employees, there is no duty to warn all such users directly.

In Bryant v. Hercules, Inc., 325 F.Supp. 241 (W.D.Ky.1970), an action for deaths sustained by miners, it was held that a manufacturer of explosives need only warn the purchaser's supervisory personnel regarding the proper location of dynamite during blasting. The manufacturer could not reasonably be expected "to go beyond its written warnings and personally warn every miner" where warnings had already been given to supervisory personnel, and where government mine inspectors testified that such personnel were fully aware of the danger of leaving surplus explosives near the point of blasting. Furthermore, the conduct of plaintiffs' decedents had been the subject of previous criticism by government inspectors for their violation of state and federal law on this very matter.

In Reed v. Pennwalt Corp., 591 P.2d 478 (Wash. App.1979), plaintiff contracted dermatitis when, as an employee in a food processing plant, she came into contact with caustic soda used to remove potato peels. The defendant manufacturer of the caustic soda had provided safety seminars attended by supervisory personnel invited by the operations manager of the employer. Employees such as plaintiff were not invited, since the manager felt that they suffered very little exposure to caustic soda. The court held that the manufacturer had fulfilled its duty by warning the employer, especially one "with its own safety programs and method of product distribution and where the manufacturer may have no effective means of communicating the warning to the ultimate user." Here the product when it reached the employee was "not in the original can, box, or form".

Where, however, the product is very dangerous and a warning is easily transmitted, failure to give warning to the ultimate user or consumer may be unjustified. As stated in comment b to § 397 of the Second Restatement of Torts, in such situations the supplier is "required to make the chattel carry its own directions." Thus in West v. Broderick & Bascom Rope Co., 197 N.W.2d 202 (Iowa 1972), where the plaintiff was injured because he used a wire rope sling beyond its rated capacity, the court found a jury question was presented regarding the adequacy of the warning given. Although defendant had advised plaintiff's employer of the sling's rated capacity, apparently no such warning had reached plaintiff. The evidence showed the danger was substantial, and that "without great burden, a curved tag, which would not likely be knocked off in service, could be bonded to a depression in the collar of each sling." Under these circumstances, failure of the plaintiff's employer to warn him did not supersede defendant's liability.

In Hubbard-Hall Chem. Co. v. Silverman, 340 F.2d 402 (1st Cir. 1965), the defendant's warning label on its bags of Parathion dust, an insecticide, had been approved for registration by the Department of Agriculture. Warning that the spray could be fatal, the label directed the wearing of a mask or respirator, rubber gloves, protective clothing, and goggles. The employing farmer told the court that he had relayed these instructions to two Puerto Rican migrant laborers who, because they died almost immediately after spraying with the product, were unable to confirm or deny the statements. One of the decedents could read a little English, and the other could not read at all. The court held that regardless of the compliance with the federal statute, defendant was liable under the common law of Massachusetts for failure to include "a skull and bones or other comparable symbols" that would reach the illiterate persons likely to be employed as farm laborers.

2. SKILLED WORKERS

As to warnings to skilled workers, it was held in Eyster v. Borg-Warner Corp., 206 S.E.2d 668 (Ga.App.1974), that, where it was common knowledge in the trade that aluminum wires should not be attached to copper terminals in a heating and air conditioning unit, the manufacturer of the unit was under no duty to warn of the hazard. Plaintiffs sued because of a fire which resulted from such a connection made by the installer. A review of defendant's " 'Technical Manual' substantiates that installation of the unit was not to be performed by laymen but only by trained, experienced technicians who could understand and follow the detailed specifications and who as a part of their trade education should have acquired knowledge of the risk of an aluminum-copper connection."

3. SUCCESSIVE HANDLERS AND ULTIMATE CONSUMERS

Under some circumstances there may be a duty to warn successive handlers or even to assure that such handlers warn the ultimate consumers. Thus in Brizendine v. Visador Co., 437 F.2d 822 (9th Cir. 1970), a boy stumbled just as he was about to open a glass door in a busy church lobby. His hand went through the glass and shattered it so that a flying piece lodged in his eye. The court held that the Pittsburgh Plate Glass Company was under a duty to warn that the glass was unsafe for use in high traffic areas. This duty was owed to the manufacturer of the door "lite," to the cabinet shop that made the completed door and to the church. A warning sticker on the glass might have fulfilled this purpose, the court said.

In Griggs v. Firestone Tire & Rubber Co., 513 F.2d 851 (8th Cir. 1975), a mismatched rim assembly exploded in the face and head of a repairman, causing serious and defacing injuries. The mismatching had been done by a former owner of the truck. Defendant had distributed catalogs with safety information to parts distributors and vehicle manufacturers, but had not made sure that such information would reach the local service stations. In view of the fact that a rim "probably will have to be disassembled at least once a year . . . and the practical fact that, at least in come cases, repair is bound to be undertaken, as here, by those not familiar with the particular dangers of these multi-piece rims, the jury could find that Firestone's assumption [that the warning would be conveyed by middlemen] was unreasonable and that it had failed its duty of care."

Defendant in Suchomajcz v. Hummel Chem. Co., 524 F.2d 19 (3d Cir. 1975), supplied to Christie, a fabricator of fireworks assembly kits, a chemical which was harmless in itself but dangerous when combined with other chemicals. Hummel knew of the use to which it would be put and knew that the kits would be shipped to minors in defiance of federal injunctions. Hummel was held liable for the wrongful death of two children and serious injury to four others when a portion of the kits abandoned in a bottle exploded as someone threw a match into the bottle. The court held it was a jury question whether Hummel violated its duty "to warn users of the potentially dangerous nature of its products."

On the other hand, a component part manufacturer is not liable where the defect arises after the product leaves his hands owing to circumstances over which he has no control. Thus in Walker v. Stauffer Chem. Corp., 96 Cal.Rptr. 803 (Cal.App. 1971), the manufacturer of bulk sulfuric acid was not liable in strict tort for injuries sustained in an explosion of a drain cleaner containing the acid but compounded with other ingredients by a subsequent seller, where the acid itself was without defect when it left the manufacturer's hands. The cleaner as compounded consisted of 50% acid and 50% alkaline base, rendering it dangerously defective since it carried no adequate warning of its highly volatile condition. The court stated: "We do not believe it realistically feasible or necessary to the protection of the public to require the manufacturer and supplier of a standard chemical ingredient such as bulk sulfuric acid, not having control over the subsequent compounding, packaging, or marketing of an item eventually causing injury to the ultimate consumer, to bear the responsibility for that injury."

4. DOCTORS OR PATIENTS

It has generally been held that, as to prescription drugs, only the doctor, not the patient, need be warned of possible side effects and contraindications. Two exceptions have been developed to this rule. Lindsay v. Ortho Pharmaceutical Corp., 637 F.2d 87 (2d Cir. 1980), notes that the FDA requires the pharmaceutical industry to include informational leaflets in eleven different prescription drugs. Another is a common law requirement, supported by several cases, that recipients of the Sabin vaccine in mass immunization programs be warned of the possibility for a small and unidentifiable class that the vaccine might cause the disease rather than immunize against it. Such was the holding in Reyes v. Wyeth Laboratories, 498 F.2d 1264 (5th Cir. 1974), where an eight-month-old baby contracted polio-myelitis slightly more than two weeks after she

[*197*]

had received the oral vaccine. On the issue of causation—that Mrs. Reyes, if warned, would not have brought her baby in to receive the vaccine—the court referred not only to the presumption that a warning would be read and heeded, but also to the availability of a safer alternative. That Mrs. Reyes might have taken preventive steps was buttressed by "the testimony of Reyes' expert . . . that some pediatricians in Hidalgo County, at least by the time of trial, had begun administering killed-virus vaccine to infants in order to build up their level of antibodies before feeding them the live-virus drug."

E. ADEQUACY AND TIMELINESS

If a warning, although given, fails to cover a foreseeable contingency, a finding of inadequacy will generally be sustained. Thus in Murray v. Wilson Oak Flooring Co., Inc., 475 F.2d 129 (7th Cir. 1973), the plaintiff was severely burned by an explosive fire starting from a floor he had just covered with Latex, distributed by the defendant. Although the warning in large bold type said "DO NOT USE NEAR FIRE OR FLAME," it was held a jury question whether the word "near" was sufficient to warn plaintiff of danger from a pilot light four feet away behind a closed door, or from stove pilot lights eight feet away and three feet off the floor.

That a danger must be clearly identified if a warning is to be deemed adequate is illustrated by the case of Wallinger v. Martin Stamping and Stove

Co., 236 N.E.2d 755 (Ill.App.1968). A cabin owner and his four guests died during the night of carbon monoxide poisoning from a gas heater installed a month previously by the cabin owner himself. He had failed to extend the vent pipe higher than the peak of the roof, thereby causing "incomplete exit of the combustion products." A four-page pamphlet had given minute instructions on installation and had additionally warned that to "conform to local codes this heater should be installed by a licensed gas appliance installer and inspected by the local gas inspector or utility inspector." In reversing a directed verdict for the defendant, the court observed that "the instructions were ambiguous in so far as they indicate the necessity of installation or inspection by professional installers or that the installation should conform to local codes, there being no local codes applicable. The instructions do not include any reference to the proper height of the vent pipe or the consequences of failing to elevate the vent pipe to an appropriate height, i. e., above the peak of the roof, except insofar as the cutaway drawing may be related thereto."

Instructions and warnings buried inconspicuously in a manual accompanying the sale of a product have rarely been held to be adequate. So in Stapleton v. Kawasaki Heavy Indus., Ltd., 608 F.2d 571 (5th Cir. 1979), plaintiff homeowner sued the motorcycle manufacturer and distributor for damages to her home when her son's motorcycle accidentally tipped over while he was cleaning it in the basement. Gasoline leaked from the tank and was ignited by a pilot light in a heater. It was for the jury to determine whether a warning of the danger on page 13 of the manual in ordinary type was sufficient. Plaintiff's son testified that he had glanced through the manual to note anything exceptional but had not "read it from cover to cover. . . . The jury could conclude that the danger posed by gas leakage was sufficiently great that the warning should have been presented in a way immediately obvious to even a casual reader."

Occasionally a warning is so watered down by ambiguous statements that it lulls the user into a false sense of security. A similar inadequacy occurs when the warning is weakened by representations of safety. Thus in Maize v. Atlantic Refining Co., 41 A.2d 850 (Pa.1945), where a supplier of carbon tetrachloride placed on all four sides of the can, in large letters, the words "Safety-Kleen," with only much smaller letters to warn of the grave danger from use of the product in a poorly ventilated place, the warning was inadequate. In Harris v. Solna Corp., 307 N.E.2d 434 (Ill.App.1974), warning requirements for the same dangerous product were met. There the label included a skull and crossbones and a warning that inhalation could be fatal. To plaintiff's contention that "adequate ventilation" should have been more precisely defined, the court replied: "In effect, the label warned that the vapor should not be inhaled at all and the adequacies of the ventilation [are] measured by the standard of a poison that could be fatal if inhaled."

Over-the-counter drugs must be accompanied by a warning on the container itself, and usually on an insert, of any danger from prolonged use without consulting a physician either because the drug might produce harmful side effects or because the patient should not continue with an ineffective treatment. In Torsiello v. Whitehall Laboratories, Div. of Home Products Corp., 398 A.2d 132 (N.J.Super. 1979), involving defendant's product Anacin, the court held that it was for the jury to determine whether a warning to consult a physician if pain persisted for ten days or redness developed was sufficient when the drug proved to be a gastric irritant for the plaintiff.

In Michael v. Warner/Chilcott, 579 P.2d 183 (N.M.App.1978), where plaintiff suffered kidney damage after taking an over-the-counter tablet for sinus congestion recommended by his physician, the adequacy of the warning was held for the jury. The court observed: "The 'warning' given by defendants states that 'This medication *may* damage the kidneys.' (Emphasis added.) [By the court.] It does not apprise the consumer of the fact that it *will* damage the kidneys. It states 'when used in *large* amounts.' (Emphasis added.) The term 'large' is vague and indefinite to a consumer. It does not state that 'Phenacetin' is a dangerous drug. The lettering is so tiny it might require a consumer to read the words with a magnifying glass." A concurring opinion considered that the drug was of "defective design" with "risks that outweigh benefits so far that no warning could provide adequate protection for the consumer." In support of this belief, the judge quotes plaintiff's expert nephrologist that no drug containing phenacetin, like this drug, should be available for over-the-counter sale. "No layman could be expected to medically evaluate the seriousness or the risk of kidney damage, even with specific data."

A warning to physicians regarding a prescription drug may also be inadequate. In Bristol-Myers Co. v. Gonzales, 561 S.W.2d 801 (Tex.1978), defendant failed to warn in its package insert, or in the privately published Physician's Desk Reference (PDR) which through annual supplements reflects any change in the inserts, that the drug Kantrex could cause deafness. Moreover, a statement in the 1970 PDR implied that the doctor could safely use the drug for curing an infection and for irrigating a surgical wound. As to the approval of the insert by the FDA, the court found that the "fact that the approved insert did not adequately warn of potential dangers to the users of this drug was known to the proper officials of Bristol-Myers long before the inadequacy became known to the government officials and a change in the warnings and instructions was required in the package insert."

Drug manufacturers have been required not only to give adequate warnings, but also to use every reasonable means to reach physicians promptly. A package insert may be unavailing, since it may reach the physicians only through the first sample or through republication somewhat later in the PDR while the package itself may contain enough of the product to cover several years of normal use for rare diseases. If, in the meantime, a dangerous side effect is discovered, the manufacturer may be required to send a "Dear Doctor" letter to all physicians. In Sterling Drug, Inc. v. Yarrow, 408 F.2d 978 (8th Cir. 1969), the evidence showed that at the time plaintiff's vision was reduced to 20% as a result of taking Aralen for her rheumatoid arthritis, the manufacturer knew of this dangerous side effect. The court held that, with this knowledge, it was not enough to warn physicians through product cards, the Physicians Desk Reference and a "Dear Doctor" letter mailed to "all physicians and hospital personnel in the United States." There was professional testimony that physicians received so much literature on drugs that they did not have time to read all of it; and that the most effective method of warning, through the detail men that regularly called on physicians, should have been but was not followed by the manufacturer. In other cases, for example, Incollingo v. Ewing, 282 A.2d 206 (Pa. 1971), it has been held that if detail men "over-promoted" a drug, de-emphasizing its recognized side effects, any warning could be found inadequate by the jury.

It should be clear from the drug cases given so far that the timeliness of a warning is of prime importance. As soon as the defendant manufacturer knows or should know as an expert of any possible danger from his drug he must warn all physicians, by the most efficient and speedy method, of the danger and of any contraindications which might assist the physician in determining whether the drug is safe for his patient. The defendant, however, will not be liable until he does have some reason to know of the danger. In Leibowitz v. Ortho Pharmaceutical Corp., 307 A.2d 449 (Pa.Super.1973), plaintiff's doctor had prescribed defendant's oral contraceptive for the regulation of menses. The patient, who had a previous history of thrombophlebitis, suffered a recurrence of the affliction. Defendant's lengthy package insert reported that some patients taking the drug had contracted venous thrombosis but that no evidence supported a causal relationship. It warned, however, that a previous history of thrombotic disease was a contraindication to the use of the drug. In denying recovery, the court said: "In no reported case has a court imposed liability on a prescription drug manufacturer on the basis of facts or discoveries made subsequent to the date a particular cause of action accrued. To do so would be to fatally choke the industry in its marketing and development procedures. A drug manufacturer would virtually become an insurer against all possible consequences, which at some future date prove to be 'caused' by the use of its product. It would cause drug companies to hesitate and prolong the time before precious, beneficial, and long-awaited drugs were put on the market."

Recovery was allowed in McEwen v. Ortho Pharmaceutical Corp., 528 P.2d 522 (Or.1974), where plaintiff was blinded in one eye and injured in the other as a result of hemorrhaging from the use of two oral contraceptives manufactured by two different defendants. Even after plaintiff complained of eye trouble, her physicians continued to recommend the use of the pills since, on reading defendants' package inserts, they found no warning against their use in plaintiff's circumstances. The court said: "Considering this testimony, the gravity of the risk involved, and the evidence of plaintiff's cumulative symptoms, there was substantial evidence that if adequate warnings had been timely given to plaintiff's treating physicians by either defendant, plaintiff's use of the oral contraceptives would have been discontinued before her injuries had become irreversible."

F. EFFECT OF STATUTE

It is clear in *Hubbard-Hall* and in *Bristol-Myers*, both given above, that compliance with statutes or with regulations pursuant to statutes does not exempt defendant from common law liability. In some cases, compliance may show that the product is free from defect or that its manufacturer is free from negligence; but it is not a conclusive defense. Compliance with statutes was unsuccessful as a defense in Rumsey v. Freeway Manor Minimax, 423 S.W.2d 387 (Tex.Civ.App.1968), involving roach poison containing thallium consumed by a three-year-old boy. The mother had placed the poison in bottle caps on a high shelf, as directed, but it was consumed by the boy when the caps were removed by an older playmate. The warning label included the word "poison" and a red skull and crossbones. As an antidote, the label stated: "Give a tablespoonful of salt in a glass of warm water and repeat until vomit fluid is clear. Have victim lie down and keep warm. Call a physician immediately!" The child was taken to a doctor within a few minutes after the accident; but the doctor lost precious time in a vain search for a specific antidote to thallium. A stomach pump was not used until after a fatal amount of the poison had been absorbed.

A verdict was directed for the defendant on the ground that all federal and state statutes and regulations had been obeyed. On appeal, however, it was held that a jury could find negligence in failure to warn that no specific antidote existed. The court found a common law duty to warn of the full extent of the danger, adding that "certainly a poison for which there is no specific antidote has more potential for harm than does a poison for

which there is a specific antidote." Had a warning
as to the absence of a specific antidote been given,
the mother or the physician probably would have
had the child's stomach emptied more promptly.

On the other hand, violation of statute may be
negligence per se, requiring no further proof. Such
cases are, however, relatively rare; even when a
negligence per se count is included, it is often only
one of two or more grounds of recovery. In
Gonzalez v. Virginia-Carolina Chem. Co., 239 F.Supp.
567 (E.D.S.C.1965), injuries received by a pilot from
a crop-dusting chemical were greatly aggravated
because of a 12-hour delay in finding out what
antidote was available for the spray. The defendant
manufacturer was unable to enlighten the doctor,
who finally learned what to do from a college
professor of chemistry. The court held the defendant negligent per se in failing to obey the
applicable federal and state statutes concerning
economic poisons. The label on defendant's bags of
dust had failed to meet three requirements: a skull
and crossbones, the word "poison" in red on a
distinctly contrasting background, and a statement
of the antidote.

G. CONTINUING DUTY

As is now widely known in the case of motor
vehicles, a continuing duty to warn of defects
discovered after the vehicle has been sold arises
under the National Traffic and Motor Vehicle

Safety Act of 1966. Recalls of children's toys with sharp edges, of Christmas tree lights that short-circuited, and other dangerous household products have been required under the Consumer Product Safety Act.

There are also a few cases which have imposed a common law duty to warn of any dangerous defects discovered after the product has been supplied. In Comstock v. General Motors Corp., 99 N.W.2d 627 (Mich.1959), it was discovered after thousands of cars had been sold that a design defect in those cars might result in a sudden loss of brake fluid. Dealers were supplied with kits to replace the defective units, but no warning was sent to car owners. Even if the jury found no negligence as to defective design, it nevertheless might find a negligent failure to warn "those into whose hands they had placed this dangerous instrument and whose lives (along with the lives of others) depended upon defective brakes which might fail without notice."

In Braniff Airways, Inc. v. Curtiss-Wright Corp., 411 F.2d 451 (2d Cir. 1969), a plane having one of defendant's engines, then about two years old, crashed. Examination after the crash "revealed that the number eleven cylinder had failed, that it had separated from the engine, and that its wall was scuffed." For about eight months before the crash, Curtiss-Wright had known of this scuffing problem and of other instances of cylinder failure. The court held that a manufacturer under these circumstances had a duty either to remedy the defects "or, if complete remedy is not feasible, at least to give users adequate warnings and instructions concerning methods for minimizing the danger."

The duty imposed in *Braniff* would presumably extend only to those whom the supplier could reasonably be expected to reach by warning, although strict liability for supplying a dangerously defective product might attach without regard to the feasibility of giving a warning to the users or others involved. Where a continuing duty to warn is imposed, an action may lie that would otherwise be time-barred under a statute of limitations.

H. THE SPECIAL PROBLEM OF ALLERGIC USERS

1. DEFINITION AND THE PROBLEM OF CAUSATION

Medical descriptions of allergic reactions are complicated and incompletely developed. It is clear, however, from a legal standpoint, that an allergic reaction is one suffered by only a minority of the persons exposed to a substance known as a "sensitizer." Ordinarily the allergic reaction does not occur upon first exposure to the sensitizer, but only at the time of a subsequent "eliciting" exposure at least five days later. A sensitizer is thus distinguished from a "primary irritant," which produces harm to the majority of normal persons, and takes effect upon first application.

In the early allergy cases the action often was dismissed on the ground that the plaintiff's sensitivity rather than the product was the sole proximate cause of the harm. The difficulty with this oversimplified approach is that the sensitizer contained in the defendant's product is also a proximate cause of the harm, and the defendant often is more aware of the risk from the product to allergic users than is the plaintiff.

This does not mean that a plaintiff can establish causation simply by showing that his illness followed use of defendant's product. Ordinarily he must point to a particular sensitizer that harmed him. Where, however, the plaintiff cannot identify the sensitizer, he still may be able to establish his case by excluding other causes. Such exclusion of other possible causes can be established by competent professional testimony. In this connection, it is important to secure a physical examination of the plaintiff in order to determine not only the extent of the injuries, but whether the injuries are of a kind likely to have been caused by defendant's product, rather than by cosmetics, soaps or the like which the plaintiff may have been using along with the defendant's product. Often the defendant's medical experts are thoroughly conversant with the injuries that may or may not be caused by its own products.

Ordinarily no duty exists to alter the formula of a product that is safe for normal use, in order to avoid the risk of injury to allergic users or consumers. A product containing even a rather strong sensitizer, that is, one affecting a substantial number of persons, will ordinarily be regarded as free from defect if it is accompanied by an adequate warning. This duty to warn may arise on negligence grounds or on strict liability principles.

2.   LEGAL BASIS OF THE DUTY TO WARN

a.   NEGLIGENCE

It is clear that no duty to warn on negligence principles can arise unless the defendant knows or should know of the danger. Actual knowledge of the possibility of allergic reactions is not required in recent decisions. The defendant is deemed to have the knowledge and skill of an expert in his field; and if as an expert he should realize the danger from his product to a substantial class of allergic users, he must give a warning to avoid liability for negligence.

Ordinarily no duty to warn exists unless the product creates a risk of harm to a substantial class of users. However, in Braun v. Roux Distributing Co., 312 S.W.2d 758 (Mo.1958), the court found negligence in failure to warn of a severe but admittedly quite isolated reaction to hair dye. This holding was in spite of evidence that during a period

when over 50 million packages of the dye had been
distributed, there had "never been either a reported
or an established case of periarteritis nodosa" caused
by hair dye of this kind.   Less unusual is the holding
in Merrill v. Beaute Vues Corp., 235 F.2d 893 (10th
Cir. 1956), where, again, grave harm was involved,
this time in the use of a hair-waving preparation.
But since only three persons were affected out of
500 million sales of the product, no duty to warn was
found.

The leading negligence case is Wright v. Carter
Products, Inc., 244 F.2d 53 (2d Cir. 1957).   There a
deodorant contained aluminum sulfate, and testimony indicated that some persons are allergic to
this substance.   The percentage was quite small;
during a four-year period prior to plaintiff's injury,
when over 82 million jars of the product were sold,
defendant had received only 373 complaints of skin
irritation.   The trial court's dismissal of the complaint because of the small percentage harmed
was reversed by the appellate court.   Recognizing
that only a "minuscule" percentage of users was
involved, the court found that the statistical analysis
of injury "so heavily relied on by the trial court"
was only one factor in the determination of defendant's duty to foresee and warn of possible
harm.   In addition to the percentage of persons
susceptible, the trial court was directed to consider
the gravity of possible injuries, and the defendant's
expert status, as bearing on foreseeability of the

harm to users of the product. As a further factor, the trial judge was instructed to consider "the difficulty, if any, of embodying an effective precaution in the labels or literature attached to the product."

Although the percentage and the size of the "substantial" allergic class are declining, many negligence cases denying the duty to warn reveal the uncertainty that still exists as to the requirement. In attempting to establish a substantial class, the plaintiff will seek to obtain disclosure of other complaints, as he can under federal discovery rules or comparable state court rules. If any changes have occurred in the product, the defendant will attempt to restrict such complaints to ones made about the product while it had the identical formula, and while it was being used under the same conditions. Where evidence of earlier complaints is admitted only to show notice of the danger, the discovery may be restricted to complaints prior to the date of plaintiff's purchase of the product.

b. STRICT TORT AND WARRANTY

A duty to warn of allergic reactions may be imposed on the basis of strict liability as well as negligence. Where recovery is based on strict liability, plaintiff must show that he is a member of an appreciable class of potentially allergic users, but he may not be required to establish that defendant knew or should have known of the risk involved. In

Crotty v. Shartenberg's-New Haven, Inc., 162 A.2d 513 (Conn.1960), where plaintiff sustained an allergic reaction to a hair remover called "Nudit," the court held that plaintiff was entitled to recover for breach of implied warranty against the retail seller of the product. Breach of implied warranty is sufficiently shown, the court stated, if the plaintiff establishes "that the product contains a substance or ingredient which has a tendency to affect injuriously an appreciable number of people," and if plaintiff can show "that he has, in fact, been injured or harmed by the use of the product." As to the defendant's position as a retailer only, the court held that he should bear the same risk as the manufacturer if he "sells the article to a prospective user who, relying on the retailer, is entitled to believe that the article is reasonably fit for the purpose for which it is sold."

Comment j to § 402A of the Second Restatement of Torts, interpreting the strict liability of that section, states that the seller of a product is required to warn of "an ingredient to which a substantial number of the population are allergic," where the danger is not generally known or reasonably expected by the consuming public, if the seller "has knowledge, or by the application of reasonable, developed human skill and foresight should have knowledge, of the presence of the ingredient and the danger." Allergy cases based on breach of warranty have generally tended to stress the presence or absence of defendant's knowledge of the risk. Requiring proof in all allergy cases, however, that the seller knew or should have known of the danger means that strict liability and negligence are treated as essentially the same in such cases. This treatment seems contrary to the underlying bases for imposing strict liability.

Where a seller expressly warrants his product, he may be liable for a breach of such warranty if an allergic reaction occurs, regardless of whether the seller knows or should know the product is harmful and of whether the plaintiff is shown to be a member of an appreciable class of persons allergic to the product. In Drake v. Charles of Fifth Ave., Inc., 307 N.Y.S.2d 310 (App.Div.1970), plaintiff was injured when she applied to her fingernails a product represented by defendant as being "completely safe," "used by millions," and "easy to use; safe." The court concluded that an allergic reaction as a defense was "proper as to a cause of action based upon an implied warranty," but was not a defense if the jury found that the defendant had "expressly warranted that the product was safe for anyone who purchased it." The language used "in no way alerted a purchaser that there might be a small fraction of potential users who would suffer an allergic reaction to the product not common to the normal person."

3. NATURE OF THE WARNING

For some sensitizers definite labeling and warning requirements are laid down by consumer legislation, such as the Federal Pure Food and Drug Act and the Federal Hazardous Substances Act. Compliance with such statutory requirements, however, may not constitute a sufficient defense, since more adequate instructions or warnings may be required under common law principles.

As held in Arata v. Tonegato, 314 P.2d 130 (Cal.App.1957), where a patch test is an effective means for detecting an allergic reaction, directions for taking such a test must be given whether or not required by legislation. Since patch tests are sometimes but not always revealing, it was held in Erny v. Revlon, Inc., 459 S.W.2d 261 (Mo.1970), that a warning may be inadequate if it fails to point out the nonconclusiveness of the test.

In *Braun*, cited above, it was held that the warning must specifically describe the possible adverse reaction. The defendant's warning had stated that the ingredients of his product might "cause skin irritation on certain individuals," but failed to warn of the possibility of the grave systemic injury suffered by the plaintiff. The court held that a jury could find the warning inadequate because of this failure.

In D'Arienzo v. Clairol, Inc., 310 A.2d 106 (N.J.Super.1973), plaintiff's hair, scalp, and face were damaged when she applied defendant's hair coloring. The literature accompanying the product said: "BEFORE YOU COLOR MAKE THESE TWO EASY TESTS." The label was in compliance with the federal statute. The court said that the instructions "undeniably" required that the patch tests be performed before each application. Plaintiff admitted that after two years' successful experience with the product she did not consider that the directions required her to make a test before every application. Although defendant had explained in general the reasons for patch testing, the court found that the defendant might have further emphasized the reason for repeated testing—that a user could develop sensitivity after repeated use of the sensitizing agent. Also, defendant might have emphasized, *before* reaching the instructions for the performance of the test itself, the unfavorable results that such a test might reveal. Whether defendant's instructions were in fact sufficiently emphatic was for the jury.

CHAPTER VII

CAUSATION, FORESEEABILITY, AND THE AFFIRMATIVE DEFENSES

A. CAUSE–IN–FACT

1. PROOF PROBLEMS

In products liability cases proving cause-in-fact may be less difficult than in some other torts—for example, medical malpractice. Once a defect has been shown to exist, and once reasonable although not entirely conclusive grounds for excluding other causes have been submitted, the court will often let the case go to the jury. The strong deterrent force behind products liability has resulted in little tolerance for potentially dangerous defects.

Some courts, however, have been more exacting than others in the requirement that plaintiff must eliminate alternative causes. Thus in Jakubowski v. Minnesota Mining & Mfg., 199 A.2d 826 (N.J.1964), the plaintiff failed to establish a prima facie case against the manufacturer of an abrasive disc which snapped in half and struck plaintiff in the stomach as he was using it in his employment. The court stated that while it was possible that the disc broke because of a manufacturing flaw or design defect, "it is just as possible that mishandling by the prior user or users or use beyond the expected life span of the disc was responsible."

In Scanlon v. General Motors Corp., Chevrolet Motor Div., 326 A.2d 673 (N.J.1974), plaintiff was driving his station wagon, nine months old and with 4,000 miles use, on a clear dry day when it accelerated uncontrollably and crashed into a telephone pole. A part claimed to be defective by the plaintiff proved to be intact when photographed. Plaintiff after the accident told the police he had "simply lost control." Plaintiff produced no evidence as to proper maintenance, no testimony of the service station owner who had serviced the car, and no subpoena of the station's records. His wife, who did most of the driving, did not appear as a witness. The court held that plaintiff failed to negate alternative causes of the accident, and affirmed a directed verdict for the defendant. A dissent contended that the majority had simply indicated how the plaintiff might have strengthened his proof; that here, reasonable men could differ. "It is the jury which passes on what 'human experience tells us' as to why an accident such as this occurred, given whatever ambiguities and gaps exist in a plaintiff's case. That defendant's case is stronger or that plaintiff's case is inconclusive or, at best, weak, does not justify taking a case from the jury. . . . We are not faced here with merely the happening of an accident. Sudden uncontrollable acceleration followed by heavy brake application and 563 feet of skid marks surpass 'mere surmise or conjecture'. . . . These undisputed facts are consistent with a product defect and more than sufficient to support a finding by a jury in strict liability."

It was stated in Foley v. Pittsburgh-Des Moines Co., 68 A.2d 517 (Pa.1949), that "the law does not require the elimination of every possible cause of the accident other than that on which the plaintiff relies, but only such other causes, if any, as fairly arise from the evidence." Thus in Greco v. Bucciconi Engineering Co., 407 F.2d 87 (3d Cir. 1969), the plaintiff was permitted to recover against the manufacturer of a magnetic metal sheet piler, where retractable "fingers" of the piler malfunctioned and caused sheet metal to fall on plaintiff's right hand, amputating his fingers. Defendant contended that plaintiff failed to negate alternative causes such as a defect in the control panel, not manufactured by defendant. There was testimony, however, that the operators of the piler had "never had a problem with the control panel" and that "they were unable to duplicate the malfunction or discover its cause;" and since defendant "presented no evidence" in support of its contention of alternative causation the jury was justified in finding that the defect was attributable to the piler itself.

As might be expected, causation problems frequently arise in the case of prescription drugs or other products used in medical treatment. Thus in Tomer (Estate) v. American Home Products Corp., 368 A.2d 35 (Conn.1976), plaintiff's decedent died of liver disease allegedly contracted as a result of two operations within twelve days using defendant's anesthetic Halothane. The trial court excluded all expert testimony concerning the danger of Halothane as revealed after the death of plaintiff's decedent. The Supreme Court held that such testimony, insofar as it tended "to show the scope of duties owed could have been properly limited to scientific knowledge existing at that time.

"The actual cause of a person's death, however, unlike the scope of duties owed by a person alleged to have caused that death, does not depend upon the state of scientific knowledge on the date of that death. To the contrary, once a person dies, or once any other event transpires, the cause or causes of that death or event remain the same forever, although man's knowledge or understanding of those causes may become more sophisticated and accurate, or more blurred, as time passes. The cause of any death is a physical fact, and like any other physical fact, is subject to proof after the fact by the testimony of experts based upon all available knowledge in existence after as well as before the death. A rule of evidence, therefore, which would limit a trier of fact to a consideration of knowledge in existence at the time of death for the purpose of determining its cause has no basis in reason or logic. We conclude that the court erred in limiting the basis of all expert testimony to knowledge possessed by the experts in 1967."

A defect has sometimes been clearly shown at the same time that it is equally clear that the defect did not cause the accident. In Stewart v. Von Solbrig Hosp., Inc., 321 N.E.2d 428 (Ill.App.1974), a surgical pin known as a Rush pin broke in plaintiff's leg after he had walked upon the leg in violation of the surgeon's instructions. The pin was intended to stabilize the fracture, not to bear the body's weight. "The plaintiff did present evidence that the Rush pin in question had inclusions and scratches which reduced the pin's strength. However, none of the evidence pointed to the fact that this alleged defect was the cause of the break. Even if the pin had no defects whatsoever, the evidence showed that the pin would have broken if the plaintiff walked on it after his cast was removed. The plaintiff walked on it after his cast was removed by his own admission."

In Price v. Ashby's Inc., 354 P.2d 1064 (Utah 1960), plaintiffs produced insufficient evidence of defect in the car to get to the jury. The evidence showed a tendency, owing to a part negligently installed by General Motors, for the front portion of the car, after it had been standing a short time with the ignition turned off, to "drop down until there was not over about three or four inches clearance from the ground. . . . After the car had settled . . . if the motor was started, the right front portion would always regain its proper altitude or level without much delay." Finally the car, driven by the plaintiff owner at a speed of 50–60 miles an hour, went off the road at a curve and into a barrow pit. The court held that the evidence "does not provide a basis upon which it could reasonably be found that the defect in the car was the probable cause of the accident."

Warning cases often involve proof of causation, as in the motorcycle case previously given where there was evidence that plaintiff might not have read even an adequate warning. The court will, however, consider any lack of conspicuousness or intensity as factors in plaintiff's failure to read, and then may hold that a proper warning might well have attracted plaintiff's attention and prevented the injury. Courts have realized, as in the motorcycle case, that *all* of the literature accompanying the product will very likely not be read. Most consumers will assume that a product is usable and safe for the purpose for which it is conspicuously advertised on the label. Any warning to be effective must be equally conspicuous.

On the other hand, warnings in some situations beyond the control of the plaintiff have been considered futile so that their absence is not the cause of the accident. For example, in Greiner v. Volkswagenwerk Aktiengesellschaft, 429 F.Supp. 495 (E.D.Pa.1976), the trial court, upon remand, found that as a matter of law defendant's failure to warn that a Volkswagen had "a propensity to overturn on sharp steering maneuvers" was not a cause of the accident. Plaintiff's driver found herself on the wrong side of the road facing an oncoming car. She turned sharply to the right, then found herself headed toward the concrete railing of a bridge and made another sharp turn to the left. The court found that even if the warning had been given and read it would not have prevented the accident. "Even giving Nickel the best possible reading of the evidence, at 30 miles per hour, she would cover ten feet in approximately one-fourth of a second. It is simply not within the bounds of human reason to suppose that, had there been a warning, Nickel would have recalled it, considered it and then intentionally crashed head-on into a concrete rail." As to the argument that a warning might have caused Nickel not to buy the car at all, the court held any such suggestion to be mere conjecture.

Where a plaintiff knows of the danger from some other source, the defendant's failure to warn will not be considered the cause of the accident. In Nelson v. Brunswick Corp., 503 F.2d 376 (9th Cir. 1974), defendant sanded and lacquered the lanes at a bowling alley managed by the plaintiff. Fumes from the lacquer exploded as plaintiff picked up some electrical appliances that arced. Since plaintiff admitted he knew of the explosive nature of the fumes, the court held that defendant's failure to warn was not the cause of the accident. Sometimes plaintiffs' actions in similar situations have been regarded as contributory negligence, barring recovery.

2. INTERRELATIONSHIP OF CAUSE AND DEFECT

A problem may arise when the defect itself cannot be proven *unless* it caused the injury. Only results can determine whether a few cans of insecticide, completely used up in spraying a crop, contained a defect. If a product unaccountably malfunctions, can it be free from defect? On the other hand, if the alleged defect did not cause the accident, it may not be a defect at all. For instance, a product may not be defective for lack of a safety device, if such a device was entirely unnecessary for its intended use and would, in fact, preclude such a use.

In Henderson v. Cominco American, Inc., 518 P.2d 873 (Idaho 1974), plaintiffs testified that most of their peppermint crop, sprayed with defendant's herbicide, died, while a small portion of the crop on which they used another spray, flourished. Neighbors who did not use defendant's Sinox PE had no trouble with their crops. The court said: "To infer that Sinox PE was the cause of the injury on the basis of this evidence would be speculative and unreasonable." Plaintiffs' witnesses did not preclude other possible causes, such as differences in watering, soil characteristics, and age of the peppermint. Also, plaintiffs failed to explain why some of their crop, sprayed with Sinox PE, although diminished, was harvestable; while other portions were destroyed. Since Sinox PE was not identified as the causative agent, there was also no proof of defect, lacking any other evidence such as analysis of the damaged crops. Therefore defendant's requests for involuntary dismissals of both the warranty and negligence actions should have been granted.

On the other hand, in Savage v. Peterson Distributing Co., 150 N.W.2d 804 (Mich.1967), plaintiffs' ranch mink died allegedly from defendant's contaminated feed. The trial court had directed a verdict for the defendant, observing that no analysis of the feed and no autopsy of the mink carcasses were offered in evidence. In reversing, the supreme court observed that situations occur where the plaintiff "cannot obtain a scientific analysis of the involved product," but should nevertheless be allowed to rest his case on "evidence of the existence or occurrence of similar facts, conditions or events under the same or substantially similar circumstances." The evidence on which plaintiffs relied consisted of testimony from "other mink ranchers (some 11 in all), the substance of which was that each experienced the same difficulty at the same approximate time as suffered by plaintiff after having fed their animals defendant Ralston's cereal mink food." In addition, the minks on the experimental ranch of another defendant in the case, when fed the cereal, experienced the same problems; examination of these minks and of the feed revealed the presence of a harmful substance described as "type 'A' salmonellae." This proof, said the court, "suggests a permissible inference that the facts thus brought forth amounted to something more than a series of disconnected and purely coincidental occurrences," so that "the jury might conclude that there was a pattern of causally connected carelessness" in defendant's manufacture.

Where only an unusual combination of circumstances causes a product to malfunction, a court is likely to hold that no defect exists. For example, in Greiten v. LaDow, 235 N.W.2d 677 (Wis.1975), two parallel angle irons attached to a printing press for the purpose of holding a plywood board, on which the printed material was deposited, were designed to retract when the power was cut off. The board and the paper on it would then "drop a minimal distance onto the wooden skid of the press." In order to change a loaded skid, the press crew had pushed a hand truck under the skid. When the truck became stuck, plaintiff reached under the skid to shake the truck loose and in so doing accidentally opened a circuit breaker which cut off the electricity, causing the angle irons to retract and the board with its load to fall onto plaintiff's head. A directed verdict for the defendant was affirmed, the court noting that the machine had been used daily for six years without accident.

3.   CONCURRENT CAUSES

Where the evidence is sufficient to support a finding of several causes for only one of which the defendant may be liable, it has been held appropriate to submit the issue of causation to the jury if the cause attributable to the defendant may have been a "substantial factor" in bringing about the plaintiff's injury. The cause attributable to the defendant need not be the only cause, or even the last or immediate cause, if it concurs with other causes of the injury. A good example of this is presented in Vlahovich v. Betts Machine Co., 242 N.E.2d 17 (Ill.App.1968). There the plaintiff was injured while removing a light bulb lens that broke allegedly because of an unreasonably dangerous condition of the lens. The defendant manufacturer of the lens sought to show that the breaking may also have been caused by failure of the plaintiff to follow directions, by improper maintenance of a ring around the lens, and by pressure exerted in removing the lens. On these facts, the court held that the trial judge erred in not charging the jury that the defect attributed to the defendant need only have been a concurring cause of the injury.

In Basko v. Sterling Drug, Inc., 416 F.2d 417 (2d Cir. 1969), plaintiff was blinded after taking two of defendant's drugs. Aralen was taken before the risk of blindness was known to the defendant, Triquin after the risk was known. The court found reversible error in the failure of the trial judge to instruct the jury that, if it found no breach of duty to warn in respect to Aralen, but a breach in respect to Triquin, and if either drug alone would have caused the injury, then plaintiff was entitled to recover from the defendant. The analogy given was that of the two fires that merge to destroy a house, one fire owing to defendant's negligence, the other of unknown origin. If the fire caused by negligence was a "substantial factor" in producing the damage, then defendant should not be relieved of liability because of another all-sufficient innocent cause.

4. BURDEN OF PROOF

In a few cases involving multiple defendants and an injury to the plaintiff from the product or negligent act of at least one of them, the courts have shifted the burden of proof to the defendants to show which of them caused the harm. In the absence of such proof, each defendant may be held jointly and severally liable for the entire harm. In Hall v. E. I. Du Pont De Nemours & Co., Inc., 345 F.Supp. 353 (E.D.N.Y.1972), a number of children were injured by playing with blasting caps that carried no warning as to their dangerous nature. Since the manufacturers of individual caps could not be identified, damages were sought from all the manufacturers of such caps along with their trade association. The court in upholding the cause of action placed great emphasis on plaintiffs' allegations that the defendants jointly controlled the risk. "The complaint states that the defendants had actual knowledge that children were frequently injured by blasting caps, and, through the trade association, kept statistics and other information regarding these accidents. . . . Moreover, defendants are said to have jointly explicitly considered the possibility of labeling the caps, to have rejected this possibility, and to have engaged in lobbying activities against legislation which would have required such labeling."

In Anderson v. Somberg, 338 A.2d 1 (N.J.1975), emphasis was placed on the fact that the defendants had far greater access to the evidence than the plaintiff who was unconscious during the surgery that resulted in injury. The tip or cup of a rongeur, a forceps-like instrument, broke off in plaintiff's spinal canal. Plaintiff sued the surgeon, the hospital directly furnishing the instrument, the distributor, and the manufacturer. The jury had found no cause as to each defendant. The court held that, in the given situation, "the burden of proof in fact does shift to defendants. All those in custody of that patient or who owed him a duty, as here, the manufacturer and the distributor, should be called forward and should be made to prove their freedom from liability. . . . Since all parties had been joined who could reasonably have been connected with that negligence or defect, it was clear that one of those parties was liable, and at least one could not succeed in his proofs.

"In cases of this type, no defendant will be entitled to prevail on a motion for judgment until all the proofs have been presented to the court and jury. The judge may grant any motion bearing in mind that the plaintiff must recover a verdict against at least one defendant." On remand, the jury found in favor of the plaintiff and against the manufacturer and distributor of the instrument. This verdict was affirmed, 386 A.2d 413 (N.J. Super.1978), upon appeal by the manufacturer.

Occasionally an opinion breaks such new ground that it cannot be ignored even though its ruling may be forever confined to one jurisdiction. Possibly Sindell v. Abbott Laboratories, 607 P.2d 924 (Cal.1980), may prove to be the beginning of a trend. Here, plaintiff Sindell and other similarly situated women brought class actions against five drug manufacturers who, during the time when the various plaintiffs were in the wombs of their mothers, sold a drug, DES, designed to prevent miscarriages. Whatever its utility in that regard— plaintiffs alleged that the drug was ineffective—it did have the effect for a certain number of women whose mothers took the drug of producing, years later, a vaginal and cervical growth of a cancerous nature, requiring radical surgery followed by repeated and painful biopsy or colposcopic examinations. Over 200 companies had marketed the drug, and no plaintiff had any way of discovering what manufacturer made the drug administered to her mother. With the case brought a generation after the treatment, the defendants equally had no way of tracing, through wholesalers or retail druggists, their sales to the various maternal patients. The court held, however, that if the five defendants are shown to have a substantial share of the market—plaintiff asserted 90%, but the court refrained from settling a precise minimum figure—then it was reasonable in the context "to measure the likelihood that the defendants supplied the product which allegedly injured the plaintiffs by the percentage which the DES sold by each of them for the purpose of preventing miscarriage bears to the entire production of the drug sold by all for that purpose." As to apportionment among the defendants, each one "will be held liable for the proportion of the judgment represented by its share of that market unless it demonstrates that it could not have made the product which caused plaintiff's injuries." A sixth defendant had already been dismissed from the action because its manufacturing of DES began after the plaintiff was born.

A dissent observes that although "the majority purports to change only the required burden of proof by shifting it from plaintiffs to defendants, the effect of its holding is to guarantee that plaintiffs will prevail on the causation issue because defendants are no more capable of disproving factual causation than plaintiffs are of proving it. 'Market share' liability thus represents a new high water mark in tort law."

B. PROXIMATE CAUSE, FORESEEABILITY, AND STRICT LIABILITY (IN GENERAL)

Some confusion has arisen because of the use of the word foreseeability in strict liability cases. Foreseeability determines liability for negligence. A negligent actor is liable only if he foresaw or should have foreseen that his act, or failure to act, could cause harm. He is not liable for totally unpredictable results of his actions. In strict liability, foreseeability is determinative of defect. A manufacturer is not required to produce a product that will stand up under all contingencies. His product is free from a dangerous defect if it proves safe under any foreseeable use, whether intended or not. If, on the other hand, the product proves dangerous only after it has undergone an unforeseeable modification or is used in an unforeseeable way, such a product is not defective. Not everyone really wants a chair that can be used as a weapon in a family fight. Should it break so that a nail or sharp splinter causes more harm than contemplated by the temporary belligerents, the manufacturer will hardly be held liable.

In Galvan v. Prosser Packers, Inc., 521 P.2d 929 (Wash.1974), the court says that foreseeability in strict liability is only foreseeability of use. Once the use and its foreseeability is determined and a defect as one cause of the injury is shown, foreseeability of the harm from the defect is irrelevant. There the plaintiff was using the farm machine as intended when, as he investigated some smoking gears, he slipped and fell into an open rear cross-auger attached to the machine. The court sustained plaintiff's exception to the following instruction: "When we say that an act or omission must be a proximate cause of an injury, we mean that the injury must be the natural and probable consequence of the act or omission and one which might have been foreseen by a man of ordinary prudence and intelligence, though not necessarily in the precise form in which it occurred." Plaintiff's counsel observed: "I feel that this permits the defendant, Food Machinery Corporation, to argue that 'well, how would we ever know this guy would fall into that machine?' Now this isn't an element of our proof, and it's not an element of their defense."

In Newman v. Utility Trailer & Equipment Co., Inc., 564 P.2d 674 (Or.1977), where plaintiff was injured when a semitrailer turned over on a curve, the court held erroneous an instruction which included the words: "Should the manufacturer or seller have foreseen the harm which the product would cause to the user under the circumstances of the case"? The court observed: "In a defective design case the essential difference between a negligence action and a products liability action is that in negligence the foreseeability of the harm by the manufacturer or seller is submitted as a question of fact to the jury, whereas in strict liability the knowledge of the article's propensity to inflict harm as it did is assumed regardless of whether the manufacturer or seller foresaw or reasonably should have foreseen the danger. . . . It is obvious that trial courts are experiencing difficulty in distinguishing *foreseeability of use* from *foreseeability of the risk of harm.* Before a manufacturer or other seller is strictly liable for injury inflicted by a product, the product must have been put to a foreseeable use."

In Eshbach v. W. T. Grant's & Co., 481 F.2d 940 (3d Cir. 1973), the plaintiff was injured when, after jumping on a riding mower behind her older brother, age nine, her foot became entangled in the unguarded chain and sprocket. The driver stopped the machine only by taking his foot off the pedal. The machine had no brakes and no ignition switch. The jury returned a defendant's verdict although plaintiff offered expert testimony on defective design while defendant offered no testimony on that issue. The court remanded the case for error in the trial judge's instructions on foreseeability. "When the trial judge here stated that liability under § 402A was dependent upon 'whether the injury could be foreseen by an ordinarily intelligent man as the natural and probable outcome of the act complained of', he improperly introduced due care as a standard upon which the liability of the seller might depend. This is clearly not so. . . . When the court instructed the jury that Grant's was to be liable only if it—in substance—anticipated or fore-saw the individualistic behavior patterns of the Eshbach children when using the lawnmower for the purpose for which it was designed—to cut grass—it subverted the intention of § 402A by permitting a vendor to avoid liability on the basis of being unable to anticipate the precise manner in which the injury occurred. . . . Similarly, the use of foreseeabil-ity by the trial court with reference to the 'foreseeability' of injury or harm is improper, for it is foreseeability as to the use of the product which establishes the limits of the seller's responsibility."

Perhaps much of the difficulty which trial courts have faced on the foreseeability issue in strict liability cases, and which has hardly been resolved by confusing appellate court decisions, could be avoided by making it clear that foreseeability is simply a factor that may assist in determining a causal defect. *Eshbach*, perhaps, makes the issue clearer than in many other cases. Here the primary inquiry, made by the plaintiff but ignored by the defendant, was whether the absence of guards, ignition switch and brakes was a defect. If plaintiff's evidence showed that there was a defect —that a feasible change in design would have prevented the accident—such evidence should be sufficient for strict liability.

C. INTERVENING ACTS

1. BASIS OF LIABILITY

Whether or not a defendant may be liable when an intervening act is a more immediate cause of injury depends upon the foreseeability of that act. Such an act is usually one by a third party, although occasionally it may involve the operation of a natural force. Since foreseeability here is determinative of liability, most of these cases are grounded in negligence. An exception is where the intervening act is a "use" and hence may be determinative of freedom from defect if shown to be unforeseeable. In such a case the sole cause-in-fact of the accident is the intervening act.

The leading cases involving intervening causation, even in the products field, were decided before a strict tort action was recognized. A manufacturer was held negligent if he foresaw or should have foreseen that a third party might use or modify a product in a way that would cause injury to the plaintiff if the manufacturer did not take feasible steps by way of warning or design change to avoid such injury. On the other hand, he was not liable if the injury, even though foreseeable, could not reasonably have been prevented by any act of the defendant.

In a strict tort action, if a proven defect contributed to the accident, it is difficult to see how an intervening negligent actor could relieve the manufacturer of liability to the plaintiff. More likely, the manufacturer, after he has fully compensated the plaintiff, will be entitled to contribution from the intervening actor, at least in those jurisdictions permitting contribution where the grounds of liability differ.

Since so many of the negligence cases involve employees whose recoveries against their employers are sharply limited in amount by workers' compensation statutes, proving the foreseeability of the employer's negligence and hence the manufacturer's negligence liability will be of vital importance to the plaintiff. On the other hand, the manufacturer may well feel an injustice where he is obliged to compensate the plaintiff fully while the employer's liability is limited to an amount which may bear little relationship either to his culpability or to the causal effect of his conduct. These troublesome inequities, hardly adjusted by any clear-cut legal rule or statute, may account for the wide variety, if not positive inconsistency, in the decisions involving intervening acts.

It is not necessary that a particular intervening act be foreseeable. Liability may be established if intervening conduct of the same general sort as that which occurred is foreseeable. Thus in Noonan v. Buick Co., 211 So.2d 54 (Fla.App.1968), an automobile manufacturer was found liable for injuries sustained when plaintiff was thrown against the frame and roof of his car because his driver's seat was not properly affixed. It was so held even though the grabbing of the steering wheel by plaintiff's three-year-old son had caused the car to go into a skid. Plaintiff then quickly turned the wheel to adjust for the skid and was rendered unconscious when he struck the roof, with the result that the car left the road and rolled over. Since any sharp turn of the wheel could have loosened the inadequately secured seat, the unusualness of the particular mishap was considered incidental.

2. INTERVENING NEGLIGENCE OTHER THAN PRODUCT MODIFICATION

Where intervening negligence is involved, any generalization as to what will relieve a defendant of liability for his defective product would be misleading. In McLaughlin v. Mine Safety Appliances Co., 181 N.E.2d 430 (N.Y.1962), the minor plaintiff was severely injured when heat blocks manufactured by the defendant were applied directly to her body to revive her after she nearly drowned. A nurse was given the blocks by a fireman who had removed them from their containers, on which was a warning that they should be wrapped in insulating material such as a towel or a blanket before application to the body. The blocks had been sold by the defendant to the local fire department, and their use fully demonstrated to several firemen by defendant's representative at the time of sale. Adequate warnings had also been conveyed to the fireman, as well as placed on the containers. The court held that "the jury might have found that the fireman not only had the means to warn the nurse, but further that, by his actions, he prevented any warning from reaching her, and, indeed, that he actually had some part in the improper application of the blocks. Such conduct could not have been foreseen by the defendant."

On the other hand, in Comstock v. General Motors Corp., 99 N.W.2d 627 (Mich.1959), the manufacturer of an automobile with defective brakes was held liable for injuries sustained by the plaintiff, an automobile repairman, when a co-employee forgot that the brakes were defective and drove the car into the plaintiff who was working on another car. The driver, moreover, had failed to follow the dealer's own precautionary rule that a "no brake" sign be placed on the car while it was awaiting repair. Such forgetfulness, the court held, was foreseeable. The court was evidently influenced by the fact that a "modern automobile equipped with brakes which fail without notice is as dangerous as a loaded gun." In spite of this great danger, defendant manufacturer had deliberately refrained from warning car owners but instead had instructed its dealers to make the necessary replacements only when cars were brought in to be serviced.

In Drayton v. Jiffee Chem. Corp., 395 F.Supp. 1081 (N.D.Ohio 1975), a small child received extremely severe burns when defendant's liquid drain cleaner was spilled upon her. The father, after pouring half of the contents into a bathroom drain, placed the uncapped bottle on the back of the sink and almost immediately heard the child scream. The child had come into the bathroom unnoticed by him. The court rejected the defendant's contention that the father's failure to supervise the child and his leaving the bottle uncapped constituted a superseding cause. Again, as in *Comstock*, the court may have been influenced by the extreme danger of the product, as noted in the previous chapter, when it was doubtful that even the strongest of warnings could justify its marketing.

The plaintiff in Steagall v. Dot Mfg. Corp., 446 S.W.2d 515 (Tenn.1969), was denied recovery from the defendant manufacturer of a highly corrosive drain solvent even though the defendant had failed to give the warning required by federal law. Plaintiff suffered severe burns when he accidently tipped over an uncapped bottle of the solvent. The bottle had been placed on an upper shelf of a dark storeroom by one of the plaintiff's assistants. Plaintiff alleged common law negligence in defendant's failure to provide a safe container and to warn adequately of the bottle's corrosive contents, and especially its failure to place on the label the signal word "danger" as required by the Federal Hazardous Substances Act. The court found the allegations irrelevant in causing plaintiff's injuries, since both he and all his kitchen helpers were aware of the solvent's corrosiveness. The bottle, without its cap, had been placed on the shelf despite plaintiff's warning that it should be kept on the floor. No evidence was presented that anyone except plaintiff and his helpers ever had access to the storeroom where the acid was kept. Under these circumstances the court concluded that the presence of a label on the bottle warning of the solvent's corrosiveness would have made no difference, since whoever placed the bottle on the shelf presumably knew of the danger. It was therefore held that the act of placing the uncapped bottle on the shelf was the sole cause of plaintiff's injury.

The court in Gordon v. Niagara Machine & Tool Works, 574 F.2d 1182 (5th Cir. 1978), affirmed the trial court's judgment for the plaintiff, reprinting that opinion as its own. The case had been in the courts for some years, as indicated by an earlier opinion of the appellate court handed down in January, 1974, when the cause was remanded. Plaintiff had lost four fingers of her left hand when the punch press she was operating unexpectedly recycled as she was manually feeding materials into it. Defendant knew of this danger when it sold the machine to plaintiff's employer, Poloron, in 1954, fifteen years before the accident. The only warning it gave was in a service manual issued to plaintiff's employer, and there was evidence that this warning was not passed on to employees. Moreover, if the service manual had been furnished to employees, they would not have understood its technical language. The court said: "Because of the high degree of grave harm apt to befall operators ignorant of the double tripping proclivity of Niagara's press, the substantial number of serious industrial accidents occurring to press operators and known to the power press industry in 1954 and long prior thereto, and since it was not reasonable for Niagara to expect the limited warning discernible only in a technical service manual furnished with the press would be communicated to press operators, we find as a fact that Poloron's failure to issue proper warnings to its press operators was reasonably foreseeable by Niagara."

3.   MODIFICATION OF THE PRODUCT

Most of the cases contending that a later modification of a product relieves the defendant of liability have involved efforts to remedy an initial defect. A few of them do not involve so much an intervening cause as a sole cause with the original product free from any dangerous defect. Thus in Hanlon v. Cyril Bath Co., 541 F.2d 343 (3d Cir. 1975), plaintiff's fingers were severed by a press used to bend, form, or punch metal. While he was trying to remove a piece of metal that had lodged in the machine he accidentally moved his foot so that it pressed down an electrical foot switch lying on the floor and thus activated the ram. Plaintiff's employer had substituted this easily activated switch for the starter supplied by the manufacturer, a treadle some eight inches above the floor and requiring a downward pressure of approximately 65 pounds. The court held that "in relation to danger of accidental activation, this substitution of a significantly different and much more sensitive starting mechanism was a 'substantial change in the condition in which [the press brake was] sold', within the meaning of § 402A."

In Robinson v. Reed-Prentice Div. of Package Machinery Co., 426 N.Y.S.2d 717 (N.Y.Ct.App. 1980), plaintiff was injured when his hand was pulled through holes that his employer had punched in a safety gate guarding the operating area of a machine for molding plastic. The court found that the employer's alteration of the machine, in order to adapt it to its specific purpose of manufacturing plastic bead necklaces, was the sole cause of the accident. It said: "Where the product is marketed in a condition safe for the purpose of which it is intended or could reasonably be intended, the manufacturer has satisfied his duty." A dissent reasoned that the manufacturer should have been held liable for negligence, since it not only foresaw the adaption of the machine to the buyer's use, but actually knew, through its sales representative, that such dangerous adaptions were being made in the several machines that had been purchased. Moreover, in response to the purchaser's request that the machine be modified to safely fulfill his needs, the manufacturer refused to make any change, even though there was testimony that such a change could have been made at relatively little cost.

Some of the cases involving modification of the product are decided upon strict liability grounds. The issue in such cases is not foreseeability but cause-in-fact. Did the original manufacturing defect or the defective modification cause the injury? Thus in Rios v. Niagara Machine & Tool Works, 319 N.E.2d 232 (Ill.1974), the defendant manufacturer sold plaintiff's employer a punch press without safety devices, expecting the purchaser to add whatever was best adapted to the work. The employer did add a Posson safety device which was attached to the operator's wrists and pulled his hands away when the ram started to descend. Plaintiff was injured when the device broke down. The court held that the employer's intervening modification of the machine relieved the manufacturer of liability. "Once this device had been attached to the machine, whatever unreasonably dangerous conditions existed when it left the defendant's control by reason of the absence of safety devices were fully corrected."

Cause-in-fact may, of course, also be the issue in a negligence case. Thus in Humble Oil & Refining Co. v. Whitten, 427 S.W.2d 313 (Tex.1968), plaintiff sued the defendant for negligence in furnishing his employer with a sixteen-foot-high portable oil storage tank that was unequipped with a ladder or gauge for the purpose of ascertaining the contents of the tank. The court found that this alleged negligence was superseded by the conduct of plaintiff's fellow employee, who placed a wooden ladder on the side of the tank with a rope tied at the top so that the ladder misleadingly appeared to be secured to the tank. This act of a third party created "a new and hidden dangerous condition" which caused plaintiff to fall when he attempted to climb the wooden ladder.

Foreseeability was the issue where the intervening employer was unsuccessful in his attempt to remedy a defect originally the result of the defendant manufacturer's negligence. In Guffie v. Erie Strayer Co., 350 F.2d 378 (3d Cir. 1965), the defendant negligently designed and constructed overhead bins of a concrete batching plant in such a way that sand, rock, and stone occasionally fell from the bins onto the maintenance platforms some thirty feet below. To protect against the danger from such spillage, plaintiff's employer constructed a roof over the maintenance platforms. Plaintiff was injured when, as he worked on one of the platforms, the roof collapsed under the weight of one and one-half tons of accumulated spillage. Even assuming the negligence of plaintiff's employer in constructing and maintaining the roof, the court found that the issue of defendant's liability for negligence in the design and construction of the bins presented a question for the jury since "reasonable minds" could differ on foreseeability.

Again, foreseeability was the issue where the intervening employer modified an apparatus not to correct a defect, but to increase its utility. In Kennedy v. Custom Ice Equipment Co., Inc., 246 S.E.2d 176 (S.C.1978), plaintiff's left arm was injured when it was drawn into an overhead conveyer belt used in a plant for producing crushed or "party" ice. The belt was used to convey ice to storage bins, from which the ice would later be removed by opening trap doors in their undersides. Plaintiff's job was to break up with a garden hoe any ice that had become solidified in the bins so that it did not fall when the doors were opened. For this purpose he walked along a catwalk which had been installed alongside the bins by his employer, George-town. Defendant, the manufacturer of the over-head screw conveyer, contended that it was placed high enough so that it was unforeseeable that anyone would come in contact with it and that therefore protective shields were unnecessary. The court held it was for the jury whether the manufacturer should have foreseen the installation of a catwalk close to the conveyer. There was testimony that the manufacturer had actual knowl-edge of the common practice in the industry to break up ice with a garden hoe. Furthermore, "the jury could have determined that the construction of the catwalk by Georgetown was a foreseeable circumstance that required the incorporation of protective shields in the design of the conveyer."

In Finnegan v. Havir Mfg. Corp., 290 A.2d 286 (N.J.1972), plaintiff was injured when an electrical foot pedal on a punch press was accidentally activated. The employer had increased the risk of accident by replacing a mechanical foot treadle. It was held for the jury if this was such a substantial change as to relieve the defendant manufacturer of liability when a two-hand pushbutton device was available at the time and would have prevented the injury to plaintiff's hand altogether.

Most of the cases involve an employer as the intervening party; but that others might be involved is illustrated by Wyatt v. Winnebago Indus., Inc., 566 S.W.2d 276 (Tenn.App.1977). Here, the plaintiff, when the motor home of a friend would not start, instructed his friend to sit at the controls with the gear selector in "park" while he got under the vehicle to connect the battery to the starter, thus bypassing safety switches. He was then run over as the vehicle started up, indicating a defective gear selector. The trial court's denial of summary judgment for the defendant was affirmed.

Closely related to the issue of subsequent modifications is that of nondelegable duties as designated in *Vandermark*, discussed in chapter 3 under Assemblers. In Alvarez v. Felker Mfg. Co., 41 Cal.Rptr. 514 (Cal.App.1964), the manufacturer of an unassembled concrete cutting machine was liable for injuries sustained as a result of a distributor's defective installation of a blade in the machine.

Even though the distributor was not the agent of the manufacturer, it was held that a "manufacturer of a completed product" is liable for defects in the final product as received by the ultimate purchaser "regardless of what part of the manufacturing process it chooses to delegate to third parties."

In Bexiga v. Havir Mfg. Corp., 290 A.2d 281 (N.J.1972), the supreme court reversed an intermediate court decision which held that because it was "the custom of the trade that purchasers rather than manufacturers provide safety devices on punch presses", the manufacturer was not liable to the purchaser's employee whose hand was crushed by a press lacking such devices. Instead, the supreme court held that "where there is an unreasonable risk of harm to the user of a machine which has no protective safety device, as here, the jury may infer that the machine was defective in design unless it finds that the incorporation by the manufacturer of a safety device would render the machine unusable for its intended purposes".

On the other hand, the court in Biss v. Tenneco, Inc., CCH Prod. Liab. Rptr. par. 8370 (N.Y.Supreme Ct.App.Div.1978), affirmed the dismissal of a claim against the manufacturer of a construction loader without a roll bar that overturned on a slippery highway killing plaintiff's deceased, where defendant had informed the deceased's employer of the availability of roll bars for the machine. The "danger increases or lessens according to the job and site for which the equipment is purchased and used. . . . If knowledge of available safety options is brought home to the purchaser, the duty to exercise reasonable care in selecting those appropriate to the intended use rests upon him."

D. UNUSUAL USES THAT ARE FORESEEABLE

1. DESIGN CONSIDERATIONS

Just as a foreseeable intervening cause will not relieve a defendant of liability if a defect in his product is a concurring cause, an unusual use by the plaintiff will not relieve the defendant of liability if that use is foreseeable. At the least he must warn against such a use, even if he does not see his way to design the product so that it will be safe under any foreseeable use. Thus both design and warning considerations are involved, although inadequacy of warning is perhaps the more frequent issue.

In Green v. Volkswagen of America, Inc., 485 F.2d 430 (6th Cir. 1973), an eleven-year-old girl lost her right ring finger when she was running past a parked VW bus and the finger became caught in a body vent containing a sharp, concealed piece of metal. The court held that the foreseeability of such a "use" and of the parking of the vehicle in an area where children were playing was for the jury.

In Reid v. Spadone Machine Co., 404 A.2d 1094 (N.H.1979), it was held foreseeable that if a "hot knife," or electrical device for cutting up plastic while still in the molding pan, could be used by two men, it would be so used in the interest of efficiency. The machine was fed from the front but activated by buttons at the side. Plaintiff lost three fingers of his left hand when, as he was pushing a cut mold back through the machine, his fellow worker at the buttons activated the machine. Aside from holding that the employer's failure to prevent this two-man operation was a foreseeable intervening cause, the court also held that the defendant could have foreseen two-man use and guarded against it. The defendant manufacturer could have placed "one button on each side facing out, thus requiring inward pressure in opposite directions. This design would have discouraged two-person use because the operator would have had to occupy the feeding area while pushing the buttons. In comparison, positioning the buttons to one side not only left open the feeding area for a second person, but required extra effort and time on the part of the single operator. The natural tendency being to save unnecessary effort and time, two-person use was facilitated."

In Troszynski v. Commonwealth Edison Co., 356 N.E.2d 926 (Ill.App.1976), either a design or a warning change would have averted the injury. When plaintiff was playing ball with his children in a backyard a ball broke the already cracked glass window of an electric meter attached to the rear wall of an apartment building. To retrieve the broken glass plaintiff slipped his hand into the box and received an electric shock. The shock, combined with the effort involved in pulling out his hand, produced such severe injuries to plaintiff's left hand and wrist as to require nine operations.   Plaintiff's expert witness testified that, besides other feasible design changes, insulation could have been provided for the line terminals for less than a dime; a printed warning attached to the box would also have averted the accident, he testified.

2.   WARNING CONSIDERATIONS

In warning cases, courts have generally required manufacturers to foresee a wide variety of uses and to forestall the danger.   In Moran v. Fabergé, Inc., 332 A.2d 11 (Md.1975), the court held that a manufacturer of cologne containing 82.06% alcohol and having a flash point of 73° Fahrenheit could be found liable to a little girl who was severely burned by a flash fire when her friend poured the cologne onto a lighted candle in an effort to scent it.   There was evidence "which if accepted as true, tends to show that Fabergé's Tigress cologne possessed a latent danger of flammability;   that Fabergé, through its officials, knew or should have known of this danger;   that it is normal to find in the home environment both flame and cologne;   that it was reasonably foreseeable to Fabergé that the flame and the cologne may well come in contact, one with the other, so as to cause an explosion which injures a person who happens to be standing nearby—Nancy; and that a reasonably prudent manufacturer, knowing of its product's characteristics and propensities, should have warned consumers of this latent flammability danger."

In Frey v. Montgomery Ward & Co., 258 N.W.2d 782 (Minn.1977), a space heater purchased by the plaintiff for use in his house trailer—which was the home, in fact, of hundreds of chinchillas that the plaintiff was raising commercially—greatly overheated. As a result he lost over three hundred chinchillas that either died or became so sick they had to be disposed of. Montgomery Ward had been advised by the plaintiff of the purpose for which he was buying the heater, so a directed verdict against the retailer for breach of the implied warranty of fitness was affirmed. As to the manufacturer, its booklet had failed to state that the space heater should not be used in poorly insulated and tightly enclosed spaces such as house trailers. Whether "the risk for which there was no warning was a reasonably foreseeable one was properly a jury question."

Spruill v. Boyle-Midway, Inc., 308 F.2d 79 (4th Cir. 1962), embraced a more common, though hardly an intended, use—the consumption by infants and little children of products ordinarily considered repulsively inedible or undrinkable. Here a child of fourteen months died after he had ingested some furniture polish which his mother had left capped on a bureau near his crib. The manufacturer was held liable for not giving a warning that could be read by the child's supervisors. Stress was laid on the product's household use. A manufacturer must "be expected to anticipate the environment which is normal for the use of his product and where, as here, that environment is the home, he must anticipate the reasonably foreseeable risks of the use of his product in such an environment." The defendant's furniture polish has since been provided with a "child-proof" cap as well as emphatic warnings.

In Boyl v. California Chem. Co., 221 F.Supp. 669 (D.Or.1963), the plaintiff used a liquid weed killer, Triox, frequently sold to ordinary consumers for garden use. The label warnings by the defendant included the avoidance of breathing the spray mist, of contact with eyes, skin, or clothing, and the necessity of washing after using. It also warned that "[l]ivestock and poultry will be poisoned if allowed to feed on treated areas", which the court noted as indicative of the defendant's knowledge of the product's "earth-contaminating potentials." Furthermore, the label warned that when the container had been emptied it should be both washed thoroughly and destroyed, indicating defendant's knowledge of the poison's stability. Plaintiff, after applying Triox to her driveway, then rinsed the spray tank with her garden hose and poured out the rinse water upon a rough grass area of her back yard. Five days later she lay down in this area, scantily dressed, for the purpose of sunbathing. As a result of absorption into her skin of Triox remaining in the rinse, she was hospitalized for three days for a critical condition and she required medical treatment for some eighteen months. The court held that in view of "its experience and expertise the defendant knew or should have known" of the danger and that "the defendant was negligent towards plaintiff in failing to give any reasonable notice or warning of a risk or danger to her personal safety from contact with earth lately contaminated with the Triox solution, and that such negligence on the part of the defendant was the proximate cause of plaintiff's resulting physical malfunctioning and disabilities."

The case of Simpson Timber Co. v. Parks, 388 U.S. 459 (1967), rev'g mem. 369 F.2d 324 (9th Cir. 1966), illustrates the difficulty courts have had with unusual and unintended uses that nevertheless can be foreseen. There a manufacturer packaged its doors for shipment abroad. The doors had openings in them for glass, and were stacked evenly in bundles so that the openings made a well. Each bundle was then covered by cardboard, except for the ends, so that the doors appeared to be pieces of solid wood. The label read "fine doors," with no warning that the cardboard covered a well. When the doors were stowed for shipment, the long-shoremen used bundles already laid down as a floor in stacking the next layer. While carrying a sack of flour for placement as a stabilizer between bundles in the top layer of doors, a stevedore stepped on the cardboard and fell into the cavity.

In a suit for resulting injuries, there was testimony that many manufacturers knew of the custom of walking on the doors, and warned of this danger either by cutting holes in the packaging to expose the well or by placing a warning notice on the bundles. The plaintiff recovered in trial court, after an instruction that negligence could be found if the manufacturer "knew or in the exercise of reasonable care should have known" that workmen might walk on the packaged doors, and if the method of bundling used by the defendant created a dangerous situation which a person of ordinary prudence would have guarded against by warning or otherwise.

The court of appeals first affirmed this decision, but on a rehearing en banc decided that the case should go back to the jury with the instruction that the defendant was liable only if it actually knew of the practice of walking on the cargo. It was conceded that if used "as a floor, or walking surface, the bundle of doors was a trap," but it was also thought that in the case of "such an ordinarily harmless item" as a package of doors, as distinguished from things apt to explode, ignite, or cause illness, there was no duty to warn against an unintended use not known to the defendant.

The Supreme Court reversed, relying on a decision that ordinarily actual knowledge of a peril is not essential to liability where a dangerous situation is foreseeable. This holding seems clearly correct. The court of appeals decision is unduly occupied with the concept of "inherent" and "intrinsic" danger, and focuses too little attention on the basic issue of whether an unreasonable danger has been created. As the dissenters in the court of appeals decision remarked, very little effort on the defendant's part would have disclosed both the risk and the simple precautions needed to avoid the harm.

E. ABNORMAL OR UNFORESEEABLE USES

Abnormal use, presumably unforeseeable, has generally been held a superseding cause, even if the product is defective. Such cases have been relatively rare, however. In Amburgey v. Holan Div. of Ohio Brass Co., 606 P.2d 21 (Ariz.1980), plaintiff was injured while working in a bucket attached to the boom of a truck crane. He claimed that an electric current had passed through the boom to the interior of the presumably insulated bucket. A fellow employee testified, however, that plaintiff was not inside the bucket but that he "had his left leg on the rim of the bucket when it made contact with a live wire." The court held that if the jury believed this witness "it would be compelled to return a verdict against [the plaintiff] because, irrespective of any defect in the boom or bucket, the proximate cause of the accident was not the defect but the manner in which the product was being utilized." It would seem that the reasoning in this case does not differ greatly from that in Stewart v. Von Solbrig Hospital, given under cause-in-fact at the beginning of this chapter.

In Kay v. Cessna Aircraft Co., 548 F.2d 1370 (9th Cir. 1977), the court employed the word "misuse" rather than "abnormal use" in affirming a judgment n.o.v. for the defendant. Plaintiff's decedent was killed when his private plane crashed during takeoff. Plaintiffs alleged defective design in that when the rear engine of the twin-engine plane failed, no obvious indication was given to the pilot. Defendant's instruction manual, however, indicated various circumstances under which the pilot should check for such failure and how such checks could be made. Plaintiff's decedent disregarded the instructions even though "the plane sat on the runway for several minutes *before* takeoff and *after* the rear engine failed. Both the Skymaster manual and basic principles of aircraft safety dictate that the pilot be alert at the time for potential problems. . . . It is unreasonable to expect Cessna to have anticipated such misuse." It would seem that in this case plaintiff failed to prove any defect in the product, since the instructions were apparently adequate and the danger of ignoring them obvious, if not specifically pointed out by the defendant.

Some courts, perhaps unrealistically, have regarded as unforeseeable that children will be permitted by their elders to play around farm machinery. In Winnett v. Winnett, 310 N.E.2d 1 (Ill.1974), a child's hand was drawn into a moving conveyer belt of a forage wagon manufactured by the defendant Helix Corp. Her fingers were caught in holes large enough to admit only a child's fingers. The court said: "It cannot, in our judgment, fairly be said that a manufacturer should reasonably foresee that a four-year-old child will be permitted to approach an operating farm forage wagon or that the child will be permitted to place her fingers in or on the holes in its moving screen."

In Richelman v. Kewanee Machinery & Conveyor Co., 375 N.E.2d 885 (Ill.App.1978), a child of two years and nine months fell into an auger and lost a leg. In allowing recovery, the court distinguished *Winnett* where the holes in the conveyor were so small that only a child's fingers could be admitted. Here the gap between the bars of the guard was sufficient to admit an adult foot. The design engineer testified that he had used his own exceptionally wide foot as a standard for spacing the guards and had deliberately chosen the least safe of three types of guards in order to increase the grain intake of the machine and thereby increase sales. The court held that foreseeability of injury to someone tripping or falling near the auger was for the jury.

Some confusion attends the so-called "defense" of misuse. It is often not the misuse itself which constitutes a defense, since most misuses, like most unintended uses, are foreseeable enough. To anticipate that a user of a product will always use it as instructed or intended would be the height of folly, matching the user's own folly. Misuse, rather, may serve as a rebuttal of plaintiff's argument either as to causation or as to defect. A product is hardly defective simply because it fails to withstand misuse. If a specific defect is shown, and a misuse that is foreseeable is also shown, defendant will be liable for resulting injury. But if a defect is not clearly identified, and a misuse is shown, it would appear that the product is not defective. On the other hand, even if the product is defective, as in the surgical case given in the section on cause-in-fact, but the misuse rather than the defect is the cause of the accident, plaintiff loses his case. As stated in General Motors Corp. v. Hopkins, 548 S. W.2d 344 (Tex.1977): "The misuse may bear upon the issue of whether the product was defective when it left the hands of the supplier or the misuse may bear on the issue of what caused the harm." Although referred to as a defense by some courts, the issue of misuse is said in Hughes v. Magic Chef, Inc., 288 N.W.2d 542 (Iowa 1980), "rather to be treated in connection with the plaintiff's burden of proving an unreasonably dangerous condition and legal cause."

According to the New York Times, the various makers of Agent Orange—a product alleged to have caused numerous injuries to veterans of the Vietnam War, including birth defects in their off-spring—have responded to a class action suit against them by filing an action against the government for misuse of their efficient and allegedly defect-free defoliant.

Theoretically the many references to misuse or abnormal use as an affirmative defense presuppose that the product is indeed defective. But many of these cases could be decided on the basis that plaintiff has failed to prove defect. For example, in Strimbu v. American Chain & Cable Co., Inc., 516 F.2d 781 (6th Cir. 1975), plaintiffs installed in their home a dumbwaiter with a hoist manufactured by the defendant. The cab was improperly aligned in the dumbwaiter shaft. When the cab stopped at the first floor of the house instead of going down to the basement as intended, plaintiff placed some additional laundry in the cab with the result that under the added weight the dumbwaiter suddenly dropped to the basement causing serious and permanent injuries to plaintiff's hands. Plaintiff contended that the hoist should have included a " 'slack chain device' which would have prevented the accident." Initially, however, the hoist, intended for industrial use, had included an equally effective deadman's switch which was removed before the home installation. The court concluded "that appellee's hoist was not a proximate cause of the accident in question." It "was reasonably safe when used in its normal industrial application. Its adaption to another use cannot impose an additional duty on the manufacturer to include a safety device incompatible with its normal industrial application."

Two sharp-edge cases illustrate the relation between defect and misuse. In Schneider v. Chrysler Motors Corp., 401 F.2d 549 (8th Cir. 1968), plaintiff injured his right eye when it came into contact with the left front vent window of his automobile. Although the court apparently assumed the window was defective because it "had a sharp edge not in compliance with the industry's custom and practice," nevertheless recovery was denied because "it is overstraining a manufacturer's duty to foresee" that a person would inadvertently hit his eye on the wing vent window of a parked automobile. In Tibbetts v. Ford Motor Co., 358 N.E.2d 460 (Mass. App.1976), on the other hand, recovery was denied because of the absence of a defect. Plaintiff injured his fingers on a sharp burr on the inner edge of a decorative slot in an automobile wheel cover which he was trying to remove with his hands although "he knew the proper way to remove the wheel cover was to pry it off at the edge with a tire iron or similar device." The court found "nothing uncommon or inherently dangerous about a slotted wheel cover", which is "not defective simply because it is foreseeable that it may cause injury to someone using it improperly."

F. THE AFFIRMATIVE DEFENSES: CONTRIBUTORY NEGLIGENCE AND ASSUMPTION OF THE RISK

1. THE RESTATEMENT POSITION

In the leading case of Williams v. Brown Mfg. Co., 261 N.E.2d 305 (Ill.1970), the court adopted comment n to § 402A of the Second Restatement of Torts as the law of Illinois in strict tort cases. This comment reads: "*Contributory negligence.* Since the liability with which this Section deals is not based upon negligence of the seller, but is strict liability, the rule applied to strict liability cases (see § 524) applies. Contributory negligence of the plaintiff is not a defense when such negligence consists merely in a failure to discover the defect in the product, or to guard against the possibility of its existence. On the other hand the form of contributory negligence which consists in voluntarily and unreasonably proceeding to encounter a known danger, and commonly passes under the name of assumption of risk, is a defense under this Section as in other cases of strict liability. If the user or consumer discovers the defect and is aware of the danger, and nevertheless proceeds unreasonably to make use of the product and is injured by it, he is barred from recovery."

In adopting this comment the court noted that "all other jurisdictions which have adopted the theory of strict liability have reached substantially the same conclusion". Here the plaintiff was injured when a trenching machine struck an underground pipe. Plaintiff was guiding the machine from a position between the handlebars at the rear. When the teeth suddenly slipped off the pipe the machine lurched backward. Plaintiff claimed that no warning was given as to the danger of operating from the rear, and that the drive belt should have been more easily adjustable. Defendant contended that it was customary to operate the machine from the side, and that adequate instructions were given in the manual as to the adjustment of the drive belts so that they would slip upon meeting an obstruction and so avoid shock. Following the Restatement, the court held that assumption of the risk but not contributory negligence was a defense. Since the jury could reasonably find that plaintiff, an experienced "operating engineer," had assumed the risk in operating the machine from behind, and especially in failing to follow the instructions concerning the drive belt, the case was remanded for trial on that issue.

In Hensley v. Sherman Car Wash Equipment Co., 520 P.2d 146 (Colo.App.1974), the same Restatement principles were applied in an action for breach of express warranty. Here plaintiff, an employee in the car wash, stepped into an opening in a "hookless conveyer" manufactured by the defendant. Defendant in its information sheet had stated that "personnel are assured safe working conditions on all areas of the vehicle by the pivoted safety hood at exit end [which] . . . eliminates all possibility of persons stepping into an open pit." Plaintiff knew that the safety hood had not been operating perfectly at all times; but she had been assured that morning by a representative of the defendant that the problem had been corrected. The case was remanded on the assumption of risk issue. The jury instructions should include one to the effect that if plaintiff had, with reasonable justification in view of her own observation, relied on the repairman's assurance, then she had not assumed the risk.

In Smith v. Smith, 278 N.W.2d 155 (S.D.1979), plaintiff, a farm laborer, cut the fingers of his left hand when a band saw he was using to cut iron unexpectedly started up, with plaintiff unable to explain why. The court remanded the case because of an erroneous instruction by the trial judge on contributory negligence as a defense to a strict liability action against the manufacturer and the retailer of the machine. The court said: "We believe it is inconsistent to hold that the user's negligence is material when the seller's is not."

In Vizzini v. Ford Motor Co., 569 F.2d 754 (3d Cir. 1977), it was held that the failure of plaintiff's decedent to fasten his seat belt was the equivalent of contributory negligence and therefore not a defense to a strict liability action.

2. ASSIMILATION OF THE DEFENSES

Recently some courts have assimilated the two defenses. Insofar as assumption of the risk had rarely been allowed except when such assumption was unreasonable it was held that the standard did not differ from the negligence standard, since reasonableness is presumably decided objectively— what the ordinarily prudent person would have done. Only if the plaintiff had acted unreasonably in assuming the risk was he barred from recovery and such action was only a form of contributory negligence, a failure to use due care for one's own protection. The tendency toward assimilating the two defenses was strengthened by the adoption of comparative negligence.

In general the assimilation of the two defenses posed a problem for products liability law. Texas confined the assimilation to negligence cases, holding in Rosas v. Buddies Food Store, 518 S.W.2d 534 (Tex.1975), that the two defenses remained separate in strict liability actions. New Jersey, one of the states which assimilated the two defenses before comparative negligence was adopted, distinguished two kinds of contributory negligence in a products liability case, Cartel Capital Corp. v. Fireco, 410 A.2d 674 (N.J.1980). Here defendant's fire extinguisher failed to function when needed to put out a fire that defendant contended was negligently started by the employees of the plaintiff restaurant. The distinction made by the court paralleled that made in comment n to § 402A, although the phrase "assumption of the risk" was avoided. In strict product liability actions, the court said, "a defendant must show that the plaintiff with actual knowledge of the danger posed by the defective product voluntarily and unreasonably encountered the risk. . . . Applying this test, we find as a matter of law that there was not an unreasonable and voluntary exposure to a known risk. . . . Plaintiff had no forewarning that the system whose purpose was to extinguish fires, irrespective of cause, would fail to function as a consequence of a design defect. Defendant did not meet his burden of proof." Therefore, the court held, under New Jersey's recently adopted comparative negligence act, in a strict liability case "only contributory negligence in the more limited sense may bar or mitigate damages".

In some states, however, the effect of abrogating assumption of the risk as a separate defense has been to force a decision in strict liability products law. Was there to be *no* affirmative defense, thus retaining the rule that contributory negligence was not a bar to recovery, or was contributory negligence to be allowed as a defense? A few states have ruled that the defense should be allowed.

3. EFFECT OF COMPARATIVE NEGLIGENCE

With the adoption of comparative negligence and a consequent mitigation of the harshness of the defense, quite a number of states decided to allow contributory negligence as a defense, as well as assumption of the risk if still viewed as separate, in strict liability actions. Yet a logical difficulty still remains: how to compare negligence, a fault, with no-fault or strict liability? As a result, some states, like Colorado in Kinard v. Coats Co., Inc., 553 P.2d 835 (Colo.App.1976), have ruled that a state's comparative negligence statute "has no application to products liability actions under § 402A."

The reader will recall that the adoption of comparative negligence raised similar problems in cases of contribution where one party was negligent and the other strictly liable.

In Wisconsin, one of the earliest states to adopt comparative negligence, the court ruled in Dippel v. Sciano, 155 N.W.2d 55 (Wis.1967), that strict products liability was a kind of negligence per se. "Strict liability in tort for the sale of a defective product unreasonably dangerous to an intended user or consumer now arises in this state by virtue of a decision of this court. If this same liability were imposed for violation of a statute it is difficult to perceive why we would not consider it negligence per se for the purpose of applying the comparative negligence statute just as we have done so many times in other cases involving the so-called 'safety statutes.'" Furthermore, "a safety rule can trace its origin to a court decision as well as a statute."

Thirty-five states as of the end of 1979 had followed Wisconsin in adopting comparative negligence, four by court ruling, the remainder by statute. Although there may be a tendency, not yet entirely clear, among such states to apply comparative negligence to strict tort products cases, the Wisconsin negligence per se approach has not generally been followed. The California Supreme Court, in Daly v. General Motors Corp., 575 P.2d 1162 (Cal.1978), was not troubled by what it referred to as a "forfeit [of] a degree of semantic symmetry" by comparing the negligence of the plaintiff with the strict liability of the defendant. It referred to the strict liability for a vessel's unseaworthiness and the longstanding application of comparative principles in maritime law. Here juries were asked to indicate to what extent unseaworthiness was a contributing cause as compared with plaintiff's own negligence as a cause. The court also assimilated assumption of the risk to contributory negligence, thus bringing it under comparative negligence principles.

Daly involved a one-car collision with a metal divider fence where the driver was killed when the door flew open and he was forceably ejected. Plaintiff claimed that the ejection, which was acknowledged to be the cause of the seriousness of the accident, was owing to a defective door lock. Defendant claimed that plaintiff's decedent had been negligent in not using either the car's seat belt-shoulder harness or its door lock, and also in driving while intoxicated. The court's ruling on comparative negligence was not made retroactive; and the trial court's admission of evidence on these contentions was declared prejudicial. Upon retrial, however, the new ruling would apply and the evidence of contributory negligence would be admissible.

The logical difficulty, which the California court dismissed rather cavalierly, is perhaps solved by a relative causation approach as in the maritime cases referred to in *Daly*. In Murray v. Fairbanks Morse, 610 F.2d 149 (3d Cir. 1979), the jury had returned a two million dollar verdict for the plaintiff, from which 5% was subtracted for plaintiff's contributory fault. He had received numerous injuries when he fell from a platform on which he was installing an electrical control panel manufactured and shipped by the defendant Beloit Power Systems. Beloit had affixed two iron cross members to the open bottom of the unit to stabilize it during shipping. One of these broke when Murray put his weight upon it while "leaning over the open space at the bottom of the unit to bolt it to the platform." He fell ten feet to the concrete floor with consequent severe spinal injuries, making him incontinent and sexually dysfunctional.

Although the comparative negligence statute of the Virgin Islands where the accident occurred specifically referred only to "any action based on *negligence*," the court held that, since an application of comparative negligence to strict liability actions was not expressly forbidden, it should as a helpful and fair principle be applied by the court as a rule of common law. The court acknowledged, however, that although it might "term a defective product 'faulty', it is qualitatively different from the plaintiff's conduct that contributes to his injury. . . . We believe that if the loss for a particular injury is to be apportioned between the product defect and the plaintiff's misconduct, the only conceptual basis for comparison is the causative contribution of each to the particular loss or injury. In apportioning damages we are really asking how much of the injury was caused by the defect in the product versus how much was caused by the plaintiff's own actions." The court concluded: "Because we believe that a pure comparative fault approach utilizing causation as the conceptual basis for apportioning damages is appropriate in § 402A actions, we judicially recognize these principles for strict products liability actions in the Virgin Islands."

In both *Daly* and *Murray* the court emphasized the compatibility of apportionment with the basic policy of products liability. Said the *Murray* court: "When plaintiff's conduct is faulty, i. e., he exposes himself to an unreasonable risk of harm which causes part of his injuries, the manufacturer should not be required to pay that portion of the loss attributable to the plaintiff's fault. Under a comparative system, the future cost of the defendant's product will accurately represent the danger it has caused and not the danger caused by plaintiff's own fault."

In Thibault v. Sears, Roebuck & Co., 395 A.2d 843 (N.H.1978), the court adopted the causal approach to the extent of ruling that "the trial court should not read [the comparative negligence statute] in a jury charge on the strict liability count, but rather should instruct the jury that it is to compare the causal effect of the defect in the product or design with the affirmative defense of misconduct of the plaintiff and allocate the loss as hereinafter indicated."

If the jury finds that plaintiff's proof meets the requirements of § 402A, and if it finds that plaintiff's misconduct has contributed to his injuries, then it must reduce the damages by the percentage that such misconduct has contributed provided it is not greater than defendant's fault. If greater, plaintiff's recovery will be barred altogether. As of the end of 1979 some thirteen states had adopted this form of comparative negligence; while eleven states barred all recovery if plaintiff's fault was "as great as" that of the defendant. These forms are referred to as "modified" comparative negligence. A few states have adopted the "pure" form of comparative negligence, whereby the damages are to be reduced strictly in proportion to plaintiff's contributory fault, whether it is 1% or 99%.

Except possibly in the states adopting the "pure" form, the effect of comparative negligence when applied to strict liability actions has been to increase the harshness of the contributory negligence rule instead of mitigating it as in negligence cases. Where, under comment n to § 402A, contributory negligence was no bar at all to recovery, it will now be a complete bar in some of the states that hold the comparative negligence rule applicable in strict liability actions. On the other hand, assumption of the risk, which was formerly a complete bar, will serve only to reduce recovery as long as the plaintiff's fault does not equal or exceed that of the defendant.

Another issue is whether plaintiff's fault is to be compared with each defendant, or with all defendants together, in a modified comparative negligence jurisdiction where there are multiple defendants. Reviewing the authorities, the New Jersey Superior Court in Van Horn v. William Blanchard Co., 414 A.2d 265 (N.J.Super.1980), held that a comparison with each defendant was statutorily compelled, although a vigorous dissent disputed this conclusion and contended that the more equitable method was to compare the plaintiff's fault with all defendants together.

As has been observed, not all jurisdictions have held comparative negligence principles applicable to strict tort actions. On the other hand, a few jurisdictions, notably New York, held contributory negligence to be a defense in strict tort actions even before the legislature passed its comparative negligence statute.

The Connecticut Supreme Court, in Hoelter v. Mohawk Serv., Inc., 365 A.2d 1064 (Conn.1976), upheld an instruction on contributory negligence as a defense where there was evidence that plaintiff was driving his car at about 80 miles an hour when it went out of control. Plaintiff alleged that the cause of the car hitting a guard rail and then a median divider was the improper way that studs had been inserted in the snow tires. The court emphasized plaintiff's "misuse" of the car. Might not the court have stressed, instead, that such misuse tended to show that no defect existed, or if the alleged defect did exist it was not the cause of the accident? Either way the incongruity of allowing a contributory negligence defense in a no-fault cause would have been avoided. In 1977 the Connecticut legislature passed Conn.Gen.Stats.Annot. § 52–572*l* (1980) providing that in all actions based on strict tort liability, contributory negligence and comparative negligence are not a bar but the defenses of product misuse and assumption of the risk remain available.

4. CONTRIBUTORY NEGLIGENCE AND IMPLIED WARRANTY

Courts have differed on contributory negligence as a defense in a breach of implied warranty action.

The more general view, however, is that of Kassouf v. Lee Bros., Inc., 26 Cal.Rptr. 276 (Cal.App.1962), where plaintiff, who was reading her paper, began eating a candy bar without looking at it, although she noticed that it "didn't taste just right." After consuming about a third of the bar, she looked at it and "saw that it was covered with worms and webbing." The court met the defendant's argument that, since an implied warranty sounds in tort, contributory negligence is a defense, by pointing out that in two other types of tort cases such negligence is similarly no defense. These examples are "an absolute liability because of ultra-hazardous activity" and cases involving fraud and deceit. Whether California might overrule the case in view of its recently adopted policy on comparative negligence and strict tort remains to be seen.

In Timmerman v. Universal Corrugated Box Machinery Corp., 287 N.W.2d 316 (Mich.App.1979), the court not only denied the defense of contributory negligence in an implied warranty action, but ruled out such a defense altogether in employee safety cases. It observed that the Supreme Court of Michigan in Tulkku v. Mackworth Rees, Div. of Avis Indus., Inc., 281 N.W.2d 291 (Mich.1979), had concluded that "contributory negligence is no defense to a plaintiff's recovery where evidence has been presented of a defendant's causal negligence in the design or manufacture of a safety device." The purpose was to promote the protection of the worker by encouraging the manufacturer to take all reasonable precautions. Here plaintiff produced evidence that the manufacturer of a "printer-slotter" machine had negligently failed to equip the machine with readily available and low-priced safety devices.

5. ASSUMPTION OF THE RISK AS A BAR

Assumption of the risk as a complete defense, barring recovery altogether, is still available in many jurisdictions. In Heil Co. v. Grant, 534 S.W.2d 916 (Tex.Civ.App.1976), plaintiff's decedent was killed when a dump truck owned by his brother descended upon him as he was working beneath the raised bed. The court held that the trial judge had wrongfully excluded, under the Dead Man's Statute, testimony of the brother that he "told Decedent that if he hit the pullout cable, the bed would come down." The jury found that the death was caused by defective design of the dump truck mechanism, as well as the company's "failure to provide bracing instructions." The court remanded the case on the issue of assumption of risk. The excluded statement of his brother was "some evidence that Decedent knew of the specific danger in hitting the pullout cable." Also, regardless of any evidence of defects as producing causes, the "assumption of the risk defense is based upon the injured person's awareness of the danger of injury rather than an awareness of the producing causes of the injury. . . . We hold that since Vernon Grant may have warned Decedent of the danger, the jury's finding of Heil

Company's failure to do so did not render the assumption of risk defense inapplicable." Furthermore, although there was "some evidence that Decedent might not have appreciated the danger of hitting the pullout cable . . . by reason of Decedent's information, age, and experience, we conclude that there was some evidence of probative force that he did appreciate that danger. Thus, an issue for the jury exists."

In Brown v. Link Belt Corp., 565 F.2d 1107 (9th Cir. 1977), an assumption of the risk defense as applied to a bystander was upheld. A workman was killed when he entered the immediate area of an operating crane. Plaintiff alleged that the lack of automatic signals was a defect. The court held that at least in the case of a machine purchaser's employee, who is obligated to work near the machine, "there appears to be no logical reason for limiting the defense to users alone."

Where assumption of the risk has been allowed as a separate defense, the courts have frequently raised the patent-latent issue once so important in design cases. In fact, since New York in *Micallef* ruled out obviousness as an excuse for dangerous design, the courts seem to have given instructions on assumption of the risk more frequently than before. Even in *Micallef* the court held that upon retrial the jury might consider whether plaintiff had assumed the risk, thus barring his recovery. Such a holding makes sense in that the chief reason for safeguarding open machinery is to protect the inadvertent, the harried or the not fully competent user of the machine, not the one who is alert and aware of all its dangers.

In Stark v. Allis-Chalmers & Northwest Roads, Inc., 467 P.2d 854 (Wash.App.1970), plaintiff's decedent was operating a front-end loader tractor to level a lot. Without any orders from his supervisor, he chose to operate the loader high up instead of improving the tractor's stability by keeping the loader close to the ground and carrying smaller loads at slower speeds. "The jury was entitled to find Stark made his choice to operate the machine as he did knowingly and without any outside compulsion."

Plaintiff in Ralston v. Illinois Power Co., 299 N.E.2d 497 (Ill.App.1973), was injured when a power driven rod for boring holes under streets for the installation of gas lines buckled up after it hit hard material. The "plaintiff stood on the exposed part of the rotating rod pursuant to an order given him by his supervisor. While [he was] standing on the rod, the operator of the trenching device reversed the direction of the rotating rod, thereby causing the plaintiff's pantleg and foot to become entangled in the rotating rod." As a result his leg had to be amputated. Plaintiff said he knew the procedure he was ordered to follow was dangerous, and he had protested to his foreman several times. The court said: "An employee cannot exculpate himself from the legal consequences of his acts on the grounds that he is fearful of losing his job if he does not comply with his superior's orders."

6. LIMITATIONS ON THE ASSUMPTION OF THE RISK DEFENSE

The majority of courts have held that an employee does not voluntarily assume the risk of his job. They have been mindful of the 19th-century origin of assumption of the risk in just such cases, with the employee compelled to suffer any hazard of employment an unscrupulous employer might foist upon him. A recent decision of the United States Supreme Court, Whirlpool Corp. v. Marshall, 100 S.Ct. 883 (1980), upheld a ruling of the Secretary of Labor under OSHA that an employee "ordered by his employer to work under conditions that the employee reasonably believes pose an imminent risk of death or serious bodily injury" may, if there is insufficient time for redress through other means, "refuse to expose himself to the dangerous condition, without being subjected to 'subsequent discrimination' by the employer." It has been suggested that the decision might cause some revival of the assumption of the risk defense under the common law, where plaintiff fails to take advantage of the privilege afforded by the rule. It would seem incongruous, however, that a decision which was designed to improve the employees' lot should have the effect of worsening it under products liability law. Also, in view of the subjective nature of assumption of the risk, the objective rule that everyone is presumed to know the law would perhaps not be applicable if, as a matter of fact, the employee was not acquainted with Supreme Court decisions or with this particular rule among the multitude of rules issued under OSHA.

The subjective element is clearly brought out in Haugen v. Minnesota Mining & Mfg. Co., 550 P.2d 71 (Wash.App.1976), where plaintiff was blinded in one eye when a grinding wheel of defendant's manufacture exploded in three pieces. Although safety goggles were available in the shop, he was not wearing them because he thought his eyeglasses would provide adequate protection against dust or small particles which he assumed were the only danger. The court held that if the plaintiff "assumed any risk at all," it was only of this latter danger. "He was obviously not aware of the latent defect in the structural integrity of the disc itself and the danger posed by that defect. This latent defect was not and probably could not have been known by the plaintiff. Plaintiff, therefore, could not have assumed the risk engendered by the defect."

In Sweeney v. Max A. R. Matthews & Co., 264 N.E.2d 170 (Ill.1970), plaintiff's lack of experience enabled him to recover. He was injured when, in his work as a carpenter, a special-purpose concrete nail purchased from the defendant shattered so that a piece struck him in the eye. The defendant sought reversal on assumption of risk grounds of a $45,000 verdict based on the defectiveness of the nail. The evidence showed that heads of the first several nails plaintiff attempted to use had broken, and plaintiff testified that as he was working "the thought entered his mind that either he was doing something wrong or that something was wrong with the nails themselves." Nevertheless, he continued using them, and did not stop to put on safety glasses, although his employer had instructed its carpenters to use these glasses when hammering concrete nails. As he struck either the fourth or fifth nail, the injury occurred.

In affirming a verdict for the plaintiff, the court stated that the trier of fact could consider such factors as "the user's age, experience, knowledge and understanding, as well as the obviousness of the defect and the danger it poses." It noted that the plaintiff was only 19 years old and that, although he held a journeyman's card, "he had never worked as an apprentice and had no experience as a carpenter" before his present employment.

The relevance of experience as a factor in determining assumption of risk is further illustrated in Sperling v. Hatch, 88 Cal.Rptr. 704 (Cal.App. 1970). Plaintiffs, husband and wife, sued the defendant dealer for personal injuries resulting from a defect in the brakes of a used car purchased from the defendant. Shortly after the purchase, they experienced trouble with the brakes "grabbing."

Although they took the car back to defendant on several occasions for servicing, the problem continued. On the last servicing before the accident, the car was delivered to the wife by defendant with a statement that the problem was "all in her head." The husband had taken a four-year course in auto mechanics, with another course in the service, and did some brake work on his own cars. On the day of the accident, the wife told her husband about the continuing brake difficulties. He drove the car, noticed that it "pulled" to the right when the brakes were applied, and warned his wife that the brakes might "grab" suddenly at a speed of 40 to 45 miles per hour. Later the same day, while the wife was driving the car at 45 to 55 miles per hour, with her husband as a passenger, she applied the brakes, they grabbed, and the car went out of control injuring both husband and wife.

The court held that the wife's case should go to the jury, since evidence of "her knowledge of the risk and appreciation of its magnitude was neither direct nor unequivocal," and defendant's employees had assured her the brake problem was "a figment of her imagination." Dismissal of the husband's claim was affirmed, however, since he "was knowledgeable about and experienced with automobile brakes," had tested the car's brakes on the day of the accident, knew and was concerned about the defect, and nevertheless voluntarily rode in the car with his wife. The decision as to the husband may be questionable, since arguably neither he nor his wife would have ridden in the car if they had actually known how serious the malfunction of the brakes was. The case illustrates, however, the importance of the factor of experience in determining whether assumption of risk constitutes a bar as a matter of law.

Plaintiff in Elder v. Crawley Book Machinery Co., 441 F.2d 771 (3d Cir. 1971), knew of the danger of allowing her fingers to protrude even slightly into a dangerous opening of a paper pressing machine, where they might be severed by the blades. Yet when she lost two of her fingers in just this way, the court concluded that her action was not assumption of the risk but simply the result of "inadvertence, momentary inattention or diversion of attention."

Sometimes knowledge of danger on the part of plaintiff is dispelled by defendant's assurances. The *Sperling* case, discussed above, shows how a statement to the plaintiff that there was nothing wrong with the defective product helped to relieve the plaintiff from the consequences of knowledge of the defect.

Sometimes the plaintiff is aware of a defect and of the consequent danger, but does not fully appreciate the magnitude of the risk. Whether such awareness constitutes an assumption of risk may present a question of fact for the jury. In Karl v. Spedding Chevrolet, Inc., 498 P.2d 1164 (Colo. App.1972), plaintiff purchased a new car with brakes that pulled to the right. He twice took the car back to the dealer for repairs, and each time the problem was supposedly corrected. After the second attempted repair, plaintiff discovered that the brakes were still pulling. When he was injured in an accident caused by the defect, the court held that summary judgment should not be directed on the basis of assumption of risk since there was "no direct evidence" of plaintiff's "appreciation of the magnitude of that risk." Although it was clear that plaintiff knew of the defect, it was not clear that he fully realized the defect could lead to loss of control of the car and a resulting accident.

As observed at the beginning of this section, most courts as a matter of public policy hold that an employee does not assume the risk of his employment. Thus in Rhoads v. Service Machine Co., Inc., 329 F.Supp. 367 (E.D.Ark.1971), it was found that an employee did not voluntarily expose herself to danger from a large punch press when she accidentally lost her balance so that her hand and arm slipped into the machine. The court noted that the "'voluntariness' with which a worker assigned to a dangerous machine in a factory 'assumes the risk of injury' from the machine is illusory."

In Suter v. San Angelo Foundry & Machine Co., 406 A.2d 140 (N.J.1979), plaintiff was operating a machine with three long rollers designed to flatten metal sheets and curve them into cylindrical shapes. While the rollers were stopped, but the power still on, plaintiff reached over to pull a piece of slag out of a cylinder. He accidentally brushed against a gear lever which activated the rollers, so that his hand was drawn into them with consequent injury. Plaintiff's expert testified that either a rotary guard should have been placed around the lever or the lever mechanism should have been placed on top of the gear housing—both methods in use at the time of the manufacture of this machine. The court, overruling an earlier case, held that the employee had not assumed the risk in operating a machine without safety devices and therefore was not completely barred from recovery. It held, however, that the comparative negligence act was applicable and that the jury was to "ascertain the extent to which plaintiff's negligent conduct was a proximate cause of the accident."

CHAPTER VIII

PROOF OF DEFECT AND OF NEGLIGENCE

A. QUANTUM OF PROOF OF A DEFECT

1. THE FACT OF THE ACCIDENT

In general, circumstantial evidence will be enough in products cases. Also, it will be sufficient to show that it was more probable than not that the causal defect existed at the time the product left the defendant's control.

In a few cases the fact of the accident itself will allow the issue of liability to go to the jury. In Cornell Drilling Co. v. Ford Motor Co., 359 A.2d 822 (Pa.Super.1976), the appellate court reversed the trial court's compulsory nonsuit where a newly purchased truck, with only 35 miles on the odometer, caught fire as it was parked with the engine off, the doors and windows closed, and with no one in the area, where the defendants stipulated that "there was no evidence of an external cause for the fire." Plaintiff's expert admitted "that he could not determine the cause of the fire because 'everything was burnt beyond the possibility of the identification of it.'" The court found "that this is not the type of accident (under the facts of this case) that would occur without some type of defective condition in the truck."

The court in *Cornell* cited Bombardi v. Pochel's Appliance & T.V. Co., 518 P.2d 202 (Wash.App. 1973), where a television set that was not being used at the time caught fire during the night, with resulting personal injury and great damage to the house and furniture as well as the complete destruction of the set itself. The only expert testimony concerned "possible" defective components. The court, however, noted that "there are some accidents as to which there is common experience dictating that they do not ordinarily occur without a defect, and as to which the inference that a product is defective should be permitted."

Plaintiff in Stewart v. Budget Rent-A-Car Corp., 470 P.2d 240 (Hawaii 1970), driving one of defendant's rental cars along a straight and level road on a clear day, suddenly found the car veering uncontrollably to the left. Applying the brakes only caused the car to jerk further to the left and overturn, seriously injuring Mrs. Stewart. The car had been driven only 2829 miles and rented just four times since its purchase by the lessor. The only testimony at the trial was Mrs. Stewart's own, and that of a master mechanic who examined the car after it had been partly "cannibalized." He found two parts of the steering mechanism which had been broken. He admitted, however, his inability to determine whether the damage occurred before the accident or as a result of it. The court held the quantum of evidence sufficient to go to the jury, and affirmed a verdict awarding plaintiff $90,500.

In Moraca v. Ford Motor Co., 332 A.2d 599 (N.J.1975), it was held that circumstantial evidence was sufficient to go to the jury even though plaintiff could not identify any specific defect in the car. He sustained serious injuries when the steering mechanism suddenly locked and the vehicle skidded off the road and into a tree. Plaintiff was driving at a speed of 45–50 miles in the right hand lane of a major highway. The court concluded that "plaintiff's proofs were sufficient to negate other likely causes of the steering malfunction thereby permitting the inference that it was the result of an unreasonably dangerous condition which existed at the time the vehicle left the manufacturer's hands." Furthermore, said the court, a "new Lincoln Continental properly operated and maintained should not in normal experience develop a critical malfunction in the steering mechanism in six months and after being driven about 11,000 miles. When this happens a jury could reasonably infer that the malfunction was due to some manufacturing defect."

In Marathon Battery Co. v. Kilpatrick, 418 P.2d 900 (Okl.1965), a new battery exploded as plaintiff was using it for the normal purpose of testing electric light bulbs. The court was unimpressed by defendant's testimony that its carefully manufactured battery, with safe components, could not possibly explode when, in fact, it did. "It is settled law that the weight to be given to expert testimony is for the jury, who may follow their own experience, observation and common knowledge and reject the opinion of experts."

Plaintiff in Agostino v. Rockwell Mfg. Co., 345 A.2d 735 (Pa.Super.1975), was operating a power saw of defendant's manufacture that had been used only about ten times. The saw "was constructed so that after the completion of a cut, a telescopic guard would be automatically released from the housing, covering the blade and thereby preventing the user from being cut." Nevertheless, after plaintiff had severed a board and was starting to put the saw on a rear bench, "the blade grabbed his trousers and cut deeply into his thigh. . . . As he moved away . . . he noticed that the telescopic guard was not covering the blade, but was 'jammed' in the housing." The court held that with "no evidence of abnormal use or secondary causes," the jury could infer a malfunction owing to a defect.

2. WITH LAPSE OF TIME

Obviously plaintiff's difficulties of proof will become greater, perhaps insurmountable, with lapse of time. Warning failure or inadequacy is an exception. Thus recovery was allowed for an injury that occurred fifteen years after the sale of the machine in Gordon v. Niagara Machine & Tool

Works, 574 F.2d 1182 (5th Cir. 1978), where defendant had confined its warning to a highly technical booklet instead of placing a decal on the machine.

Where a safety device intended to last the life of a machine or other product wears out before the end of that life, plaintiff may be able to recover. So in Miller v. Bock Laundry Machine Co., 568 S.W.2d 648 (Tex.1977), the minor plaintiff recovered when he lost an arm because an extractor in a coin laundry machine continued in motion so rapid that it was capable of sucking the boy's arm into the machine after the lid was opened. The machine had been manufactured eighteen years earlier, but was expected to last much longer, perhaps thirty or forty years. Experts testified that the failure of the safety device was owing to the deterioration or shrinkage of rubber pads covering the ledge upon which the operating mechanism rested. The shrinkage caused the mechanism to slip down about an eighth of an inch, with the result that the safety device that prevented the opening of the lid was no longer properly located in relation to the rotating basket. Experts testified that at the time the machine was manufactured it was known that rubber would deteriorate when in contact with oil and ozone given off by the electric motor, and that pads of neophrene or chloroprene should have been used instead.

On the other hand, in Larson v. Thomashow, 307 N.E.2d 707 (Ill.App.1974), the court rejected plaintiff's contention that "[d]rive shafts are not supposed to fall out after two years and four months of use involving approximately 24,000 miles." It held that such an occurrence "is not sufficient to draw the inference that the product was defective when it left General Motors' control."

When a part is protectively sealed or hidden, lapse of time may not prevent the attribution of a defective condition to the manufacturer. Thus in Holloway v. General Motors Corp., 271 N.W.2d 777 (Mich.1978), the court on rehearing reversed its earlier decision that a ball joint assembly had failed only after the car hit a ditch, then a utility pole. The car was then four years old, and had been driven 47,000 miles by three different owners. Plaintiff's expert had testified that the failure occurred as a result of the car's running over a number of chuckholes in the road. Defendant's own counsel acknowledged that the break in the ball point assembly was "fresh, metallurgically clean, and due to an impact failure," not to fatigue. The case was remanded for jury trial, since such a break was "consistent with and, indeed, probative of the Holloways' theory of manufacturing defect."

B. EXPERT TESTIMONY

It should be clear from many cases given throughout this book that expert testimony is usually necessary to identify the defect. In Cronin v. J. B. E. Olson Corp., 501 P.2d 1153 (Cal.1972), the plaintiff was able to establish a prima facie case through expert testimony that the aluminum composing the hasp which held bread trays in place in the rear of a truck "contained holes, pits and voids, and lacked sufficient tensile strength to withstand the impact" of an accident. Plaintiff, the driver of a delivery truck sold by the defendant to plaintiff's employer, was injured when he attempted to pass a pickup truck which turned suddenly to the left, forcing plaintiff off the road and into a ditch. The impact of the collision broke the safety hasp behind the driver's seat so that the trays slid forward and knocked plaintiff through the windshield of the truck. In this case the mere fact of the accident, occurring as it did after the truck had seen nine years of service, would scarcely have proved defectiveness. Nor could a jury be expected to know the normal strength of such a hasp, or detect the porousness of the one involved even when placed in evidence.

As to the qualifications of plaintiff's expert witnesses, defendants in products cases, like those in medical malpractice, have urged upon the court restrictions that would require that witnesses share the narrow experience of the defendants themselves. Courts have tended to take a broader view. In Trowbridge v. Abrasive Co. of Philadelphia, 190 F.2d 825 (3d Cir. 1951), the plaintiff's expert testified that the defendant manufacturer of grinding wheels, like others in the industry, tested only for centrifugal stress and failed to make feasible tests for stresses caused by vibration and impact. Both these stresses were important in plaintiff's snagging operation where the wheel suddenly shattered into pieces that tore through plaintiff's legs. The defendant contended that plaintiff's witness, a graduate engineer with a specialty in the strength of materials and a one-time instructor at Massachusetts Institute of Technology, was not qualified as a witness because of his lack of experience in the abrasive wheel industry. The court held that the "qualification of an expert is a matter peculiarly within the discretion of the trial judge. . . . We note in passing, however, that the wider perspective of the broad specialist may be of invaluable assistance to the trier of fact; the narrow specialist, on the other hand, may be limited by occupational myopia." As to the relative weight to be given the opinion of three experts then employed by manufacturers of grinding wheels as against plaintiff's expert, that was for the jury.

In Holmgren v. Massey-Ferguson, Inc., 516 F.2d 856 (8th Cir. 1975), it was ruled that the trial court had erroneously struck the testimony of plaintiff's witness because he had never been a design engineer. He was a professor of mechanical engineering and had been frequently involved in "consulting work in the fields of machinery design, structure and mechanics." He was familiar with farm machinery and gave his opinion that the auger of a corn picker machine into which plaintiff had fallen could have been more safely designed in several specific ways. The court said: "We deem it too strict a standard that one must have manufactured or previously designed machinery to understand principles of safe design. . . . General technology within scientific disciplines is not shared by so few."

The courts will, moreover, sometimes admit testimony by those whose qualifications may fall short of the professional or scientific expert. Thus in Netzel v. State Sand & Gravel Co., 186 N.W.2d 258 (Wis.1971), where plaintiff was burned by standing as a "puddler" in concrete mixed and delivered to the job site by the defendant, the court admitted the testimony of the job foreman as a "lay expert." In his 35 years of experience working with concrete he had learned that the substance could burn but had never before observed a burn under similar conditions.

In Lynd v. Rockwell Mfg. Co., 554 P.2d 1000 (Or.1976), plaintiff lost a portion of his index finger while operating a table saw of defendant's manufacture. He alleged negligent failure to design and test a moulding insert so that it would not fly out and strike the operator with its sharp edge. While asserting that in a design defect case, expert testimony is usually "an indispensable element of plaintiff's case," such testimony is not essential "when the issues presented relate to matters which require only common knowledge and experience to understand them."

C. EXPERIENCE WITH SIMILAR PRODUCTS

Plaintiff may show that a product is defective by testimony that similar products of the defendant have proved to be unsafe. Conversely, defendant may wish to prove freedom from defect of a specific product by showing a history of safe use of similar products manufactured or sold by him. Evidence both of safe and unsafe use of other products may be admissible for these purposes, provided it is sufficiently related to the facts in litigation.

Such evidence was presented in Becker v. American Airlines, Inc., 200 F.Supp. 243 (S.D.N.Y.1961). The suit involved wrongful death actions, brought on behalf of passengers killed in an airplane accident, against the owner of the airplane (American), its assembler (Lockheed), and the manufacturer (Kollsman Instrument Corp.) of two altimeters used in the plane. The altimeters' defectiveness allegedly caused the accident. American sought by pre-trial order to secure evidence of similar Kollsman altimeter malfunctions, known to Lockheed and Kollsman but not to American, in order to show negligence on the part of Lockheed and Kollsman in not warning American, and in order to establish "a basis for an inference of malfunction" of the two altimeters in question. The court held that the evidence was admissible for these purposes, since the "malfunction of identical devices is relevant;" but that the defendants "must have full opportunity to explore the reasons for the alleged malfunctions," in an effort to negate any adverse inferences. The court also held that these defendants should be allowed to offer evidence of "instances of proper functioning of this type altimeter," to support inferences of nondefectiveness and due care.

The decision limits evidence of safe and unsafe history of similar products to instances prior to the accident, for purposes of trial convenience and because the post-accident occurrences were "in great measure merely cumulative of the proof" furnished by the prior occurrences. There is, however, no general limitation on use of evidence of post-accident occurrences, when offered for purposes of establishing a defect, although such evidence would be irrelevant to establish negligence arising from prior notice of the defect. Thus in Gall v. Union Ice Co., 239 P.2d 48 (Cal.App.1951), it was held that evidence of the explosion of a sulfuric acid drum produced and delivered by the same defendants, occurring on the same day as the explosion of the drum that injured plaintiff, was admissible "for the purpose of showing the propensity of these drums to burst and hence their dangerousness." Similarly, in Ginnis v. Mapes Hotel Corp., 470 P.2d 135 (Nev.1970), it was held that where plaintiff was injured by the malfunctioning of an electric door in a hotel, subsequent accidents involving the same door, and "repair orders for other doors" in the same hotel, whether the orders were given "prior or subsequent" to the accident in litigation, were admissible in a strict tort action should they "tend to prove the faulty design or manufacture or any other necessary element of that cause of action."

Since evidence of defects in similar products may be collateral and therefore distracting, it may be excluded in the discretion of the trial court. Collateralness may be present especially when defendant attempts to offer proof of safe history as evidence of lack of defect, since numerous instances of safe use of similar products may have only slight probative value. Thus in Hessler v. Hillwood Mfg. Co., 302 F.2d 61 (6th Cir. 1962), it was stated that proof of the general "excellence" of defendant's product is "not relevant on the issue" of whether a particular product has "been defectively manufactured." On the other hand, as discussed in the chapter on warnings, absence of known complaints may be peculiarly relevant in determining defectiveness where allergies are involved since the victim must be a member of an appreciable or identifiable class of allergic users in order to recover.

Evidence of safe or unsafe history must usually be based on firsthand knowledge of the witness to avoid problems of hearsay and conjecture. Although evidence of the presence or absence of complaints prior to the accident in litigation may be relevant and admissible to establish the existence or nonexistence of notice or of foreseeability on the part of the defendant, such evidence is hearsay and conjectural if offered to prove whether the specific product is defective.

Proof of substantial similarity may provide sufficient basis for admission of evidence, and countervailing proof of some dissimilarity will then go only to the weight of this evidence. So in Jones & Laughlin Steel Corp. v. Matherne, 348 F.2d 394 (5th Cir. 1965), an action for wrongful death resulting from defendant's negligent manufacture of a fitting on a pendant line supporting the boom of a crane, where cracking or splitting of the fitting caused the boom to fall on the deceased, plaintiffs were permitted to show that another of defendant's fittings had broken under "substantially similar" conditions. This evidence was admitted to show "the harmful tendency or capacity" of defendant's fittings. The court noted that "some of the conditions" in the two occurrences were dissimilar, in that neither the weight of the cranes nor the load being moved was the same, and "the prior use or condition" of the other crane was not described. The defendant, however, "had ample opportunity to explore these differences," either "upon cross-examination or by its own witnesses," but it chose not to do so. Such differences "could have been developed to go to the weight" of the evidence, but they did not render the evidence inadmissible.

In Walker v. Trico Mfg. Co., Inc., 487 F.2d 595 (7th Cir. 1973), plaintiff appealed from a jury verdict for the defendant manufacturer of a blow-mold machine that crushed her left hand when she accidentally tripped a limit switch of allegedly defective design. It was held that the trial court had erred in admitting Trico's evidence of the absence of any prior accidents with these machines, of which it had sold about 45. The record failed to "disclose how many of those machines had the limit switch located in the same position as the switch on the machine in question or whether there were any other material differences in such machines. Nor did the testimony identify any of the other users of the machines or give any foundation evidence whatsoever with regard to the frequency or conditions of use of such other machines."

Occasionally, as in Darrough v. White Motor Co., 393 N.E.2d 122 (Ill.App.1979), evidence of safe use of the same product by others may be useful to the defendant. Here the plaintiff fell in climbing out of a truck tractor. Evidence that others had used the ladder without incident was admissible to show safety of design.

D. POST–ACCIDENT REMEDIAL MEASURES

It has been widely held that in negligence cases, remedial measures taken by the defendant *after* the accident cannot be admitted into evidence. Such evidence is regarded as irrelevant to defendant's knowledge or actions before the accident and moreover its admission might deter post-accident improvements or repairs if defendant felt that such remedial measures might be used against him. However, a substantial number of jurisdictions have recently refused to apply the rule in strict liability actions. In the leading case, Ault v. International Harvester Co., 528 P.2d 1148 (Cal.1974), the court said: "The contemporary corporate mass producer of goods, the normal products liability defendant, manufactures tens of thousands of units of goods; it is manifestly unrealistic to suggest that such a producer will forego making improvements in its product, and risk innumerable additional lawsuits and the attendant adverse effect upon its public image, simply because evidence of adoption of such improvement may be admitted in an action founded on strict liability for recovery on an injury that preceded the improvement."

In Caprara v. Chrysler Corp., 417 N.E.2d 545 (N.Y.App.1981), the court noted the development of strict tort liability and observed: "[T]he very economic realities that shaped these legal changes— among others, the growing market share of the mass manufacturer, the well-nigh universality of insurance, the escalation of governmental regulation— undermine any assumption that it is necessary to pay the price of sheltering defendants in strict products liability litigation from evidentiary use of their product changes in order to persuade them to make improvements to which self-interest must propel them in any event." Here plaintiff attributed the accident to the excessive play of a ball joint. There was testimony that subsequent to the accident, Chrysler modified its ball joints by adding a plastic insert which eliminated end play or movement.

It remains uncertain to what extent *Ault* will be followed. In Phillips v. J. L. Hudson Co., 263 N.W.2d 3 (Mich.1977), the court held the policy reasons for excluding evidence of post-accident repairs "to prove negligence are equally applicable where the fact to be proven is a product defect."

On the other hand, *Ault* was followed not only in respect to a design change but also where a warning change was involved, in Good v. A. B. Chance Co., 565 P.2d 217 (Colo.App.1977). Here a warning decal for an aerial boom device which had caused the electrocution of plaintiff's decedent had been prepared one year before the accident but not distributed until afterwards. The court said that this evidence "tended to establish Chance's knowledge of the defect in its product, the feasibility of giving a warning, Chance's duty to warn, and its breach of that duty." The plaintiffs' "evidence of post-accident warnings had a direct bearing on the liability issue."

In Harless v. Boyle-Midway Div., American Home Products, 594 F.2d 1051 (5th Cir. 1979), a fourteen-year-old died from sniffing Pam, intended to prevent food from sticking to cooking surfaces.

Defendant had notice of 45 deaths from the misuse of the product in the four years before the death of plaintiff's child. About three months before that death, it affixed to its cans a label warning that inhalation of the contents could be fatal. No effort was made to recall inadequately labeled cans. The trial court erroneously excluded evidence that no deaths from the newly labeled product had occurred. The Court of Appeals held that this evidence should have been admitted to rebut defendant's contention that no matter what type of label was used, teenagers would not heed it.

In Schaeffer v. General Motors Corp., 360 N.E.2d 1062 (Mass.1977), plaintiff collided in 1964 with an oncoming car as his own 1963 Cadillac shot uncontrollably across the road. Plaintiff had purchased the car with a controlled differential as optional equipment. No warning was given that the equipment might cause the car to slide sideways under slippery conditions. The court sustained the trial judge in his admission of warnings given in owners' manuals five, six, and seven years after plaintiff purchased his car, when it was agreed that the design of the differential had not changed. The judge had correctly instructed the jury that "the manuals cannot ordinarily be considered as admission of prior negligence or fault. But this rule of evidence has given rise to numerous exceptions. The evidence was also admissible to prove the practical possibility of giving cautionary warnings. . . . Such evidence would bear directly on the question whether . . . the defendant had done all that was practicable to prevent such an accident as occurred."

On the other hand, in Smyth v. Upjohn Co., 529 F.2d 803 (2d Cir. 1975), post-injury warnings of a drug's side effects were held not admissible to determine defendant's ability to write a stronger warning, when such ability was uncontroverted.

In LaMonica v. Outboard Marine Corp., 355 N.E.2d 533 (Ohio App.1976), the court declared categorically that evidence of changes in a product subsequent to an occurrence was not admissible in a negligence action, but was admissible in a strict tort action for the limited purpose of showing feasibility. Where other evidence of feasible alternatives was before the jury, the evidence of changes that had been excluded by the trial judge was cumulative and therefore the exclusion was harmless error.

Despite *LaMonica,* the trend seems to be toward allowing evidence of post-accident remedial measures even in negligence cases for certain limited purposes. In the leading case of Sutkowski v. Universal Marion Corp., 281 N.E.2d 749 (Ill.App.1972), involving a giant strip-mining shovel, as tall as a ten-story building, evidence of the post-accident installation of a barrier against rocks and other debris sliding down the spoil bank underneath the machine was held admissible. The installation by the defendant followed a recommendation made to the mining company, not to the defendant, by plaintiff's expert witness, a mine inspector. "The offer of proof substantially discloses the witness would have testified to design alternatives which could and should have been installed at the time of manufacture of the machine. . . . If the feasibility of alternative designs may be shown by the opinions of experts or by the existence of safety devices on other products or in the design thereof we conclude that evidence of a post occurrence change is equally relevant and material in determining that a design alternative is feasible."

Evidence of post-accident changes or warnings may be admitted for impeachment purposes. In Dollar v. Long Mfg., North Carolina, Inc., 561 F.2d 613 (5th Cir. 1977), plaintiff was killed when he was crushed between the control panel of a backhoe and the rollbar canopy of the tractor to which it was attached. The design engineer of the defendant testified that "the backhoe was safe to operate while affixed to a rollbar-equipped tractor." The court held that it was erroneous to have excluded the post-accident letter sent to all Long backhoe dealers "warning them about the death dealing propensities of the Long backhoe when used in the fashion employed here." The sound policy that dictated exclusion of post-accident remedial measures to prove negligence was not appropriate here when such evidence was "offered for another purpose, such as proving ownership, control, or feasibility of precautionary measures, if controverted, or [as in the case at bar] impeachment." The court did "not think *unfair* prejudice to the defendant would have resulted from his having been confronted by his own letter warning of exposure to death by such use."

In general, recall letters are now admissible to show defect, especially when the letter describes the same risk described by plaintiff's witnesses. Thus in Carey v. General Motors Corp., 387 N.E.2d 583 (Mass.1979), plaintiffs' experts described three defects, any one of which might have caused the throttle to stick. One of these was a fast-idle cam which was improperly made of a plastic-metal combination. A recall letter had indicated that a piece of the cam might become lodged in the throttle linkage and prevent it from closing. The court discounted any suggestion that admitting such evidence would discourage recalls, since they were mandated by law. In Barry v. Manglass, 389 N.Y.S.2d 870 (App.Div.1976), it was said that recall letters were relevant in letting the jury "know that the existence of the defect in a particular model of vehicle was likely and that said likelihood was greater as to such model than it was as to other models." However, since vehicle recall letters seldom imply that *all* cars of a certain model have the suspected defect, they cannot be received as an admission that plaintiff's particular vehicle was defective.

E.   STANDARDS OF THE INDUSTRY

1.   RELATIONSHIP TO LIABILITY

As indicated in the chapters on design and warning, adherence to the prevailing standards of the industry will not be conclusive evidence of due care. Considerable weight, however, can be given such evidence; and some recent products liability statutes provide that it creates an inference or even a presumption of due care. Ordinarily, however, the testimony of expert witnesses that the standard fails to assure safety and that precautionary measures are feasible will permit the jury to find negligence. An early example is Marsh Wood Products Co. v. Babcock & Wilcox Co., 240 N.W. 392 (Wis.1932), where two college professors testified that testing procedures not then practiced in the industry and not required by the state Boiler Code were essential for determining the suitability of steel for boiler tubes. "Obviously," said the court, "manufacturers cannot, by concurring in a careless or dangerous method of manufacture, establish their own standard of care."

In strict liability actions, where due care is not at issue, courts have differed as to whether or not the standard of the industry has any relevance in determining the existence of a defect. Here again, some state products liability statutes authorize the use of such evidence in determining defectiveness.

Since such standards usually involve design, rather than production defects, they have already been discussed in chapter 5, especially in the introductory sections dealing with feasibility, state of the art, and risk-benefit analysis.

2. ADMISSIBILITY OF EVIDENCE

a. IN GENERAL

Problems of proof arise in determining just what is the standard of the industry, assuming that such a standard has some bearing upon either negligence or defect. These problems are largely those of the admissibility of evidence where courts have differed on relevancy and hearsay issues.

b. INDUSTRY CODES

In Union Supply Co. v. Pust, 583 P.2d 276 (Colo.1978), the court upheld the trial judge in admitting two conveyer safety codes drawn up by industry-sponsored associations. It felt that this exception to the hearsay rule was justified by the requirement "that the safety standards be introduced through an expert witness" giving the adverse party "a fair opportunity to cross-examine the expert on any inconsistencies, misrepresentations or other limitations of the standards." The court found the codes relevant, especially in design cases like the one at bar. "By reason of the nature of the case, the trier of fact is greatly dependent on expert evidence and industry standards in deciding whether a defect is present."

In Nordstrom v. White Metal Rolling & Stamping Corp., 453 P.2d 619 (Wash.1969), the defense submitted evidence of its compliance with the safety standards set up by the American Standards Association for Metal Portable Ladders. The court held such evidence admissible even though none of the numerous and widely representative compilers of the code was available as a witness. The court considered the code itself both relevant and trustworthy. A vigorous dissent would have followed the majority rule that such evidence was hearsay especially when, as here, "there was no declarant but rather a committee speaking through a formalized document and leaving the declarants unidentified and unresponsible for its contents."

In Clary v. Fifth Avenue Chrysler Center, Inc., 454 P.2d 244 (Alaska 1969), the court admitted into evidence manuals of competitors which, unlike defendant's manual, warned that carbon monoxide might enter the open windows of parked station wagons if the engine was running.

c.   GOVERNMENT CODES

As to government codes, it was held in Pyatt v. Engel Equipment, Inc., 309 N.E.2d 225 (Ill.App. 1974), that Health and Safety Rules of the Illinois Industrial Commission should have been admitted over the objections of the defendant. As an out-of-state manufacturer of the machine, not the employer of the plaintiff, the rules were not applicable to him. The court upheld plaintiff's contention that the "rules are admissible into evidence for the limited purpose of establishing some evidence of standards of machine design." In Bunn v. Caterpillar Tractor Co., 415 F.Supp. 286 (W.D.Pa.1976), safety regulations issued under OSHA and the Maine Enforcement and Safety Administration were admitted even though they were not applicable to defendant. The jury was instructed that the regulations could be used "as you may decide they determine a standard of conduct."

In d'Hedouville v. Pioneer Hotel Co., 552 F.2d 886 (9th Cir. 1977), it was held no error to admit government regulations regarding the flammability of fabrics that were issued after Monsanto's sale of the fibre used for carpeting. The court conceded that such standards would be irrelevant to show negligence in their violation, but in this strict liability case defendant's due care was not in issue.

In Stonehocker v. General Motors Corp., 587 F.2d 151 (4th Cir. 1978), it was held that the trial court in a roll-over case had improperly excluded defendant's evidence that the roof of its vehicle exceeded the standards subsequently promulgated by the Department of Transportation.

d. SCIENTIFIC LITERATURE

As to scientific literature, it was held in Kershaw v. Sterling Drug, Inc., 415 F.2d 1009 (5th Cir. 1969), that the court below had correctly allowed plaintiff "to examine her expert medical witnesses concerning the contents of medical articles about chloroquine retinopathy and to introduce the articles into evidence. While Sterling is correct in arguing that the articles were hearsay as to the existence and nature of the disease, they were properly introduced to show that Sterling reasonably should have known of the existence and nature of the disease."

F. STATUTORY STANDARDS AND NEGLIGENCE PER SE

As indicated in the chapters on design and warning, compliance with statutory requirements will not be conclusive evidence of freedom from either defect or negligence. However, such evidence may be considered by the jury. Furthermore, a number of the recent products liability statutes have required that the jury be instructed that such compliance raises a rebuttable presumption of freedom from defect.

Obviously a failure to comply with a statute or regulation pursuant thereto will be evidence of negligence, or of defect, or both. Problems of proof in such negligence per se cases will be minimal. Such cases are, however, in the products field relatively rare, perhaps because the corporate defendants, with their expert advisers, will rarely violate a government statute. However, in Zerby v. Warren, 210 N.W.2d 58 (Minn.1973), a retailer was held liable on negligence per se grounds to plaintiff whose minor decedent had died from sniffing glue sold to another minor in violation of a statute forbidding such sale.

The most likely failures are in warning labels, as in *Gonzalez* given in chapter 6, or in food where accidental foreign matter in a single can or loaf will constitute a violation of state and federal Pure Food laws against adulteration; or an article may be mislabeled by mistake rather than design. In Orthopedic Equipment Co. v. Eutsler, 276 F.2d 455 (4th Cir. 1960), defendant had indicated on its label that a surgical nail to be inserted into a medullary canal, containing the marrow, of a fractured bone was smaller in diameter than it actually was. As a result, the nail became lodged in the canal when only part way through. Two additional operations were required for its removal; and the impaction of the nail caused incurable osteomyelitis with loss of use of the leg and probably, in the future, an amputation. The court found that the nail had been misbranded and thus violated a provision of the Federal Food, Drug, and Cosmetic Act. It noted that the act did not "expressly provide a civil remedy for injured consumers. However, the statute imposes an absolute duty on manufacturers not to misbrand their

products, and the breach of this duty may give rise
to civil liability."

Violation of a statute will not, however, necessarily involve liability. The injury must be one which
the statute is designed to prevent. Thus in Kelly v.
Koppers Co., Inc., 293 So.2d 763 (Fla.App.1974),
recovery was denied where plaintiff contended that
her decedent would have been seen and rescued
before she drowned in a Holiday Inn pool if it had
not been for paint that camouflaged the decedent.
The court held that the plaintiff's reliance "upon
the violation of the Department of Health's regulation, requiring the floors and walls of swimming
pools to be light in color is misplaced as these rules
and regulations are promulgated for the purposes of
sanitation, healthfulness, and cleanliness."

On the other hand, negligence per se is usually
considered a form of strict liability, especially when
the statute is designed to protect a particular class
of persons from their inability to protect themselves.
Should plaintiff fall within that class, his contributory negligence will not be a defense although it
may reduce damages in a comparative negligence
jurisdiction.

G. RES IPSA LOQUITUR

Res ipsa loquitur is an evidentiary rule that has
been useful in products law, particularly in exploding bottle cases where a specific act of negligence
is difficult, if not impossible, to pinpoint. The rule

is defined in § 328D of the Second Restatement of Torts as follows:

(1) It may be inferred that harm suffered by the plaintiff is caused by negligence of the defendant when

(a) the event is of a kind which ordinarily does not occur in the absence of negligence;

(b) other responsible causes, including the conduct of the plaintiff and third persons, are sufficiently eliminated by the evidence; and

(c) the indicated negligence is within the scope of the defendant's duty to the plaintiff.

In Giant Food, Inc. v. Washington Coca-Cola Bottling Co., 332 A.2d 1 (Md.1975), an exploding bottle case, the court reviewed the bottler's evidence of careful procedures, wholly mechanical, at his plant and compared them with the frequent manual handling of bottles at the retailer's store. Since the bottle exploded as plaintiff was carrying it to his shopping car, his own mishandling was eliminated as a cause. Plaintiff met the requirements for invoking against the retailer the doctrine of res ipsa loquitur which included "proof that there is greater likelihood that injury was caused by defendant's negligence than by some other cause."

On the other hand, in a similar case the court refused to apply res ipsa. In Green v. Safeway

Stores, Inc., 541 P.2d 200 (Okl.1975), plaintiff was injured when a bottle fell from a carton just after she left the store where she had purchased it. It shattered explosively, and permanently injured her foot. The court observed that "the doctrine of res ipsa loquitur cannot be invoked until, as a preliminary proposition, a plaintiff establishes what caused the accident." A dissent would hold that plaintiff was required to prove only that the product "was not mishandled after it came into the injured person's possession." The judge observed that the majority position "in effect penalizes the appellee for failure to have the presence of mind to retrieve the carton in contemplation of recovering for her injury."

The rule has been applied against multiple defendants, as in Dement v. Olin-Mathieson Chem. Corp., 282 F.2d 76 (5th Cir. 1960), where the plaintiff had been injured while working with an explosive charge containing three component parts. Of these, either the blasting cap or the dynamite might have caused the accident. The court held that, for the application of res ipsa it was not necessary to sever out "one particular force. . . . Even in cases in which there is no combination as there obviously is here, the Texas courts recognize joint liability against actors completely independent and unrelated to each other in circumstances where their conduct has caused indivisible injury which cannot be accurately apportioned and identified by the plaintiff."

By its terms, the rule is a method of proving negligence. Yet the fact-of-the-accident cases given at the beginning of this chapter show that it can be adapted to a strict liability situation, where the accident is such that it would not ordinarily have happened without a *defect* in the product. In Lee v. Crookston Coca-Cola Bottling Co., 188 N.W.2d 426 (Minn.1971), another exploding bottle case, the court said: "Where res ipsa is relied upon as the theory of recovery, plaintiff is not required to allege or prove specific claims of negligence or, as in this case, a specific defect. Indeed, plaintiff's inability to determine the specific defect or cause, coupled with the fact that the defendant is in a better position to present evidence as to the cause of the accident, is itself a fundamental reason for the res ipsa rule. The same reasoning applies with equal force to excuse plaintiff from proving a specific defect when pursuing recovery on the theory of strict liability. This is especially true in exploding-bottle cases and similar situations where the product is destroyed by reason of the defect, which is also obliterated, or where the defective part alone is destroyed by the incident. In short, under the theory of strict liability plaintiff should not be required to prove specifically what defect caused the incident, but may rely upon circumstantial evidence from which it can reasonably be inferred that it is more probable than not that the product was defective when it left defendant's control."

A NOTE ON TRENDS

The extraordinary relaxation of proof requirements in the strict liability corollary to res ipsa loquitur suggests a trend toward an even more extensive liability of manufacturers and other sellers than in the past. Such cases as *Barker* and *Sindell,* where much of the burden of proof is shifted to the defendant, also suggest a trend in the same direction. On the other hand, products liability today is probably at the crossroads where any prediction would be risky. As insurance costs go up, forcing prices in the same direction, the drive toward consumer protection has lost some of its force. The recently adopted statutes in the products field may seriously lessen recoveries. The adoption of a uniform product liability act such as that proposed by the United States Department of Commerce would have the same effect. Some courts, using risk-benefit analysis, or using exterior standards such as industry codes or government regulations as a gauge of defect, have been more sympathetic to defendants, at least in design cases, than in the immediate past. In spite of the rapid development of the case law in the direction of plaintiff recoveries during the last twenty years, the future remains uncertain. All that can be said is that the basic principles of products liability law are here to stay.

INDEX

References are to Pages

INDEX

INDEX

References are to Pages

[*319*]

INDEX

INDEX

References are to Pages

INDEX

References are to Pages

INDEX

MACHINERY
See also Abrasive Disks; Design Defects, subheading Machinery; Fork Lifts; Lawnmowers

Construction, 150–151, 249–250, 257–258, 276–279, 298, 304–305

Consumer, 123–124, 131–132, 289

Factory, 100, 193, 218, 220, 227, 242–245, 289–290, 307–308

Farm, 80–81, 101–102, 112, 119, 122, 128, 265

MANUFACTURERS (GENERAL DISCUSSION)
See Assemblers; Component Part Manufacturers; Successor Corporations

MINORS, INJURIES TO, 145–148, 164, 183, 196, 229–230, 252–253, 259

MISLABELING, 311–312

MISREPRESENTATION, NEGLIGENT
Certifiers, 67–68

Retailers, 43–44

Testers, 68

MISREPRESENTATION, PUBLIC
Economic loss, 95–96

Personal injury, 39–43

Pictorial, 42–43

MISUSE
See Unusual Uses, subheading Misuse

MOBILE HOMES, 120–121, 248

MODIFICATION OF PRODUCT
See Intervening Acts

MOTOR VEHICLES
See Automobiles; Bus; Motorcycles; Tractors; Trucks and Trailers

MOTORCYCLES, 173–175, 199–200, 223

INDEX
References are to Pages

NEGLIGENCE

NEGLIGENCE, GROSS

NEGLIGENCE PER SE

INDEX

[334]

INDEX

[*336*]

INDEX

References are to Pages

INDEX

INDEX

References are to Pages

†